Beyond the Garden Gate

Beyond the Garden Gate

THE LIFE OF CELIA LAIGHTON THAXTER

NORMA H. MANDEL

UNIVERSITY PRESS OF NEW ENGLAND

HANOVER AND LONDON

Published by University Press of New England,
One Court Street, Lebanon, NH 03766
www.upne.com
© 2004 by Norma H. Mandel

Printed in the United States of America
5   4   3   2   1

Library of Congress Cataloging-in-Publication Data

Mandel, Norma H.
Beyond the garden gate : the life of Celia Laighton Thaxter /
Norma H. Mandel.
   p.   cm.
Includes bibliographical references and index.
ISBN 1–58465–297–7 (cloth : alk. paper)
1. Thaxter, Celia, 1835–1894. 2. Thaxter, Celia, 1835–1894—Homes
and haunts—Isles of Shoals (Me. and N.H.) 3. Poets, American—19th
century—Biography. 4. Isles of Shoals (Me. and N.H.)—Biography.
5. Gardeners—United States—Biography. 6. Painters—United States—
Biography. I. Title.
PS3013.M36   2004
811'.4—dc22   2004007937

Frontispiece: Childe Hassam, *In the Garden (Celia Thaxter in Her Garden)*.
SMITHSONIAN AMERICAN ART MUSEUM, GIFT OF JOHN GELLATLY.

Designed by Angela Foote

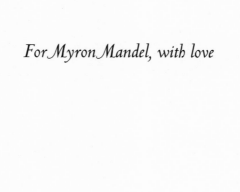

For Myron Mandel, with love

CONTENTS

ILLUSTRATIONS

ACKNOWLEDGMENTS

Writing *Beyond the Garden Gate* has been a family affair. The memory of my parents, Hannah and William Haft, has been a constant source of inspiration. They filled my childhood with a love of learning. My father's insatiable appetite for reading and his knowledge of history—and human nature—have affected my entire life. Each time I explore a new library or return to an old one for another hour of work, staying long after the time I had planned, my mother's dictum to "do a little bit extra" echoes through my mind. Had they lived, I know that at the completion of this book they proudly would have said, "We knew you could do it."

My children, Francie Mandel, Sandra and Michael Mandel, Monica and Joshua Mandel, and Nina Mandel, have all encouraged me to pursue my dream. I am grateful for their support and confidence. My grandsons, Glenn and Benjamin Mandel and Timothy Mandel, are still too young to read *Beyond the Garden Gate*, but I am confident that someday they will. My granddaughters, Claire and Julie Mandel-Folly and Hannah Mandel, have truly inspired me with their love of reading, their fresh ideas for the book, and their constant enthusiasm.

My daughter Francie Mandel deserves special thanks. Her skill as a clinical social worker, her knowledge of the women's movement, and her editorial expertise have been invaluable. From the writing of my doctoral dissertation on Annie Fields, Celia Thaxter's close friend, to the completion of this book, she has helped me over and over again.

I have often been skeptical of the phrase "without whom this book could not have been written." However, I have changed my mind because my husband, Myron Mandel, has made this book possible. He has read every word I have written (several times) and with his fine legal mind has clarified many a muddled thought. His words of encouragement have helped me through numerous stressful moments. He has traveled with me throughout New England, from Thaxter's Isles of Shoals to John Greenleaf Whittier's home in Amesbury to the Henry Wadsworth Longfellow house in Cambridge. He has attended many conferences and done legal research at the Portsmouth Atheneum. Without him this book could not have been written.

In addition to my immediate family, I am indebted to my extended family. My mother's sisters, Ruth Blank, who is eighty-nine years old, and Roselle Silverstein, who is ninety-three years old, read my entire manuscript, correcting punctuation and typographical errors that younger eyes had missed. Their love comes shining through whenever I need it.

My cousins Jean and David Farkas have graciously provided their editorial and writing expertise. My cousin, art dealer Arnold Klein, has provided valuable information about the artists who were part of Celia Thaxter's circle of friends.

My heartfelt thanks to friends and acquaintances who gave generously of their time, resources, and ideas: Ann Boutelle, Marie Donahue, Janice Finklestein, M.D., Jessica Gerson, Charlotte Goodman, Nita Klein, Roberta Mitchell, Hannah Pakula, Sharon Stephan, Judith and Stephen Sultan, Donna Marion Titus, and Nancy Woloch. I am also grateful to the staff of the following libraries: the Barnard College and Columbia University Libraries, the Huntington Library, the Houghton Library, the Morgan Library, The Portsmouth Atheneum, the Smith College Library, and the Albert Small Special Collection Library at the University of Virginia.

In September 1997, I received the following letter from Jonathan Hubbard, a great-grandson of Celia Thaxter: "I am responding to your author's query in the *New York Times Book Review* regarding Celia Thaxter. I am a descendant of Celia and have some of the biographical materials on her that my cousin, Rosamond Thaxter, used in writing her biography. Please let me know how I may be of assistance to you in your work." I met Jon soon after, and his help in my work is immeasurable. Not only did he lend me Rosamond Thaxter's extensive research, but he has introduced me to other family members, is always available for questions, has encouraged me endlessly, and has read the entire manuscript carefully and professionally. He has become a mentor, a colleague, and a friend. My gratitude to him is boundless.

Beyond the Garden Gate

> If it were ever intended that a desolate island in the deep sea
> should be inhabited by one solitary family, then indeed Celia
> Thaxter was the fitting daughter of such a house.[1]
>
> —ANNIE FIELDS, *Letters of Celia Thaxter*

A BLEAK ISLAND, AN ISOLATED FAMILY, A PROPER DAUGHTER—ANNIE FIELDS'S PREFACE TO
her collection of Celia Thaxter's letters is an appropriate introduction to this
biography as well. That Thaxter not only lived but *thrived* on her rocky islands
six miles off the coast of Maine and New Hampshire is in itself remarkable.
That she overcame the vicissitudes of a troubled marriage, the pain of caring
for a physically and emotionally disabled child, and the demands of an overly
dependent mother to become the most widely published woman poet in the
Atlantic Monthly as well as an author, artist, gardener, and ornithologist is a compelling story. Each summer she reigned over a distinguished island artistic and
literary salon; aside from Annie Fields's gatherings in Boston during the winter,
there was no similar occasion anywhere else in New England. Thaxter's circle
of friends included some of the best-known men and women in the literary,
artistic, and musical worlds. James Russell Lowell, John Greenleaf Whittier,
Annie and James T. Fields, Harriet Prescott Spofford, and Sarah Orne Jewett
were among the authors who journeyed regularly to Appledore House, the
family hotel named after the island. Childe Hassam, John Appleton Brown, and
William Morris Hunt were resident artists, and Ole Bull, Julius Eichberg, William Mason, and John Knowles Paine provided music.

Among the Isles of Shoals

The "desolate island" to which Annie Fields referred is in fact a group of nine
islands off the coast of Maine and New Hampshire. In 1873 Thaxter wrote

Among the Isles of Shoals, which has survived long after her poetry has almost (but not entirely) disappeared. The book, which originally appeared as a series of articles in the *Atlantic Monthly*, was written at the urging of Fields's husband, publisher James Fields, to capitalize on Thaxter's popularity as a frequent contributor. In picturing "her" islands, Thaxter compared them to Melville's description of the Galapagos Islands, his "Encantadas," the enchanted isles. She argued that Melville's "dark volcanic crags and melancholy beaches can hardly seem more desolate than do the low bleached rocks of the Isles of Shoals to eyes that behold them for the first time," but, she insisted:

> There is a strange charm about them, an indescribable influence in
> their atmosphere. . . . The eternal sound of the sea on every side has a
> tendency to wear away the edges of human thought and perception;
> sharp outlines become blurred and softened like a sketch in charcoal;
> nothing appeals to the mind with the same distinctness as on the
> mainland, amid the rush and stir of people and things, and the excite-
> ments of social life.[2]

The islands' name comes from the remarkable shoals, or large schools of fish, that swim nearby. The largest island is Appledore, where Thaxter's father, Thomas Laighton, built the first successful island resort in America, the Appledore Hotel. Nearby is Smuttynose, well known then and now for the bloody murder committed there in 1873. It is connected to Cedar and Malaga Islands. Star Island was home to the tiny village of Gosport, settled first by European fishermen and later by a small colony of Norwegians. A mile southwest of Star lies White Island, where Thomas Laighton, the newly appointed lighthouse keeper, brought his family to live in 1839. Lunging Island, originally called Londoners, is the most westerly and most dangerous of the islands with its sharp rocks and narrow channel. The boundary separating Maine and New Hampshire runs right through the Isles of Shoals.

Coming to the islands for the first time, "the stranger is struck only by the sadness of the place—the vast loneliness; for there are not even trees to whisper with familiar voices—nothing but the sky and sea and rocks," wrote Thaxter. "But the very wildness and desolation reveal a strange beauty to him. Let him wait till evening comes, 'With sunset purple soothing all the waste,' and he will find himself slowly succumbing to the subtle charm of that sea atmosphere." Her descriptions of the colors one sees—the "rosy" sea and sky at dawn turning golden as the sun rises, the shadows on the bleached granite rocks, the "glittering" sails dotting the horizon, the "gulls' wings reddened with the dawn"—help the reader to visualize the beauty of these isolated islands.[3] And while there are few trees, there are many varieties of wildflowers, ferns, and other plants: "the spotted jewel-weed is as rich and splendid as a flower in Doctor Rappacini's famous garden."[4]

The history of the Isles of Shoals is equally fascinating. Longtime Isles of Shoals historian Lyman Rutledge wrote that "The Shoals tradition goes back to the early explorers, and beyond them to the nameless and unrecorded fisherman of the North Atlantic. From the time of Leif Ericsson in the year 1000, fleets of fishing boats drifted from European waters ever westward in quest of better fishing grounds."[5] Although John Smith is credited with discovering the islands in 1614, it is safe to say that during the sixteenth century English fishermen sailed there every summer, giving each one a name. Smith, however, was the first European to show them on any map, and his visit furnished Shoalers with numerous stories of his adventures.

After John Smith's arrival, the fishing industry developed rapidly. Trading posts were set up; homes were built; and even an academy for boys on Hog Island (the early name for Appledore Island) was established. By 1840, Smuttynose had a courthouse and church. Rutledge wrote that "The village at the Shoals was for many years said to be stronger in wealth and resources than the New Plymouth Colony."[6] The independence of the Shoalers, reflected in Thaxter's father and in Thaxter herself, was evident from the beginning:

> Having no official recognition, the Islanders were under no government but their own. Law and order were maintained by ship's command until colonial governments were formed. Shoalers had no truck with the political life of the mainland. Orders from the Crown and from the Massachusetts Bay Colony were ignored. Even in later years, when they perforce had to accept the authority of Maine, Massachusetts, and New Hampshire, they continued to be the most independent of all colonials. Without oath or ceremony they owned first allegiance to their island empire and to the customs which had grown up among them as islanders.[7]

This rebellious spirit might have attracted pirates; however, despite stories told by old-timers, including Celia and her brother, the venerable "Uncle Oscar," pirates were not particularly drawn to the Isles of Shoals. In fact, only three were known to have visited there, the most famous of whom was Blackbeard around 1720.[8]

The Revolutionary War marked a turning point in the history of the Isles of Shoals. Early in the war, all residents were ordered to leave, partly for their own safety and partly because each side was afraid that the islanders would help the enemy.[9] Some went to Maine, others to Massachusetts, but when a few returned at the end of the war, they discovered that the fishing industry was no longer viable, and the island economy was ruined. Thereafter, life on the Isles of Shoals was increasingly difficult. In "A Woman of Star Island," Thaxter paints a picture of the fate of the island women in bleak imagery:

> Over the embers she sits,
> > Close at the edge of the grave
> With her hollow eyes like pits,
> > And her mouth like a sunken cave.
> Her short black pipe held tight
> > Her withered lips between,
> She rocks in the flickering light
> > Her figure bent and lean.
> She turns the fish no more
> > That dry on the flakes in the sun;
> No wood she drags to the door,
> > Nor water—her labor is done.
> She cares not for oath or blow,
> > She is past all hope or fear;
> There is nothing she cares to know,
> > There is nothing hateful or dear. . . .[10]

The lack of natural resources, the isolation, and the fierce storms all combined to leave the small population desolate and alone. Occasionally help came—a Miss Peabody of Newburyport taught school from 1823 to 1826, and the Reverend Origen Smith came in 1835 and remained for ten years, trying to banish liquor and restore law and order. He was followed by a Reverend Mason. None was successful in creating a prosperous economy or an "enlightened" citizenry. Indeed, the only distinguishing positive effect of the remoteness of the islands was the development of a "peculiar" language and "a shrewd sense of humor." Swearing was developed to an art, Thaxter wrote: "They seemed to have a genius for it, and some of them devoted their best powers to its cultivation."[11]

In the eyes of most people, the Isles of Shoals in the mid–nineteenth century were home to a dying community, inhabited by a derelict population scarcely earning a living from the sea. However, to Thomas Laighton, a native of Portsmouth, New Hampshire, and a shrewd businessman with some money, they were a wise investment. In 1839, he purchased Smuttynose, Malaga, and Cedar Islands, hoping to revive the dying fishing industry and open a hotel.

He moved his family from the mainland to tiny White Island, where he had become the lighthouse keeper. Eight years later, with the help of Celia's future husband, Levi Thaxter, he opened a resort hotel that eventually became an extremely popular watering spot for New Englanders. At the same time, the islanders began to turn their lives around: "Now there is not a vestige of those dilapidated buildings to be found," wrote Thaxter in the 1870s; "almost every- thing is white and square and new; and they have even cleaned out the cove, and removed the great accumulation of fish-bones which made the beach so curious."[12]

All Thaxter's oeuvre relates to the Isles of Shoals: her poetry, her books, her popular magazine articles about the murder at Smuttynose. The impact of the islands, from her arrival at age four to her marriage at sixteen, and then for the rest of her life, cannot be overstated. In a discussion of artistic creativity, author May Sarton wrote, "Place as well as person was instrumental."[13] This is particularly true for Celia Thaxter. The Isles of Shoals were the controlling force in her life—they inspired her, overwhelmed her, invigorated her, and in her final years provided the setting for one of her most cherished achieve- ments, her island garden.

Celia Thaxter died suddenly on August 25, 1894, at her cottage on Apple- dore Island; she was fifty-nine years old. She was buried on the island in a coffin bedecked with flowers and attended by her family and closest friends. Her brother Oscar wrote, "As I saw Celia lying there, the thought came to me that surely anyone so gifted and beloved could not be lost forever."[14] He was right; as one of the most talented women of the nineteenth century, she remains a figure of enduring interest.

Childe Hassam, *Lighthouse*. MEAD ART MUSEUM, AMHERST COLLEGE, GIFT OF WILLIAM MACBETH, INC.

1 _Home in a Lighthouse_

Sept. 29, 1839:   Landed at White Island
Oct. 1, 1839:   Took possession of the Lighthouse
                   and other public property
Oct. 3, 1839:   Family arrived per Capt. Fall[1]

—THOMAS LAIGHTON, _Journals_

NO ONE CAN BE CERTAIN WHY THOMAS LAIGHTON LEFT PORTSMOUTH, NEW HAMPSHIRE. Many stories, mostly apocryphal, exist, but he was a taciturn New Englander who had reasons he would never reveal. The first time the citizens of that small seacoast town knew he was leaving was September 28, 1839, when a notice appeared in the _Portsmouth Journal_ announcing that "Hon. Thomas H. Laighton, Senator of District 1, has been appointed Keeper of White Island (Isle of Shoals) Light House, in room of Joseph L. Locke, Esq., who has been promoted to the charge of the Whale's Back Light, in room of Mr. Samuel E. Hascall."[2]

Thomas belonged to one of the oldest and most prominent families in Portsmouth, one that traced its ancestry back to Scotland prior to the Norman conquest. The first Laighton to come to America settled in Portsmouth in 1645. By the time Thomas was born, his father, Mark Laighton, was well established in Portsmouth's shipping business. According to Lyman Rutledge, the Laightons were exporters and importers whose "ships cruised the costal waters from Nova Scotia to the West Indies with cargoes of lumber, molasses, rum, fish, and general merchandise."[3]

Thomas was born on February 2, 1805, the third of ten children. When he was thirteen, an attack of typhus fever left him lame, and for the rest of his life he walked with a limp. As a result of this handicap, Thomas was unable to attend college; nevertheless, he organized a workingmen's reading club and became active in politics; he was elected to the school board, the Portsmouth Board of Selectmen, and eventually the New Hampshire Senate. For a time he was also co-editor of the local newspaper. But most important, he was an entre-preneur, investing in land on the Isles of Shoals, revitalizing the fishing indus-try there, and eventually establishing a thriving hotel on Appledore Island.

On June 23, 1831, Thomas married twenty-four-year-old Eliza Rymes, who devoted the rest of her life to him and to her children. Their first child, a daughter, died in infancy. Celia was born in June 1835; Oscar, in 1839; and Cedric, a year later. Little is known of Eliza's childhood, although it appears that she received no formal schooling. Rosamond Thaxter, who wrote a loving biography of her grandmother Celia, said that when Celia was expecting her third child, she "grew ever more homesick, and wrote her mother how much she needed to see and talk to her. Eliza with great difficulty replied, explaining to her daughter that letter writing was extremely hard for her since she had never had the advantage of as much education as her husband."[4] Her lack of an education was not usually such a handicap, however. In fact, Lyman Rut-ledge believes that much of the success of Thomas's hotel ventures was thanks to his wife:

> Eliza was the guardian angel during those first months and years of uncertainty . . . visitors spoke fervently of her cheerful hospitality, radiant spirit, and genial disposition; her wifely devotion and moth-erly care of her children; her competence, courage and unaffected simplicity, and her wonderful cooking—especially her wonderful cooking. So strong were these impressions that her guests paid high tribute to her character and ability but seldom commented on her appearance, yet she was known in her youth and long remembered as "exceptionally beautiful."[5]

Eliza's courage in facing the isolation and vicissitudes of island life was remarkable. Miles from shore, with few neighbors, she protected her family during storms, illnesses, and day-to-day problems. From the moment they arrived at White Island, the entire Laighton family depended upon her. Critic Perry Westbrook agreed that Eliza was a remarkable woman—"an authentic New England matriarch—almost the pioneer woman in her inexhaustible capacity to take on her own shoulders most of the vexations of family life." However, he suggested there was another side to her devotion to her family: "such women are domineering, and in their too successful efforts to shield their families from all unpleasantness, they create an unwholesome dependency upon themselves. Quite likely the desperate homesickness that all the children felt when away from the Shoals was for the mother more than for the place."[6] His observations are valid.

Her children were so dependent on her that they were unable to leave her either physically or emotionally; although both Celia and Cedric married and spent time on the mainland, they were constantly drawn back to the islands. Oscar never left. When Eliza died in 1877, the family was shattered by the loss.

Thomas, on the other hand, had a very different personality. A born Yankee trader, he and several friends organized The Portsmouth Whaling Company in 1832 with a capital stock of twenty-five thousand dollars; it later quadrupled to one hundred thousand dollars. He made other prudent business decisions as well, including the early purchase of several of the Isles of Shoals. In addition to investing, Thomas held a variety of other jobs during his younger years. Many of them were in conjunction with his friend Abner Greenleaf, a popular politician who in 1828 was appointed postmaster of Portsmouth by President Jackson. In 1833, Thomas was named assistant postmaster; three years later he and Abner became co-editors of the *New Hampshire Gazette*. Thomas also launched his own political career, beginning with what must have been a heated election in 1837, when a reporter for the *New Hampshire Patriot* observed:

> Little *Tommy Laighton* is boiling over with wrath and has raised a tremendous "storm in a tea kettle." "We defy you to defeat us," says he. There will be no occasion for that, for the little fellow will consume of his own heat, if left alone. Little *Tommy* sputters like a roasting apple.[7]

Far from being consumed, "Little Tommy Laighton" proved to be a formidable opponent. Twice he was elected to the State Senate, twice to the New Hampshire House of Representatives, and once to the Board of Selectmen of Portsmouth. He suffered only two political defeats in these years and continued to be elected to public office until 1842.[8]

There had been an unwritten understanding that when Abner Greenleaf retired as postmaster, Thomas would succeed him. In the meantime, he welcomed the chance to become the lightkeeper at White Island as an interim job: it would provide an opportunity to expand his investments and further his plans to revitalize the fishing industry in the Isles of Shoals. Nevertheless, quite a few eyebrows were raised in Portsmouth when he left for tiny White Island with his wife and two young children; Celia, who was then four, and Oscar, her three-month-old brother. Everyone knew the hazards the family would be facing—isolation, violent storms, lack of easily available food. Thomas intended to stay just two years, but when he was passed over for postmaster, he decided to remain permanently.

Some have said that Thomas was disgruntled when he left Portsmouth because he had not been appointed postmaster. But in Celia's obituary, a different point of view surfaced: "The elder Laighton, though a man of considerable native ruggedness and probity, was a bit odd and numerous are the stories told of his eccentricities." The obituary suggests that Thomas stayed at the Isles of Shoals because he enjoyed his power: "He was monarch of all he surveyed, for tradition relates that he exercised to the fullest his sovereignty, as seated, obese and choleric, on the piazza in front of his rough cottage and in stentorian tones, he ordered off the island any and all persons who ever tried to land without his consent."[9] In this respect Thomas was similar to the protagonist in Sarah Orne Jewett's "The King of Folly Island." It is entirely possible that Thomas inspired this short story since Jewett, one of Celia Thaxter's close friends, must have known the history of his departure from Portsmouth and the story of the family's isolated existence on the islands. The main character in this tale, King George Quint, is a fisherman who exiled himself to an island off the coast of Maine, where he lives with his young daughter. In a conversation between several elderly men, the reader learns that he left his hometown because of a problem with the village postmaster. An old-timer remarks: "Well, he's done a good thing sence he bought Folly Island. I hear say King George is gittin' rich. . . ."[10] King George explains his decision differently: "I always had an eye to the island sence I was a boy; and we've been better off here, as I view it."[11]

Initially the author appears to admire King George: "There was truly an air of distinction and dignity about this King of Folly Island, an uncommon directness and independence."[12] But, as the story continues, the basic selfishness of his decision becomes apparent: "There was no actual exile in the fisherman's lot after all; he met his old acquaintances almost daily on the fishing grounds, and it was upon the women of the household that an unmistakable burden of isolation had fallen."[13] Moreover, referring to him as "King" reinforces the sense of tyranny he enjoys over his island and all who live there.

"The King of Folly Island" provides a portrait of a strong-minded Yankee, an intelligent man, hospitable to guests, loving to his daughter, and, though understanding of the burdens he has placed upon his family, too stubborn to leave his island. King George Quint is a lens through which to view Thomas Laighton: two proud, independent men, willing to sacrifice their families to achieve their own goals.

But there was more to Thomas Laighton's choice, or "exile," than an obsession with power. Like his fellow New Englander Henry David Thoreau, he walked to a different drummer: "A man's life should be a stately march to a sweet but unheard music, and when to his fellows it shall seem irregular and inharmonious, he will only be stepping to a livelier measure. . . ."[14] The move to the Isles of Shoals was unconventional, but, as seen through the eyes of family friend John Albee, it was in keeping with his personality:

> Her [Celia's] father was a great doubter, a man who did his own thinking—strong and independent, with an iron will, a good and persevering hater of most accepted ideas. Yet withal he had a softer side; his sun sometimes broke through the storm clouds of the godless isle. . . .
> I received and have retained the impression that he was a man with remarkable memory and vigorous intellectual powers but exercised in a rather narrow sphere and with an independence sometimes amounting to perverseness in all of which characteristics his daughter resembled him; but in her they were modified and refined. . . .[15]

Albee's comparison of Celia with her father is intriguing. Thomas's perseverance, intellect, and independence, all the traits that she observed so closely during her childhood, were mirrored in her own adult life.

Like many men of his generation, Thomas kept journals, some of which have been preserved. Unlike Thoreau's, they are not filled with his every thought. In fact, they are sparsely written, often just accounts of financial transactions. He was a private man who had no desire to reveal his inner life. Two sets of entries reflect this reticence:

1832:

July 29: *My father walked to New Castle and navy yard.*
July 31: *Set up through the night with my father.*
        Paid 1½ cts. lb. for meat
Aug. 2: *My father died.*
        Paid my pew tax in the Universalist meeting-house.
Aug. 3: *My father buried.*

Aug. 6:   Paid for mourning articles for mother and sisters $4.00
Paid my pew tax in the Universalist meeting-house

And in 1833:

Sept. 28:   Went to Newington & carried wife. Child taken sick.
Oct 12:   Child died at 45 minutes past 11 o'clock in the forenoon. Aged
11 months and 6 days.
Oct. 13:   Child buried.[16]

What do these entries disclose? A cold, unemotional individual? Or a deeply grieving son and father? It is very possible that these losses were so profound that he was unable to express his sorrow. John Albee has written that Thomas had a "softer side," and it was this vulnerability that made it so difficult for him to find the words for his losses. In fact, in a letter written to Eliza in October 1856, Thomas did reveal that side of himself:

A week has elapsed since you left our peaceful home and to me that week, brief though it be, appears a little eternity. You cannot imagine, my dear wife, how necessary your presence is to the happiness and comfort of my life. Your absence and Oscar's is the tearing away of the best part of our home—he is the music and you the sunshine of our solitary life. But the time wears away, and then to meet you again, safe, contented and happy, what a glorious moment it will be for us all. . . . God forever bless you, my own dear wife that you may enjoy yourself and return early to your devoted friend and ever loving husband is the prayer of   Thomas B. Laighton.[17]

This was the Thomas Laighton of Celia's earliest memories, the loving father who taught her to read and write, to use the lighthouse lanterns, to accept the vicissitudes of nature.

The Laightons lived in the White Island lighthouse until 1841, when Thomas was unexpectedly elected to a two-year term in the House of Representatives. The intrepid family moved once again, this time to Haley House, a large old house on Smuttynose Island. The resourceful Eliza turned it into a comfortable and cheerful inn; it was so successful that she ran it each summer until 1847, when the family moved to their permanent home on Appledore.

Although Thomas did not write in his journals from 1840 to 1845, those days are not lost. Thaxter remembered her first years in her new home clearly

The stormy shores of the Isles of Shoals. REPRODUCED HERE BY PERMISSION OF THE HOUGHTON LIBRARY, HARVARD UNIVERSITY.

and incorporated many of her memories into *Among the Isles of Shoals*. Although time often erodes some of the rough edges of one's childhood, it is safe to say that this book presents a fairly accurate picture of her earliest days:

> I well remember my first sight of White Island. . . . It was at sunset in autumn that we were set ashore on that loneliest, lovely rock, where the lighthouse looked down on us like some tall, black-capped giant, and filled me with awe and wonder. At its base a few goats were grouped on the rock. . . . The stars were beginning to twinkle; the wind blew cold, charged with the sea's sweetness; the sound of many waters half bewildered me. Someone began to light the lamps in the tower. Rich red and golden, they swung round in mid-air; everything was strange and fascinating and new. We entered the quaint little old stone cottage that was for six years our home. How curious it seemed, with its low, whitewashed ceiling and deep window-seats, showing the great thickness of the walls made to withstand the breakers, with whose force we soon grew acquainted. A blissful home the little house became to the children who entered it that quiet evening and slept for the first time lulled by the murmur of the encircling sea. I do not

think a happier triad ever existed than we were, living in that profound isolation.[18]

Thaxter's description of "that loneliest, lovely rock" reveals her lifelong am-
bivalent relationship with the Isles of Shoals. Surely it was lonely, particularly
in the winters, which "seemed as long as a whole year to our little minds,"[19] and
yet it was also lovely as the family gathered by the fireplace surrounded by
books, playthings, Thomas's canaries, and "loving care and kindness."[20]

There were other contradictions in Thaxter's relationship to the islands. She
wrote of her family's "profound isolation,"[21] a phrase that more than any other
reveals the loneliness she experienced. Yet she also described the fun she and
her brothers enjoyed when spring came: playing on the beach, climbing on
rocks, planting a tiny garden, and visiting with neighbors from nearby islands.
It is as if the very isolation in which they lived heightened their appreciation
of the world around them: "my handful of grass was more precious to me than
miles of green fields, and I was led to consider every blade where there were
so few."[22]

Watching storms "with delighted awe"[23] is another example of Celia's ambivalence. The ferocity of the storms was a constant source of terror to her,
even as an adult. As a child, experiencing them must have been overwhelming.
She described one storm that came from the southeast, broke into the windows
of the lighthouse, knocked the dishes to the floor, and eventually dragged the
covered bridge that connected the house and the lighthouse into the sea. And
yet: "Would it were possible to describe the beauty of the calm that followed
such tempests! The 'long lines of silver foam that streaked the tranquil blue, the
tender-curving lines of creamy spray' along the shore, the clear-washed sky,
the peaceful yellow light, the mellow breakers murmuring slumberously!"[24] She
seems caught between extremes: the natural world was frightening but beautiful; her life was lonely but happy, thanks to her loving family.

Aware of the difficult life he had chosen for his family, Thomas helped them to
adjust in the only ways he knew. Thaxter often described his attempts to accli-
mate her to the realities of life on an island. For example, one night during their
first year there, he and Celia heard the booming of cannons echoing through
the air, warning ships of danger during a heavy storm. Suddenly through "a
break in the mist and spray, we saw the heavily rolling hull of a large vessel
driving by, to her sure destruction, toward the coast. It was as if the wind had

torn the vapor apart on purpose to show us this piteous sight; and I well remember the hand on my shoulder which held me firmly, shuddering child that I was, and forced me to look in spite of myself."[25] Thaxter's subsequent ability to face difficult situations had its foundation in her father's lesson: you must confront the hazards of life in order to overcome them.

As Celia grew older, Thomas gave her more responsibilities; he allowed her to help him kindle the lights of the lighthouse, happy in the knowledge that she was helping to provide safety for the unknown sailors who crossed the stormy seas. He also gave her another task at the lighthouse that she never forgot. She wrote that (not unlike King George Quint) "Often, in pleasant days, the head of the family sailed away to visit the other islands, sometimes taking the children with him, oftener going alone, frequently not returning till after dark."[26] It was her job, and one she seemed to accept eagerly, to wait by the shore for her father's return, lighting the slip for his boat with her lantern. In the clearly autobiographical poem "Watching," the child narrator says:

> How patient have I been,
> Sitting alone, a happy little maid,
> Waiting to see, careless and unafraid,
>   My father's boat come in. . . .
>
> Close to the water's edge
> Holding a tiny spark, that he might steer
> (So dangerous the landing, far and near)
>   Safe past the ragged ledge.
>
> I had no fears—not one;
> The wild, wide waste of water leagues around
> Washed ceaselessly; there was no human sound,
>   And I was all alone. . . .

Unafraid, she proclaims, "But Nature was so kind / Like a dear friend I loved the loneliness. . . ." Nevertheless, she is overjoyed when her father appears:

> Yet it was a joy to hear,
> From out the darkness, sounds grow clear at last,
> Of rattling rowlock, and of creaking mast;
>   And voices drawing near![27]

"Watching," written with the wonder of a child, paints a picture of Celia's childhood: her not-unhappy loneliness, her trust in nature, her devotion to her father.

Celia's brothers, Oscar and Cedric, although four and five years younger than she, played a significant role in her life. The children's lives were circumscribed literally and figuratively by their island existence: "We hardly saw a human face beside our own all winter."[28] The brothers, however, were isolated far longer than Celia. In a letter, written in 1876, she described how: "A steam tug came out and brought my brother Oscar; the tug came to bring people to see about the voting at Star Island, and he took advantage of the opportunity. Just think of the surprising fact that these brothers of mine, thirty years old and over, never voted in their lives and never wished to!"[29] Eventually Cedric married, but Oscar remained rooted to the islands for his entire life.

Oscar Laighton was a true character who enjoyed his role as Celia's little brother, always referring to her as "sister." "Uncle Oscar," as the visitors to Appledore affectionately called him, lived until he was almost one hundred years old, relishing every minute of his fame. He would have loved the headline on his obituary: "Uncle Oscar—His Death at 99¾ Made 100,000 Persons Mourn." The "100,000 Persons" to whom the headline refers include both the visitors to the family's resort and those who came later to the Religious and Educational Conference Center, which was established on the site of the Star Island Hotel. The obituary read:

> He was a Santa Clausy sort of person, white-whiskered, about 5 feet 9½ inches tall. He weighed about 180 pounds. He had the bluest eyes you ever saw; twinkly, like Saint Nick's. . . . He always wore a blue Windsor tie. . . . Nobody ever remembers him in any costume other than the faded blue suit which was part of his trademark. Shoalers marveled at the imperishability of this garment, yet none remember him in a new suit. . . . His real trademark was a bachelor button, properly symbolic. . . . Uncle Oscar spoke willingly about his past, but he seldom mentioned his one romance. He did admit, however, that in 1864 he proposed (by mail) to a girl; that he had been accepted; that she had never appeared for the wedding. He never told why. . . . He didn't wear glasses. His teeth were his own. His hearing became less acute with the advancing years. He didn't smoke. An occasional medicinal snifter was the extent of his alcoholism. . . . Although he had been "king" of the Isles of Shoals, a principality he had lost prior to the turn of the century, he did not mourn for the grandeur and glory of yesteryear.[30]

Uncle Oscar: "He was a Santa Clausy sort of person."
PHOTOGRAPH, COURTESY JONATHAN HUBBARD.

Cedric Laighton was only a year younger than Oscar. Rosamond Thaxter wrote that "The two brothers, so near of an age yet so different in temperament, were, in the future, inseparable companions always. Oscar, full of romance, open-hearted and improvident, Cedric with a keen business sense, frugal and cautious, were alike in their devotion to their family and the sea."[31] While a pronounced dependency upon their mother characterized all three children, in Oscar it was most extreme. He remained a bachelor, involved each summer with sophomoric romances. Much to Celia's delight, after his marriage Cedric moved to Boston for part of each year. However, like the others, he remained under the spell of the islands and returned to the Shoals each summer.

Both brothers left memoirs. *Letters to Celia*, a collection of letters Cedric wrote from 1860 to 1875, is a poignant reminder of the closeness of the family.[32] There is a sweetness and naïveté in Cedric's use of the family nicknames: Cedy for himself, Dom for his mother, Bocky for Oscar. Remembering their childhood together, he unashamedly expressed his love for his sister:

> Everything reminds me of you today. The ocean is swept by a gentle north wind; as I write I can look from the window down to Broad Cove, where we have gathered sea mosses and Irish moss so many times together. Four or five miles from the shore a Portland steamer is passing. I think of the journeys we used to make over the rough rocks about Norwegian Cove in search of mosses, and how you used to reach down into deep ponds at the risk of tumbling in yourself, after precious specimens of green moss. I think of the wonderful fairyland, over at Neptune Hall, where we used to imagine we saw magic rings drawn in the grass, where the fairies used to dance and sing, as we thought. . . . As the boat is about to start for Portsmouth, I shall have to end my letter here, so goodbye, dearest sister, and take the undying love of Cedy[33]

Oscar's reminiscences, *Ninety Years at the Isles of Shoals*, reflect his eccentric but loving nature. Along with several of Celia's poems, he included scenes from his childhood, gossip about friends and relatives who visited the island, and a description of Appledore Island, which, he proudly said, "was next to Concord, in Massachusetts, as a gathering-place for distinguished people."[34] The book ends with a history of the family after Celia's death.

Was the life of the Laighton children as idyllic as it sounds? Probably not. While Thaxter often compared herself with Miranda, even Shakespeare did not depict his heroine's life as continuously happy and uncomplicated. Children argue and get sick; parents become tired and impatient. Surely being confined to a small house day after day in the winter months was not a treat for anyone. But the love the family felt for one another was a reality, and their devotion to each other never wavered.

In her biography of Sarah Orne Jewett, Paula Blanchard provided insight into the unusual relationship between Celia and her brothers: "while the

Laighton children probably had some conventional playthings, their world was miniature and highly selective, composed of tiny samplings of the larger environment. Other people's commonplaces became their miracles."[35] And this wonder at the outside world continued throughout their lives. As an adult, Thaxter wrote about all sorts of commonplace objects—seaweed, birds, rocks —with the same awe as she described the cathedrals of Europe. Living at the mercy of nature, enveloped by family ties, isolated physically and emotionally from the outside world—the consequences of the Laighton children's circumscribed childhood can scarcely be overstated. Thaxter's love of nature stemmed from the fact that the sea and the soil provided her main playthings. The beauty of the island as well as its hardships inspired her poetry, her books, and her art.

2 Enter: Levi Thaxter, 1841-1851

How curious the thought of the past is! Nearly forty years ago
this month I was married. The moonlight on the water looked
exactly the same that evening as it does now. How many lives
we seem to live in one! I heard the cricket in the grass, the
same sound I heard to-night.[1]

—CELIA THAXTER TO ROSE LAMB,
SEPTEMBER 1889

SO MUCH OCCURS IN OUR LIVES AS A RESULT OF CHANCE; SO MUCH DEPENDS UPON FATE.
"What if . . ." is a question everyone has imagined at one time or another.
In Celia Thaxter's life, this conjecture is particularly intriguing. If Thomas
Laighton had not been elected to the New Hampshire legislature in 1841 and
moved the family to Smuttynose Island, Celia might never have met Levi
Thaxter. Events would not have occurred that necessitated her leaving her
island home and embarking on a new life on land, one filled with success and
fame as well as hardship and difficult adjustments.

But this is all speculation—what actually happened was that with Thomas's
election to the New Hampshire legislature in 1841, a temporary lighthouse
keeper was appointed, and the family moved to Smuttynose Island. There,
Eliza became the entrepreneur in the family, managing a small inn that attracted young visitors from the mainland. Their temporary home was just the
right setting for such a venture. Samuel Haley, the previous owner of the
island, had discovered four bars of silver left by pirates. He used his newly
found treasure to improve the island, including constructing a massive seawall
connected with Malaga Island. This provided a small safe harbor for boats, a
valuable asset for an island hotel. Recalling these early days, Rosamond Thaxter wrote that "many gay parties sailed from the mainland to enjoy the fresh sea
breeze, good fishing and old Jamaica rum, of which a plentiful supply was kept
on hand."[2] Another attraction was Eliza's cooking: fish chowders, broiled
mackerel, and apple pandowdy were her specialties.[3] Maria Parloa, who later

became the "pastry cook" at Appledore House, as well as at several other resort hotels, included Eliza's fish chowder recipe in her very popular *Appledore Cook Book*, subtitled *Practical Receipts for Plain and Rich Cooking*.[4]

Among the first visitors were three Harvard students: Levi Lincoln Thaxter, Thomas Wentworth Higginson, and John Weiss. Levi had come for fun, relaxation, and a respite from the pressures of making a career decision. Higginson and Weiss had joined their friend to swim, talk, and loaf on the beach. Richard Dana, Jr., who later wrote *Two Years Before the Mast*, was also a guest, as well as John Greenleaf Whittier's beloved younger sister Lizzie and her friend Margie Curzon. Although Celia was much younger than Lizzie and Margie, a friendship developed among them which lasted throughout their lives. As word of the Mid-Ocean House of Entertainment spread, other famous guests traveled there, including Franklin Pierce, then a United States senator from New Hampshire, and Nathaniel Hawthorne, an aspiring writer and Pierce's former classmate at Bowdoin.

Levi Thaxter, the young visitor who was to become Celia's husband ten years later, was born on February 2, 1824, in Watertown, Massachusetts. Although little has been written about his mother, Lucy White, we do know that his father, Levi Thaxter, Sr., was the scion of a well-known New England family. His ancestors had come from England to Hingham, Massachusetts, in 1638 and later married into another Revolutionary War family, the Lincolns. Benjamin Lincoln, an aide-de-camp of George Washington, and Massachusetts governor Levi Lincoln were among Levi's forefathers. Levi Thaxter, Sr., was a successful businessman who was on the first board of directors of the Newton National Bank and later became its president. He and his brother-in-law, Abijah White, were leading citizens of Watertown, holding every public office from tithing man, hog reeve, and selectman to representative to the legislature.

Like his father and many of the early Thaxters, Levi attended Harvard College. His correspondence with his classmates reveals a typical privileged college student: self-important, bantering, confident. His closest friend was Thomas Wentworth Higginson, to whom he once wrote: "I have survived five weeks of vacation here in Watertown and the stupidity of the place compels me to acknowledge that I am tired of it, and shall be delighted to return to Cambridge, the more so as I shall enter upon the last term of submission to the august government which reigns there supreme."[5] Higginson, known to his friends as Wentworth, later gained fame as an editor, author, leader of Negro troops in the Civil War, and confidant of Emily Dickinson. He shared Levi's enthusiasm for poetry and eagerly accepted his invitation to join an elite gathering of young people called the "Brothers and Sisters." Levi's cousin, Maria White, and her fiancé, poet James Russell Lowell, were the center of this group, most of whom were Harvard graduates from Boston Brahmin families. Levi and Wentworth joined them at Elizabeth Peabody's Foreign Book Store in Boston, where they read and discussed their own poetry as well as the work of Emerson, Browning, Tennyson, and Carlyle.[6] Levi had already become enamored of Robert Browning's poetry and recited his verses at every possible occasion.

Levi was only nineteen years old when he graduated from Harvard in 1843. He faced the decision of either bowing to his father's wishes to study law or following his own preference for acting. Some years later, Higginson provided Annie Fields with a telling description of the relationship between the father and son:

> In youth he [Levi Jr.] was a master of the revels, full of fun and frolic; and his great desire was to be an actor and he spent a year in New York studying, to his father's great dismay. You speak of his deep attachment to his parents; it may have been so to his mother, but certainly not to his father, a rather grim country lawyer whose only desire was to make Levi the same, and who clucked after him like a hen who has hatched ducks.[7]

Undoubtedly, Levi's lack of a job must have been a constant source of irritation to his hardworking Yankee father; indeed, in a letter to his daughter Lucy in 1856, he commented: "Levi appeared in good spirits but has no prospect of any employment. . . . Such a state of idleness for a young man is deplorable. What is to become of him is my constant silent enquiry."[8] Despite his disapproval, eventually he provided Celia and Levi with a home and financial assistance as well as a generous inheritance.

After graduation, Levi decided to go to New York City to study acting. He rented rooms in a boardinghouse and found what seems to have been some kind of an office job. His real ambition, however, was to study elocution with the actor Charles Kean. Another letter to Higginson reveals his enthusiasm for his new lifestyle:

> New York is a rich place: a little of everything going on — Theatricals flourish. There is a French opera . . . the orchestra is better than anything I have heard. The Keans are drawing crowded houses at the Park, myself always among the crowd applauding like the Devil. You

ought to see my office. . . . Don't you think business will bring you to New York this winter? Should you come and desire to be economical, I have a wide single bed and breakfast (very good one) can be purchased for six cents and dinner for twelve and a half. . . . You may have heard that I have dropped the Levi from my name. Perhaps I shall change it altogether. Lincoln Thaxter! How will it look on paper. . . .[9]

Unfortunately, his acting career did not succeed. At the end of the year, he returned to Cambridge and acceded to his father's wishes to study law.

In 1846, Levi rebelled against his father once more. After graduating from Harvard Law School, he returned to New York. Apparently someone at home had spread rumors about his state of mind; in a letter to Christopher G. Ripley, another classmate, he remonstrated:

I cannot resist writing you a few lines at least to express my indignation at the slanderous stories you say are circulating about me. Tell me *who* said so and so? *Who* says so and so? Who *lies*? I am *not* "heartily sick of the stage!" nor of the "idea that I would ever succeed!" I never thought so—never told anyone so, and who says I did, tells a damn'd lie. I never for the infinitesimal part of a second *"felt homesick!"* On the contrary, I never was so satisfied with any action in my life as that decisive departure. . . . As to being *homesick*—New York is not a place to be homesick in. If one felt any inclination that way—as I never have—there is enough to divert and distract. . . .[10]

Nevertheless, despite his efforts, Levi's acting career in New York never materialized. From all indications, he had only one (limited) success. He wrote Christopher Ripley another letter in which he announced: "I have just time to inform you that I have *appeared*. Saturday night was the time, and the part, the same one. It was, as far as I can hear, considered a successful first appearance, and was very satisfactory to myself."[11] Unfortunately, there is no other record of this "success," and by the summer Levi had returned home.

The first official notice of Levi's entrance into the Laighton family circle was July 26, 1846. On that date, Thomas Laighton wrote in his journal: "Mr. Howes & Mr. Thaxter dined at my house. Mr. Thaxter came to board with me. Paid Eliza for washing to date."[12] According to Higginson, Levi had come back to the Isles of Shoals that summer "there to meditate and declaim to the waves like

Demosthenes."[13] When Thomas and Levi met, the two formed an immediate bond. In August, as they sailed among the islands together, Thomas confided that he planned to revive the fishing industry in the Shoals and develop the islands as a summer resort. For Levi, who was struggling to find an occupation that would please both himself and his father, the idea was appealing. He envisioned the Brothers and Sisters meeting there in romantic isolation, reading, writing, and talking in the most natural of settings, and he eventually convinced his father to invest in the scheme. Writing to his mother, Wentworth was equally enthusiastic: "He [Levi Jr.] and Mr. Laighton have bought the most beautiful of the islands; are going to bring it under cultivation, have a boarding-house for invalids and aesthetic visitors and do something to civilize the inhabitants of the other islands."[14]

In the fall of 1846, Levi also became part of Celia's life. According to her brother Oscar:

> We were delighted one day in October when our splendid friend, Levi Lincoln Thaxter, came again to White Island. . . . We were all fond of him, and father urged him to stay with us through the winter, which he consented to do. This was an event of far-reaching importance to my sister, brother and myself, for Mr. Thaxter became interested in our education. I can appreciate at this late day our great good fortune in having such a teacher. Mother arranged a pleasant chamber for our school room. Sister was taught to write straight across the letter sheet without lines. . . .[15]

It is easy to understand the family's enthusiasm for the new tutor. In the first place, here was another adult to enliven the family's lonely winter days. Levi's credentials as a Harvard graduate certainly appealed to Thomas, who probably was happy to be relieved of his teaching duties now that he had begun planning his next venture. And Eliza undoubtedly enjoyed the prospect of caring for this romantic and melancholy young man.

Levi stayed for a few months and then returned home. The following February, Thomas mentioned in his journal that he had written to Levi and that on April 4 he again arrived at White Island. This time he was not a guest of the family, for Thomas recorded that Levi paid him twelve dollars for his board. Apparently that did not bother Levi; returning home after another month's stay, he wrote prophetically (if not pretentiously) to his host:

> And often I think of the lighthouse islands, and those who dwell there; and then come musings and wonderings about the future, and

with them what seems conviction that the mutations of life will sometime bring me to those favorite rocks as a central and lasting abiding
place. Some of my friends wonder at my excessive affection for the
Shoals, and I am myself surprised to find how much they occupy me.[16]

Within the next few months, Thomas began working in earnest on a new
undertaking, this time on Appledore Island. According to Oscar, "he ordered
lumber and building materials from Bangor, Maine . . . workmen were secured
in Portsmouth, and, by the first of August, the frame of the first Appledore
House was up."[17] In September, Thomas gave up his duties at the lighthouse,
and the family moved to Hog Island, which was renamed to the more appealing "Appledore." At the same time, Thomas was able to convince Levi to
become his partner, and Levi Thaxter, Sr., forwarded twenty-five hundred dollars to Thomas for "One undivided half of Hog Island and the buildings
thereon."[18] At the end of September, Levi's parents came to the islands, and on
October 7 the deal was finalized.

What was Celia doing during this momentous time? Living much the same life
she had been enjoying all along. At the time of the move to Appledore, Celia
was twelve; Oscar, eight; and Cedric, six. Oscar recorded (from a perspective
of many years) that the first few days there presented an adjustment for the
children, who had been accustomed to living on only six acres of land on
White Island and twenty-seven on Smuttynose. Here there were ninety-five to
enjoy: "we were cautious at first, fearing we might become lost in the valleys of
this boundless continent!"[19] Celia taught her brothers to swim, and their father
provided them with a rowboat. Together they explored the island: "With sister
we would ramble over the island until we were familiar with every spot of it.
The North Valley we called fairyland. Here, with stones and driftwood, we
built a little house, and sister would tell us wonderful fairy stories, which a
fiery-winged blackbird, swaying on a reed nearby would verify with all his
might."[20] As they had done all their young lives, the Laighton children entertained themselves, relying on the ever changing world of nature to enrich what
many would have described as a lonesome existence.

By mid-October 1847, the exterior of Appledore House was completed; the
chimneys had been built, and the plastering was finished. Inside "there were
eighty sleeping chambers on the three upper floors, with spacious public rooms
below. . . . The broad piazza, two hundred feet long, was within a stone's throw

of the water, with a fine view looking west."[21] During the winter, Thomas and his faithful helper, Ben Whaling, worked steadily on the new building while Eliza and her helper, Nancy, were busy sewing linens. Levi returned to tutor the children. Again, according to Oscar: "his knowledge of the best in literature and art made him a rare teacher. Sister was enjoying her lessons and advancing rapidly."[22] One of the first seaside resorts in America was almost ready.

The spring passed in a whirl of preparations, and on June 15, 1848, Appledore House finally opened its doors to the public. Thomas had advertised in newspapers in Boston, Newport, and Manchester and had purchased a schooner, the *Springbird*, to transport guests from the mainland.

The first guest was Levi's longtime college friend John Weiss, who was studying to become a Unitarian minister. The *Springbird* also brought six other visitors, including—much to the delight of the Laighton boys—the Stones, a family with two children. Oscar wrote, "Cedric and I had fine times with Lucy and Richard Stone, as we never had children of our own age to play with before."[23] Celia by this time was able to assume responsibilities at the hotel— responsibilities she accepted for the rest of her life. In his naïve way, Oscar painted a very revealing picture of his sister's life as a young teenager:

> Our sister Celia, at fourteen, was a fine looking girl and proved of great help to mother about the housekeeping. She also grasped the importance of education, never losing a moment she could give to study. Father was too busy to help her much, except in the winter, but Mr. Thaxter and John Weiss were greatly interested in her efforts to learn and gave her wonderful encouragement, and with the help of these masters of English literature she advanced rapidly.[24]

Levi also participated in running the resort; a rather skeptical article in the *New Hampshire Journal* of 1848 describes him during a visit to Appledore:

> We soon sighted Appledore Island with the newly built Appledore House. It has become the resort of the "Fashionables" from every quarter, who are strangely flocking there. . . . Waiting to receive us stood our hospitable friend Mr. Thaxter, a genuine specimen of a gentleman. We wonder why a gentleman of his accomplishments, a graduate of Harvard, should be content to settle on this barren remote

Island? He told us that during the summer one day there were 98 guests from all parts of the N. E. states! They come hungry and go with satisfied appetite, come feeble and go away strong. . . .[25]

The success of Appledore House illustrates an interesting chapter in American history. As early as the 1820s, wealthy Americans had begun visiting seaside resorts such as Cape May in southern New Jersey and Newport in Rhode Island. The families of well-to-do merchants, people involved in literary or artistic pursuits who could bring their work with them, and men and women of independent means were the usual visitors. Most vacationers came in search of improving their health:

> If the promotional literature were to be believed, ailments ranging from constipation to sterility, from scrofula to gout, as well as female diseases, sleeplessness, chronic diarrhea, bilious complaints, and hair loss would all succumb to the powers of the mineral waters. Those resorts that could not boast of proximity to mineral springs promoted instead the health-giving properties of their geography or climate. Newport and Cape May made claims for the ameliorative effects of ocean breezes or sea bathing. . . .[26]

Thomas Laighton was a shrewd enough businessman to know how profitable these other resorts were. Within a few years he, too, was successful and was able to enlarge his original building. An early advertisement in the *New Hampshire Gazette* read: "Dressing rooms and other improvements have been made to this establishment, securing to invalids the luxuries of sea bathing in the open ocean, without the annoyances of sand and dirt."[27] Within ten years, Thomas's success seemed assured; he had added two wings and amenities such as a floating dock, bathing pool, tennis courts, and bowling alley.

When Nathaniel Hawthorne visited Appledore House in September 1852, he recorded his impression of Thomas in his *American Notebooks*. He described a congenial, though somewhat eccentric, proprietor: "As I entered the door of the hotel, there met me a short, corpulent, round and full-faced man, rather elderly, if not old; he was a little lame. He addressed me in a hearty, hospitable tone, and judging that it must be my landlord, I delivered a letter of introduction from [Franklin] Pierce. . . ."[28] As the week progressed, they spent evenings together: "So there he sits in the sea-breezes, when inland people are probably drawing their chairs to the fireside; and there I sit with him, puffing a cigar responsive to his pipe—not keeping up a continual flow of talk, but each speaking as any wisdom happens to come into his mind."[29]

Another early visitor was Dr. Henry Bowditch, a prominent New Hampshire physician and an animated correspondent. His letters to his wife provide both an account of the vacationers' daily activities and an endorsement of the healthful advantages of life on the Isles of Shoals. He reported that even the Laightons' health had improved remarkably: when Thomas arrived he was "a confirmed dyspeptic," but "after five months residence he was totally restored." Eliza was thought to have consumption, but after two years, her cough disappeared. To emphasize his diagnosis, the enthusiastic doctor wrote: "They are both now pictures of enormous obesity, weighing over 200 a piece."[30]

In one letter, he described life at Appledore: "Our party at the hotel are the landlord and landlady . . . and their sons, all bursting with rosy health, about 50 boarders, some pale and puny, seeking health, others pleasure seekers and comparing this with Newport—but we are a simple race. We have no balls though sometimes doubtless a hop in a large hall in which is a piano."[31] The doctor's days were spent cruising the islands, studying the geology, and talking to the residents at Gosport. He also wrote of a less pleasurable day spent rowing several women to Star Island: "It was very foggy and we could scarcely see from Island to Island. The ladies, some of them, behaved like fools, and I got a little vexed. Mrs. B. is a trump. 'Vivant the married women' again I say. They are all worth 20 half women, as ancient maiden ladies usually are."[32]

At night, a variety of spontaneous activities occurred. One evening "an attempt was made to have some spiritual rappings, but unsuccessfully."[33] Another entertainment was a costume ball (Dr. Bowditch appeared as Neptune) with dancing and "burlesque." The good doctor reported, "I actually *roared and screamed* with merriment."[34]

Not every visitor to Appledore responded with the unbounded enthusiasm of Dr. Bowditch, however. John Greenleaf Whittier described his first visit to the Isles of Shoals to his friend Lucy Larcom, a poet, with less exuberance:

> My sister was urged by her physician to go to the Isles of Shoals, &
> accordingly we have been to that lone ancestral land which [James
> Russell] Lowell has immortalized. It is a very quiet, new & strange little world. The Appledore House is large, neat and admirably kept. . . .
> We were at the Shoals through the hot term—the thermometer on
> the piazza only reached 73. For myself, I prefer the Mountains but
> must confess that the sea has also its charms. The Island is a rock var-

ied with green grasses, or huckleberry bushes & wild roses, with only a light house upon it, open to "all the winds that blow."[35]

Despite his preference for the mountains, Whittier visited frequently and became one of the most important members of the inner circle of Celia's summer salon.

During the summer of 1848, Levi's whole family—his parents, his sisters, Lucy and Mary, and his brother Jonas—came from Watertown and stayed for a month. This was the beginning of a lifelong friendship between Celia and Lucy Thaxter. Other visitors included Wentworth Higginson and his wife, Mary Elizabeth Channing, who came with a party of friends. As sometimes happens, marriage had changed the close relationship between the two men. Anna Wells, Higginson's biographer, notes: "Mary did not like Mr. Laighton; she thought Levi looked anxious and overworked, and she could not even admire his reading of Browning, which seemed to her inferior to Wentworth's."[36] Even more important:

> After supper, when Mary had gone to bed, the two young men went out in a rowboat in the quiet harbor between Star and Appledore Islands, hoping for one of the long confidential talks of their Harvard days, but they found . . . that marriage had changed all that. Higginson knew that Mary would be anxious if he stayed too long, and Levi's confidences were disturbing. He had developed a romantic attachment to the thirteen-year-old Celia Laighton. Entirely apart from the absurdity of a man Levi's age falling in love with a child, Wentworth didn't like her. She seemed to him affected and silly. Levi was attempting to persuade Laighton to send her to the mainland for a year in boarding school, which seemed to his friend a good idea if only for the purpose of separating them.[37]

This was the first mention of Levi's attraction to Celia; it is plausible that Levi would have confided in his longtime friend and equally plausible that his friend would have disapproved.

In October 1848, despite the fairly successful first season that Appledore House had enjoyed, Levi and Thomas took the first steps toward dissolving their partnership. Reasons for the breakup were suggested by Mary Higginson, who understood only too well that Levi was not accustomed to manual labor:

> Mr. Laighton, Levi's partner, is extremely unpleasing . . . and Levi did
> not appear happy and satisfied. He feels great responsibility and anxiety—it is an awful life for a young man of refinement and cultivation
> . . . I pitied him very much. Mr. Laighton is lame so that Levi appears
> to do much more than his share—and while it was crowded he did
> a great deal of work—cleaning knives, etc. . . . this sort of thing can
> hardly be agreeable to him. . . .[38]

On October 7, 1848, Thomas wrote a long entry in his journal which began: "We agreed to dissolve and divide the Island equally between us. Mr. Thaxter to retain the Northerly House and I to have the public house with all buildings erected since our connexion [sic] in business. . . ."[39] Apparently satisfied with his negotiations, Thomas returned to his old taciturn self on October 8: "Pleasant day. Mr. Thaxter selected some articles from the furniture which he is to pay for at the cost."[40] Levi remained at Appledore, and for the next few weeks both men appear to have been working amicably. Thomas recorded that he had lent Levi his crowbar and hoe, that the two of them drank a quart keg filled with port wine, and that he sent the forequarters of a pig to him. But on November 22 a surprising entry appeared: "Thaxter handed me what he called a plan of the lot he wished to take—had some unpleasant words with him."[41] The entry is surprising because Thomas rarely recorded his personal feelings. The disagreement might have erupted when Levi asked for money owed his family, because the next day the matter seems to have been settled: "Called on Thaxter and paid for his father $60.00, it being the interest on his note. . . ."[42] However, Lyman Rutledge speculated that this might have been the occasion when Levi declared his love for Celia, who was then only thirteen.[43] He referred to an article in the *Boston Post* published shortly after Celia's death; although much of the information was inaccurate and conjectural, no doubt there was a grain of truth:

> There came down one day to Appledore an invalid, a young lawyer in
> the person of Levi Thaxter of Watertown, Mass. who was to give a
> new turn to this young seacoast girl's existence. Celia, although she
> afterward eclipsed her father in stoutness, is described at this time as a
> tall, stately girl with dark eyes and dark complexion, richly tinted.
> The young lawyer, intellectual, imaginative and romantic, found a

most congenial companion in the pretty, frank, open-hearted girl, and with plenty of opportunity to be together they soon became boon companions. They both became fonder of each other's society, and before the season ended, he had won her heart, if not her hand. When he proposed for her hand to her father, the latter fancying his daughter to be a mere child, flew into a rage, and the young lawyer was ordered out of the house and off the island. The lover left, but not far, however, for, after expressing a determination to wait until Celia should arrange to make legally her choice, he took up a residence in a hut on an adjacent island. The affection of the young girl was increased instead of lessened, and at last the stern father was forced to relent, reluctantly consenting to the union on condition that they wait twelve months. They waited and were married in 1851.[44]

While we must question the source of the writer's information, particularly since he concluded that "Their married life was one of perfect happiness," it certainly was possible that Thomas would have been angry if Levi had indeed announced his love for Celia to him as he had done to Wentworth. In his journal, Thomas noted that two days after they exchanged "unpleasant words" Levi went home to Watertown, where he became sick, and Thomas himself became ill for a whole week. Again, this is all speculation and circumstantial evidence —meanwhile Celia continued her peaceful existence, unaware of any conflict between the two male adults who figured so prominently in her life.

Whatever happened was resolved quickly, because Thomas received a letter from Levi on December 8 "about stock"; by the sixteenth he had returned; and on the seventeenth Thomas sent him a forequarter of beef. On Christmas day, Levi dined with the Laighton family.[45]

Appledore House opened again in the summer of 1849. Oscar reported that Levi and John Weiss came out early in April to renovate North Cottage, a house abandoned by Eliza's brother William Rymes, who had returned to Portsmouth. It had a beautiful view, large rooms, and open fireplaces. Levi's friends, including Wentworth, Henry David Thoreau, and James Lowell, had promised to visit. Levi's father and his sister Lucy also stayed there. Lucy took over the housekeeping, and soon there were lace curtains and a dining room that Oscar regarded as "a revelation!"[46] Although the 1849 season appeared successful, at the end of it Levi and Thomas dissolved their partnership completely. Rosamond Thaxter speculated that the reason was that "Levi was far too much of an intellectual dreamer to be very businesslike, and Thomas' quick and stubborn temper may have flared up once too often."[47]

In the fall of 1849, Celia began her first tentative separation from her family when she left for Mt. Washington Female Seminary, a boarding school in Boston; the term she spent there was her only formal education. Levi's friends were still dubious about the match, privately referring to Celia as "the Mermaid," but the Thaxter family seems to have grown fond of her. Higginson eventually paid her a left-handed compliment, writing in his diary: "Lucy [Thaxter] says she is by no means of a coarse nature and few girls would have borne as well her unfavorable position. Levi writes that she 'has a great deal in her.'"[48]

Unfortunately, Celia never wrote about her experiences during that year, so we are left with a gap in our understanding of her adolescence. It is intriguing to think of this teenager, away from home for the first time, among strangers and prospective in-laws. She had been home-schooled, and suddenly she was in a classroom, an outsider who had never even had a girl friend. Did she miss her family? Did she see Levi often? Did she have fun with her classmates? The only hint we have was dropped in one of Celia's early letters, a note written to Jennie Usher of Maine in the spring of 1851. In it she wrote plaintively:

> I had a[nother] friend named Jennie who was very dear to me. She was a roommate of mine at school. She never would write to me though I begged her to and now I believe she has left school for I can get no trace of her. I hope our friendship will not end so, my dear second friend Jennie. . . .[49]

In an addition to the unanswered letter, she also mentioned that her father did not like a story she had written, but "it found quite an impassioned admirer in Mr. Thaxter, which more than compensated me for the disappointment in regard to father. Perhaps you do not know who Mr. Thaxter is. He is the gentleman whose wife I shall probably be next fall."[50] This was Celia's only reference to her romance with her tutor; again we are left to speculate about the nature of their courtship: how often they were alone together, her emotions, the ways in which Levi expressed feelings. In the best Victorian tradition, Celia never wrote about this period of her life.

The following fall, on Tuesday, September 30, 1851, Celia and Levi were married. There seemed to have been little planning; Levi obtained a marriage license, and his brother Jonas hurried to Kittery to find a minister. Rosamond Thaxter's description of the wedding captured the simple joy of the day:

> Meanwhile Celia . . . gathered armsful of scarlet huckleberry leaves, bright rose-haws, wild asters and beach goldenrod to fill the room where she would be married. For her bouquet, she stripped the garden of its last, fragrant sweetpeas. Her mother had lately finished making a warm, red merino dress for Celia, and this she wore for her wedding gown. The wedding . . . took place in the gaily decorated front parlor of Appledore House. . . . The bride, slender and touchingly young, her brown hair smoothly parted in the middle and drawn back by her silver comb, held her head as always proudly high, as if to catch the sea breeze; Levi, with his full auburn beard and deep-set piercing eyes, was a distinguished looking bridegroom.[51]

Eliza, Thomas, and the boys, of course, were there, as well as Levi's sister Lucy and brother Jonas. John Weiss, not yet an ordained minister, performed much of the marriage ceremony; his wife, Sarah, and their baby as well as assorted Appledore Islanders were also present. Eliza made a wedding cake; they drank wine and champagne, and sixteen-year-old Celia began a new life.

3 *The Early Years, 1851–1860*

We had a merry time, and then I took my dear wife home in
the beautiful night, bright and clear with the stars and a growing moon.[1]

—LEVI THAXTER TO WENTWORTH
HIGGINSON, OCTOBER 1851(?)

AFTER SPENDING THEIR HONEYMOON AT NORTH COTTAGE ON APPLEDORE, CELIA AND
Levi set out for the mainland with what appeared to be no particular plans, no
income, and no home of their own. Their first stop after Portsmouth was the
Thaxter residence in Watertown, Massachusetts. Although Celia had visited
the Thaxters during her year at school in Boston, it must have been awkward
for a sixteen-year-old bride to meet a family so different from her own. Fortunately, Levi's parents, sisters, brother, and cousins who lived next door gave her
a warm welcome.[2] Her father-in-law provided the newlyweds with a temporary
home, and Celia and Levi began their married life in Watertown.

By February Celia was pregnant, and her father's reply to the news is a classic response of a loving but patriarchal father:

> Dear child, you know how very anxious I am that matters should be
> thus. I shall rejoice if it shall be a boy—but will thank God sincerely
> be it male or female. Be very careful of yourself and don't leave off the
> bag of camomile for an instant. The sooner you can conveniently
> return here the better it will be for you, for in the ocean air there is
> strength.[3]

Celia and Levi did indeed return to Appledore for the birth of their son in
the summer of 1852; he was the first baby to be born there in eighty years. A
midwife from among the women on the neighboring islands was in attendance,
but as a result of an in utero injury or a birth trauma, a complication occurred

that left Karl disabled. At a distance of almost 150 years, it is, of course, impossible to know what caused Karl Thaxter's subsequent physical and emotional handicaps. It is also not possible to know their exact nature, but it is conceivable that Karl suffered from cerebral palsy, which would account for his limp and for the realization by Celia and Levi, after a few months, that something was seriously amiss.

However, these problems were not evident immediately, so the first months were untroubled, and the lives of the happy parents, as well as impressions of Thomas Laighton, were recorded by Nathaniel Hawthorne in his *American Notebooks*. He had again traveled to the Isles of Shoals in September 1852 after an intense period of writing; he only had not completed the *Blithedale Romance* but also a campaign biography for his Bowdoin classmate Franklin Pierce, who later joined him at Appledore House. In addition, his sister Louisa had died, so he was in great need of a rest.[4] Although some of his information was inaccurate, as when he stated that Celia had fallen in love with Levi first ("his own affection did not develop itself till after hers"),[5] in general his observations of both Celia and Levi were discerning. He spent many hours roaming among the islands with Levi, whom he pictured as "very intelligent, frank and gentlemanly in manners, and quite a remarkable character to find on this solitary island."[6] He also met Celia and described "Mrs. Thaxter sitting in a neat little parlor, very simply furnished but in good taste. She is not now, I believe more than eighteen years old, very pretty, and with the manners of a lady—not prim and precise, but with enough of freedom and ease."[7] Hawthorne recognized that while Celia always had the "manners of a lady," she never could have been described as "prim." All her adult life she displayed a self-confidence that allowed her to be frank and open without being offensive. She and Nathaniel enjoyed one another's company well enough to spend several evenings in conversation:

> I spent last evening (as well as part of the evening before) at Mr. Thaxter's. It is certainly a romantic incident to find such a young man on this lonely island; his marriage with this pretty little Miranda is true romance, only too much in the beaten track of romance. In our talk, we have glanced over many matters, and among the rest, that of the stage, to prepare himself for which was his first motive in coming hither. He appears quite to have given up any dreams of that kind now. What he will do on returning to the world (as his purpose is) I cannot imagine; but, no doubt, through all their remaining life, both he and she will look back to this rocky ledge, with its handful of soil, as to a Paradise.[8]

As much as Hawthorne saw her as a "pretty little Miranda," there was nothing condescending in his portrayal of her; in fact, he seemed to admire her "freedom and ease." His concern for what would become of them when they returned to the world beyond their "rocky ledge" was realized in the years that followed. For her part, Celia did not seem awed by the famous author; instead she sang and chatted with him about the island, entertaining him with no trace of shyness.

At the end of the summer, the young family returned to the mainland, but in the spring of 1853 they were back at the Isles of Shoals, where Levi assumed the temporary position of lay minister at the Stone Chapel on Star Island. His duties included teaching the fishermen's children in the little village of Gosport. This should have been a contented time for the young couple, but Karl's behavior was disturbing. His birth, only a year after they were married, had left them little time to adjust to family life. Celia's anxiety was reflected in a letter to her friend Margie Curzon: "I can't tell you how busy I am. . . . The presence of an idiot in the house has tied my hands."[9] Her choice of the word "idiot" is jarring, but it must be remembered that the problems facing a family with a handicapped child were particularly difficult in the nineteenth century, when social services and special education were nonexistent; the child was either cared for at home or institutionalized, an alternative Celia would never consider.

In March 1854, tragedy struck the Thaxter family: Jonas, Levi's younger brother, died suddenly of typhus fever. In a letter to her friend Sarah Weiss (wife of Levi's Harvard classmate John Weiss), Celia described the devastating experience:

> It was only the day before Jonas died that we received the first shock of his danger from Ian. They had taken care not to give us any alarm in their letters. . . . His letter shook Levi more than anything that ever happened to him since I have known him, and we both felt worse because Karl was very sick for him, and we were so anxious. . . . We longed to start that day which was a lovely one, but could not, neither could we dare to go the next. . . .
>
> All this time, you know, we could not hear a word from the mainland. The next day, Friday, we tried it on the edge of a Northeast snowstorm, which increased so rapidly that before we had sailed a mile we could not see a rod about us in any direction, and we had no compass

aboard . . . it was impossible to return. . . . None of us dared to descend into the fearful little hole called the cabin. The smell was unendurable. Levi took poor Karl under his great cloak after the men contrived to fasten him to the deck. . . .

Weak and weary we were when at last they dragged us out of the boat upon the wharf . . . but we could not think of stopping then. . . . At Newburyport Levi got out and returned . . . and said to me "Jonas is dead." We kept on, and nearly dead, we reached our present haven in the afternoon. Levi dropped Karl and me into the arms of these kind Robbins women and went immediately to his father's. How weary we were. Karl was very sea sick and can scarcely walk straight yet. . . . They were all thankful indeed to have Levi. They told him how his mother had sat and watched at her window day after day for him. . . .[10]

This was one of the most compassionate descriptions of Levi that Celia ever recorded. Grief-stricken by the death of his brother, frightened by the illness of his son, and frustrated by the long journey from the islands, Levi managed to come home to comfort his parents, who had been waiting longingly for him.

After the funeral, Celia and Levi returned to the islands, but when an ordained minister arrived in Gosport in the fall of 1854, they were again homeless and jobless. They accepted the hospitality of the Curzon family of Newburyport, Massachusetts, who urged them to use their mill house, Artichoke Mills, on the banks of the Artichoke River. Much to Celia's delight, Margie Curzon, whom she knew from her visits to the Mid-Ocean House a decade earlier, was living with her parents next door. Lizzie Curzon Hoxie, who was to become another good friend, lived nearby. In November, Celia and Levi's second son, John, was born. Karl was two and a half when the second baby was born. Celia was just nineteen. From the beginning, John made his presence felt in the family; in a letter to her brother Oscar, Celia wrote:

> Levi has walked to town this morning and baby and Karl and I are having as good a time as we can under the circumstances, as baby gets more and more obstreperous every day and I have to seriously remonstrate with him. Occasionally if Karly comes within a yard of him he squeals enough to cut your head in two and looks at me as much as to say "why the deuce don't you come and pound him for daring

to approach my imperial majesty!" Sometimes when he is having a serious tantrum I take him by the shoulders and say very severely: "Now John, stop that instantly! Don't let me hear another sound!" and down goes his voice and his upper lip at the same time and he is so grieved he doesn't get over it for a while.[11]

Throughout his life, John displayed similar behavior, reflecting the problems of a middle child, sandwiched between Karl, who needed constant attention, and his younger brother Roland, the pride of the family.

"In the fall of 1855 . . . an event occurred which, though less tragic than it might have been, had a permanently disturbing effect upon the lives of Levi and Celia."[12] While Rosamond Thaxter often wrote in superlatives, here she was understated. Celia, Levi, and their children had spent a happy summer at Appledore. Shortly before they returned home, Oscar and Levi were sailing back to the islands from Portsmouth, where they had gone to buy household supplies, when they encountered an unexpected storm. Celia and Thomas spotted the endangered boat and watched, horrified and helpless. Although the two men nearly drowned, they eventually weathered the storm. However, the terror they endured had a permanent effect upon Levi. He left the islands immediately, vowing never to return (although he did in later years). He sold his father-in-law his fifty acres on the south side of the island for seventeen hundred dollars and the little cottage where they had spent their honeymoon for six hundred dollars. In his own words, he "remised, released and forever quitclaimed" his property on Appledore.[13] Although there is no record of Celia's feelings about the sale of the property, it is safe to say that she was unhappy about it. As Rosamond Thaxter observed, "this was the first rift, the opening wedge which tended as the years passed, to separate Celia's and Levi's lives, sending them along paths leading in different directions."[14]

For Celia, who had lived so long in close proximity to the sea, the near ship-wreck was frightening, but it was also a fact of life that she could accept. For Levi, the trauma so overwhelmed him that, without regard for Celia's feelings, he chose to escape from any association with the Isles of Shoals. As a result, for many years Celia traveled to the islands by herself or with the children, leaving Levi alone or with his younger sons.

The winter after the accident the family returned to Artichoke Mills, where Celia was happy with her friends, busy with her family, and still enamored of Levi. It is easy to forget how young Celia was when her children were born, hardly out of adolescence. Her letters showed a childish delight in her new surroundings and revealed the joy she was experiencing as a mother. Only her reference to "my king Levi" foreshadowed the days to come:

> Dear Oscar . . .
>
> The Merrimack is a great deal better than the land, it is like a great flat marble floor and the amount of sleighing down on it is remarkable. I tried to skate the other day but kept falling down and my king Levi laughed so that I gave up in great disgust. I keep faithful to coasting and yesterday coasted way from the top of a high hill, plump down on the frozen Artichoke all across to the other side, a long coast I can tell you. . . . I wish the winter was gone and we were all back at the dear old island again. I long for you all to see the children. I suppose every old lady thinks her own geese, swans, but I certainly do think my two little boys dear and cunning and lovely. . . .[15]

In 1856, Celia and Levi moved into their own home in Newtonville, a suburb of Boston. Celia described it to Sarah Weiss as having lovely views: "hills, woods, clustered villages with spires," and "all sorts of modern conveniences." It was large, with a cellar, kitchen, pantry, and dining room, a "splendid great-hall," "five chambers upstairs & a fine attic." Best of all, she could "let the children raise Cain as much as they like."[16] From their window they could see the Charles River, where they rowed in the summer and skated in the winter.

Levi's father provided the money to buy the house, and in his will furnished even more help. He left Levi twenty-five thousand dollars outright as well as "the use and improvement of the estate where he now resides which I purchased of Alfred Hou, also use, rent, improvement and profits of store on Commercial Street, Boston."[17] At least their home was secure, and there was a small source of income.

Celia's letters to her friend from Artichoke Mills, Lizzie Hoxie, reveal the ups and downs of her life in her new home. Only twenty-one years old, far from her loving family, with two small children, a large house, and a husband she loved, but who was unemployed, her mercurial feelings are understandable. In May 1856 she complained, "My eyes are almost shut from weariness and sleepiness."[18] Nevertheless, the following January she was all aglow after returning home from the islands, where she had been caring for one or the other of her aging parents:

> You don't know what a steady old drudge I have grown to be, and I'm happy as the day is long, and the children are perfect "gardens of paradise," and Levi is beautiful and gentle and good and unselfish as mortal man can be. And we have splendid times. Such good evenings as we have! And they are so fascinating sometimes we don't break up the meeting till past eleven, never till after ten. We draw the table up to the roaring fire, and I take my work, and Levi reads to me; first he read "Aurora" (and you're an abominable woman for not thinking it the beautifullest [sic] book that was ever written), then "Dred" . . . You don't know how entirely happy we are to be together again, with both children; it seems as if we had found each other anew and never were so substantially happy before. The children keep so well it is almost alarming. . . .[19]

Aurora Leigh, which appeared in 1856, is a long (eleven thousand lines of blank verse) poem written by Elizabeth Barrett Browning, wife of Levi's favorite poet, Robert Browning. It is a portrait of the artist as a young woman, a poet so committed to her career that she even turns down a proposal of marriage. "Aurora Leigh," Virginia Woolf has written, "with her passionate interest in social questions, her conflict as artist and woman, her longing for knowledge and freedom, is the true daughter of her age."[20] That this long and sometimes tedious poem was such a favorite of Celia and Levi's is revealing. Obviously they agreed with Barrett Browning's forward-thinking ideas, enjoyed her wonderful descriptions, and delighted in her humor. This early introduction to "Aurora" helped plant the seeds for Celia's search for independence from the traditional constraints of marriage and family.

Three months after this enthusiastic letter was written, the burdens of keeping house began to take their toll, and the first signs of tension in Celia and Levi's relationship appear. In her next letter to Lizzie, Celia complained:

> . . . I do my own washing now, and think of you all the time, and get tired to death and half dead, but unlike you I fret and worry when things go wrong, and scold and fuss. Oh, for your patience! How

mine takes wing and leaves me forlorn and ugly and horrid! How it seems as if the weary load of things one makes out to do, with such expenditure of strength and nerves and patience, goes for naught, no manner of notice ever taken of all that is accomplished; but if anything is left undone, ah me, the hue and cry that is raised. . . .

> Ever most affectionately your poor little helpless, foolish, Celia.[21]

A few months, later Celia's life seemed even more unhappy; in May 1857 she wrote to Sarah Weiss: "We are half worn out with the everlasting drudgery of existence. L. is at work from morning till night in the gardens & I in the house."[22]

Living in Newtonville as a member of the Thaxter family also involved social responsibilities that neither she nor Levi were inclined to accept; often they were burdened with pressures to conform to the lifestyle that Levi's father ("grandfather" in this letter) expected:

> To be called in the middle of the forenoon from a washtub of dirty clothes in splashed & poverty stricken gown to answer the bell & let in two elegant silked & flounced & feathered young ladies from Boston come to make a ceremonious call on "Mrs. L. L. Thaxter" is to say the least, disagreeable. . . . It is so absurd this kind of life,—so absurd in grandfather to put us here—so ridiculous keeping up an appearance we both despise so in our hearts. It is amusing to hear Mary & even dear little Lucy [Levi's sisters] saying they should admire to live as I do. Little do they imagine what it is—I rather think if they were called upon to go through with it they would squirm spiritually more than I do.[23]

Clearly Celia was unhappy with her life, but Levi did not record his feelings at this time. We know only that he did not get a job and continued to accept his father's financial help, prolonging his dependency upon him. Celia was forced to go along with this arrangement. It would take many years before they were able to follow fulfilling separate paths.

To make matters worse, disturbing signs of Karl's problems persisted. Although Celia tried to accept the situation, she confided to Lizzie Hoxie: "Karly, I think, is getting less nervous and more like a human child than he was. I try very hard to let him alone, but he is so mischievous and raises Cain continually that I can't help visiting him with small thunder occasionally, also spanks. Poor little spud! he is very loving and sometimes very sweet and gentle."[24] Unfortunately, despite Celia's best efforts, Karl's physical and emotional issues only escalated.

In January of 1858, at the age of eighteen, Cedric Laighton made his first visit to his sister, who by then sorely missed her distant family. The visit of her younger brother must have cheered Celia; they had had a wonderful correspondence for years, beginning in 1852, when Cedric wrote:

> My dear Sister,
>
> Father is writing to you and so is Oscar, and I thought I would like to write too, to tell you how much I love you and to wish you and Mr. Thaxter Happy New Year. We are all well.
>
> > good bye
> > Cedric ([age] 11)[25]

Like his brother Oscar, who had visited when he was fifteen, this was the first time Cedric saw large trees and horses. He looked around the mainland with amazement and then rushed back to Appledore. Celia never was as insular as were her brothers; she met new situations undaunted and with great aplomb, but they hurried home as soon as possible. Oscar spent the rest of his life on the islands, except for a trip to Europe with Celia, and Cedric moved to Boston only after his marriage.

Although her life in Newtonville was demanding, Celia was thrilled when Roland was born in August 1858. In a letter to Lizzie Hoxie, she wrote: "I'm fairly in raptures with this baby; never was in raptures before, always thought small of my goslings, but this baby smiles the very heart out of my breast. . . . Isn't it funny that he should be such a jolly, sweet little pleasant creature when his mamma was always so glum before he came? And he hasn't a name! Levi wants to call him David, but I despise it, and Roland, which is the only other name he will listen to, isn't exactly satisfactory either."[26] Eventually they settled upon Roland, in honor of Robert Browning's "Childe Roland," one of Levi's favorite poems, although the family called him "Lony" most of his life.

The summer after Roland's birth was spent in Newtonville rather than on Appledore. There, in addition to the care of her young family, Celia often entertained Levi's college friends. This was a mixed blessing: while it added more work to her busy schedule, it also kept her in touch with the literary world that lay at her doorstep. "I devour books whenever I get a chance, read Dante and peel squash, à la Elizabeth Brontë," she wrote Lizzie.[27] Levi's interest in Browning continued; he and his visitors, who included clergyman John Weiss, artist

William Morris Hunt, and *Atlantic Monthly* editor James Russell Lowell, spent many evenings earnestly discussing him, as well as the latest authors and poets.

Despite the joy of the new baby, Celia became more unhappy. Her letters contained fewer glowing descriptions of the children and more mention of childhood illnesses, endless days of work, and longing for her family and the islands. Celia admitted her sadness to Lizzie. Although she might have been suffering from post-partum depression, this was also an early instance of the depressive episodes that plagued her during the rest of her life:

> New baby and his brothers are in bed and asleep and I feel like being in bed and asleep too, too sleepy to have any ideas left. . . . Somehow "crude" is the word that expresses this place. It seems to be at the world's end—lonely, un-get-at-able, uninteresting, not one beloved, friendly face within reach, no children for ours to play with; but it might be a great deal worse too. . . .
>
> Tell Margie,[28] mother has half promised to come this February and see us, and that we are going to the island in March, for in the summer Levi proposes wandering off to Mount Desert or some preposterous place. There can never be such a charming sea place as the islands; how can anybody want to go further? I do not, most certainly.[29]

The happiness of Celia's idyllic childhood and the romance of her early married years were gradually replaced by the trials of her day-to-day responsibilities. Celia was desperately lonesome for her family, her islands, her childhood. In May 1860, she sent her brother Cedric a poem she had written expressing her homesickness for the Isles of Shoals. He replied: "I am perfectly delighted with the little poem you so kindly sent me, and I shall keep it as long as I live, as a sad memorial of departed days, as Bocky would say."[30] This "little poem" was destined to change her life.

4　New Horizons, 1861

Neither am I ungrateful. . . .[1]

—CELIA THAXTER, *Poems*

CELIA'S "LITTLE POEM" WAS "LAND-LOCKED," PUBLISHED IN THE *ATLANTIC MONTHLY* IN March 1861. Although in the years to come she often wrote of her longing for the sounds, sights, and scents of her childhood, there is an originality in "Land-locked" that makes it one of her most poignant and appealing works. The poem begins with dark images:

Black lie the hills; swiftly doth daylight flee;
　　And, catching gleams of sunset's dying smile,
　　Through the dusk land for many a changing mile
The river runneth softly to the sea.

In the next stanza she expresses her profound loneliness for her island home:

O happy river, could I follow thee!
　　O yearning heart, that never can be still!
　　O wistful eyes, that watch the steadfast hill,
Longing for level line of solemn sea!

Although she tries to find happiness in her present life, the memories of her islands pervade her thoughts:

Have patience; here are flowers and songs of birds,
　　Beauty and fragrance, wealth of sound and sight,
　　All summer's glory thine from morn till night,
And life too full of joy for uttered words.

Neither am I ungrateful; but I dream
>Deliciously how twilight falls to-night
>Over the glimmering water, how the light
Dies blissfully away, until I seem

To feel the wind, sea-scented, on my cheek,
>To catch the sound of dusky flapping sail
>And dip of oars, and voices on the gale
Afar off, calling low,—my name they speak!

O Earth! thy summer song of joy may soar
>Ringing to heaven in triumph. I but crave
>The sad, caressing murmur of the wave
That breaks in tender music on the shore.[2]

The poem ends with musical imagery—"the summer song of joy. . . . the sad, caressing murmur of the wave . . . tender music on the shore"—that through its cadence evokes the poet's sadness.

Whoever submitted "Land-locked" to America's leading literary magazine remains a mystery—although probably it was one of her brothers, to whom Thaxter had sent a copy of her poem the previous year. It was a complete surprise to Celia, however; in February she wrote to her family expressing her joy:

> I found a delightful letter from Mr. Folsom waiting for me . . . and also one directed to Mrs. Celia Thaxter in an unfamiliar man's hand—What can this be, thought I, opening it. I unfolded and read the following extraordinary document. Feb. 26th—C.T. Watertown, Mass. We enclose our c'k for $10 in payment for the poem 'Land-Locked' in the Atlantic Monthly for the ensuing month. Yours respectfully, Ticknor and Fields."[3]

Annie Fields claimed that the poem was delivered by "a friend" to editor James Russell Lowell;[4] many, including Rosamond Thaxter, assumed that the friend was Levi,[5] but a letter to Sarah Weiss confirmed that indeed he was not the "friend." In this letter, Thaxter modestly described a flattering note she received from James T. Fields, the editor of the *Atlantic*, in response to another poem that she had submitted. She went on to say, "And it is so nice that Levi, who always snubbed me on the subject & never saw Land-Locked till he read it in the Atlantic, is so pleased about this little thing & likes it, & carries it back to Mr. Fields who sent it to me for a name himself. . . ."[6]

These letters shed new light on Celia and Levi's relationship. The idea of Levi launching her career is erroneous; obviously he had no idea of the public appeal of her poetry until James Fields, the leader of Boston's publishing world, recognized her ability. Moreover, it was Annie and James Fields and the other men and women whom Celia met as her reputation grew who inspired her to write. Although Levi may have encouraged her eventually, it appears that initially he was jealous of her success. He never provided the financial help she needed to pursue her career without constant pressure to make ends meet. Like many other nineteenth-century women, she achieved fame without "a room of her own."

Despite Levi—or maybe because of him—the publication of "Land-locked" literally turned Celia's life around. Overwhelmed with housework, beginning to tire of her stay-at-home husband, she found her milieu in Boston's literary world. Luckily she was in the right place at the right time—living in Boston in the nineteenth century was an extraordinary experience, particularly for those fortunate enough to be included in the city's intellectual circles. Boston and its environs were home to America's most famous authors, and the cultural elite of the city were sophisticated, worldly, and well-educated men and women. They not only prized arts and letters but were instrumental in the advancement of public education, the administration of libraries, and the development of liberal arts colleges. In addition, they held editorial control of popular magazines, such as *Harper's, Scribner's*, and, of course, the *Atlantic Monthly*. Founded in 1857, the *Atlantic's* first editor was James Russell Lowell, Levi's cousin by marriage. James Fields succeeded him and was in charge when contributors included Oliver Wendell Holmes, Ralph Waldo Emerson, Henry Wadsworth Longfellow, John Greenleaf Whittier, Harriet Beecher Stowe, and now Celia Thaxter.

Among the many reasons Thaxter succeeded in this new world was that there was a uniqueness about her life that belied simple classification, an independence of spirit that set her apart. She also dared to give voice to her innermost feelings. Noting the darkness that surfaced in "Land-locked," critic Josephine Donovan has compared her with Sylvia Plath and Anne Sexton:

> At times her austere, harsh imagery anticipates that of 20th Century poets such as Anne Sexton and Sylvia Plath. Probably some of Thax-

ter's bitterness, like theirs, stemmed from the frustrations she encountered trying to play the many and conflicting roles of wife, mother, and artist.[7]

All Thaxter's poetry was not bitter, of course; her most popular poems reflected the lives of the women who read them, their hopes and dreams as well as their frustrations. Others, like her most anthologized poem, "Sandpiper," were loving reminiscences of life on the Isles of Shoals, blending her love of nature with her spiritual philosophy:

> I do not fear for thee, though wroth
> > The tempest rushes through the sky:
> For, are we not God's children both,
> > Thou, little sandpiper, and I?[8]

The first friends in Thaxter's new life were her publisher and his wife. They met in May 1863 when Annie and James came to Newtonville to visit and "brought home a carriage full of flowers and the sweet fragrance of a new friendship."[9] Thaxter must have been overjoyed. Except for her brothers, she never had playmates as a child, depriving her of a "best friend" until she found Annie. They were almost the same age, and both were married to older men, but there the similarity ended. Ann West Adams, born in Boston on June 6, 1834, was a descendant of Presidents John Adams and John Quincy Adams and the Boylstons, a wealthy Boston merchant family. Annie's father and older brother were physicians. Her mother's family, the Mays, were early colonists and social reformers. She was educated at George Emerson's School for Young Ladies, which had been founded in 1823 by a group of concerned fathers to provide classical secondary education for their daughters.

When Annie was twenty, she married James T. Fields. At the time of their marriage James, who was thirty-seven, was the junior partner at Ticknor and Fields and the most renowned publisher in America. In addition to the major American authors and poets, clients of his publishing firm included British writers, among them Tennyson, Thackeray, Dickens, and Carlyle. Van Wyck Brooks, pundit of American culture, described him in colorful terms:

> The younger partner, James T. Fields, a man of letters in his own right, was a big, jovial creature, always dressed in Scotch tweeds, with a full beard, abundant hair, keen, twinkling eyes and a hearty manner. The

Old Corner Bookstore in Washington Street, where Fields sat behind his green curtain, laughing and manufacturing reputations, was already an institution.[10]

For a man born into a family that his biographer William Tryon has called "undistinguished,"[11] James's career was an example of the American Dream. Born in Portsmouth, New Hampshire, on December 31, 1817, James was only two when his father died, and he was raised by his mother. He graduated from high school at fourteen and, like many of his contemporaries, moved from the country to the city. Through a family friend, he gained employment at Carter & Hendee's Bookstore in Boston. In 1834, the business was purchased by William Ticknor and became a Boston landmark, the Old Corner Bookstore.

James made friends easily, spent hours at the Mercantile Library, and began writing poetry, some of which was published. As a result of the recognition his poetry received, he gained entrée into the world of lecturing as well. However, the most important aspect of his life was his job at the Old Corner Bookstore. Impressed by his hard work and ability to understand the business, William Ticknor encouraged him to assume more responsibility, so that by his twenty-first birthday he was the store's senior clerk. In 1840, James persuaded Ticknor to convert the Old Corner from a bookstore into a publishing house, where his talent for attracting clients became evident. Three years later, he became a junior partner at Ticknor, Reed & Co., the precursor of Ticknor and Fields. Their clients included Whittier, Holmes, Lowell, and Longfellow. As America's most popular poets, they assured the firms' preeminent position in the world of publishing.

With James Fields's charm and William Ticknor's money, the company expanded. In 1847, James made his first trip to Europe, where he met authors who would become important social and business friends, including Mary Mitford and William Wordsworth. In 1850, he scored the greatest literary coup of his career. In an oft-repeated story, he went to see Nathaniel Hawthorne after Hawthorne had lost his job at the Custom House and asked if he had written anything since the publication of *Twice-Told Tales*. Somehow he managed to wheedle out of Hawthorne that he had another manuscript, which turned out to be *The Scarlet Letter*. The publication of *The Scarlet Letter* was one of the most important events in American literary history, and one more indication of James's business acumen.

James T. Fields's influence on the dissemination of culture in New England and the creation of an economic foundation for Boston's literary development was impressive; he was able to supply the American reading public with the quality literature it wanted, and he provided his authors with the income they needed. Unfortunately, while Fields's career was blossoming, his personal life was filled with tragedy. When he was twenty-nine, his fiancée, Mary Gannett, died; in 1850, at age thirty-two, he married her eighteen-year-old sister, Eliza, who passed away a year later. To assuage his grief, he made a second tour of Europe, during which he solidified his contacts with Thackeray, Browning, Carlyle, and Dickens.

Two years after his return from Europe, James began wooing his late wife's cousin, Annie Adams, who was seventeen years younger than he. In October 1854 they were engaged, and on November 15 they were married. While giving lip service to the tradition of subordinate roles for wives in nineteenth-century marriages, they, in fact, had a marriage that could be considered a partnership. He introduced Annie to the world of literary society, where she became the ideal hostess, advancing his career through her warmth, intelligence, and propriety. She also collaborated with him in his editorial duties by helping to attract new talent, reviewing manuscripts, and acting as an intermediary with bothersome clients. James relied upon Annie's editorial judgment, encouraged her to write, and supported her civic and charitable interests. For years, Annie wrote hundreds of poems for every occasion—anniversaries, birthdays, holidays—which she preserved in a series of blue notebooks. According to Rita Gollin, her poetry was representative of the period, "tightly structured, passionately moral, confident and humane."[12] It was published in the *Atlantic* and other magazines, receiving polite, but often unenthusiastic, reviews. She also wrote several books, including *Authors and Friends* (1922), a memoir of the many famous people she knew, including Celia. Her most important book, *How to Help the Poor* (1883), foreshadowed modern social work theory; it sold over twenty-two thousand copies within two years.

In the years after his marriage, James's career flourished as Ticknor and Fields's reputation grew. In June 1861, three months after Thaxter's "Landlocked" was published, he was appointed editor of the *Atlantic Monthly*, succeeding James Russell Lowell, who had held the position since its founding in 1857. In his new role, James made plans to broaden the readership through new, young contributors like Thaxter, whose writing had more popular appeal. His innovations were successful, and circulation rose from thirty-two thousand in 1863 to fifty thousand in 1870.[13] In addition, business at Ticknor and Fields could not have been better: five major periodicals and thousands of books were being published; throngs of customers crowded the company showroom; James was besieged with visitors. As one of Fields's favorite authors, Celia's success was assured.

For Thaxter, the most remarkable part of her new life was her invitations to the Fieldses' home at 148 Charles Street in Boston. Annie, who is remembered most for her literary salon, believed that her primary responsibility was to make her home a haven for the authors her husband represented. According to Josephine Donovan, 148 Charles Street became "a veritable hospice for aspiring, as well as established, authors."[14] Annie's celebrated breakfasts and dinner parties were the center of the social life of Boston's literati.

What did Celia Thaxter find when she entered that door at 148 Charles Street? First, she must have noticed the ambience of an earlier age. The young Willa Cather, the urbane Henry James, and the peripatetic Charles Dickens all recorded how 148 Charles Street was a link with the past, a symbol of refinement and culture.[15] It reflected a way of life that Thaxter had never known. Then, she must have been thrilled to meet many of the authors whose work she and Levi had been reading, writers who treated her with the dignity and respect they accorded one another and which she had not gotten from Levi. After the flattering reception she received, her life in Newtonville appeared even more dreary and oppressive.

Annie was the ideal hostess, eager to nurture feelings of connection and, empathy among her guests, particularly among women writers. "It was the one place that women writers, excluded from the network of male clubs, could meet on an equal footing with male writers and publishers," wrote Harriet Beecher Stowe's biographer Joan Hedrick.[16] In addition to Celia, Annie encouraged the careers of Gail Hamilton, Louise Guiney, Rebecca Harding Davis, and Lucy Larcom. As their friendship developed, Thaxter valued Annie's opinion highly and frequently sent her manuscripts to evaluate. In return, she read and commented (always favorably) upon anything Annie wrote.

The invitations to 148 Charles Street cemented Celia's relationship with Annie Fields. Here was a woman from a completely different walk of life, without the family responsibilities that burdened her, but who shared many of the same frustrations. Both—for very different reasons—had little time to write; both were greatly attached to their mothers; both cared deeply for their friends. What ensured their friendship was the gift of sympathy. The idea of a gift of sympathy, the ability to give and receive in an empathetic relationship, is central to understanding Thaxter and Fields's friendship. It is the lens through which their affection for one another is enlarged and clarified. Annie Fields was the embodiment of this idea, which explains her skill in making her home a haven for aspiring authors and illuminates her relationships with the wide variety of men and women who constituted her circles of friends. Gradually her gift of sympathy touched even more people as she became a leader in emerging educational, social, and philanthropic reforms. Her ability to empathize did not diminish as she grew older; until the end of her life, she was surrounded by loving friends.

Thaxter was blessed with the gift of sympathy as well. It was evident in her concern not only for her family and friends but for her Norwegian neighbors on the Isles of Shoals and for the unknown victims of the innumerable shipwrecks she witnessed. Becoming Annie's friend validated her feelings; in Fields, Celia found a loyal supporter and a professional, honest critic of her work. A whole new world was at her doorstep, a world she embraced with all the energy she could muster after the needs of her family were met.

During the years following the publication of "Land-locked" in 1861, Thaxter spent as much time with Annie as possible. It was difficult because these years were fraught with domestic problems and family responsibilities, yet somehow she always found time to see her friend, and their friendship flourished.

5 Coming of Age, 1862–1868

It seems as if I had made a great leap from a child into a mother.[1]

—CELIA THAXTER TO SARAH WEISS,
2 July 1852

THE EASE WITH WHICH THAXTER WAS ABLE TO LEAVE HER HOME AND FAMILY, HER "POTS and kettles,"[2] and blend into the sophisticated world of 148 Charles Street is intriguing. Like a nineteenth-century Cinderella, she was able to forget her family pressures and enjoy evenings surrounded by Boston's famous men and women at the opera, at lectures, and at Annie's salon. The drudgery of her days as a housewife and mother was in sharp contrast to her stimulating evenings.

Thaxter's most pressing day-to-day problems involved her immediate family: Karl, handicapped from birth; John, the quintessential middle child; and Roland, beloved and sickly. In addition, she was beginning to realize that she and Levi were growing farther and farther apart. Anxiety about her family exhausted her both emotionally and physically.

To understand Celia and her relationship with her children, it is helpful to envision what life was like in the Thaxter household. The difficulties with Karl were most obvious. Physically, he suffered from weak eyes and a limp, which added to his poor self-image. He was not mentally retarded: eventually he went to school, attended the opera, learned to run a printing press, and took photographs, but his behavior was unpredictable. When he was very young, Celia lived in fear that Levi would place Karl in an institution, so she assumed the major responsibility for him. However, there can be no doubt that Levi loved him and helped by taking over much of the care of John and Roland. When Karl was eight, Celia wrote from Appledore to her friend Mary Lawson:

You will wonder how I could leave Levi & my other chicks so long, but Levi wished us very much to come, especially for Karl's sake & he is thankful to get rid of the anxiety & worry of Karl himself, for a while. And an excellent girl takes excellent care of them all, so I feel quite easy about them. Karly is a different being here—living out of doors in the air which is the health of life to him, he grows sturdy & quiet & all his flying nerves are soothed into a delightful state of calm. I never saw so horribly nervous a person in my life—I'm sure he doesn't get it from me, for I haven't any nerves in the common acceptance of the word. Well, he rows in his boat all the day long & is happier than any king . . . he fishes & he drives in the flock of cows for milking & he digs his "riverlets," as he calls them, in the wet sand in the upper cove, & he sails boats & leads a life of bliss generally & is petted & praised by all his kin until his eyes are wide with amazement, that being a kind of thing he isn't at all used to, you know.[3]

At this time, Celia and Levi were working together to find a way to adjust to Karl's "nervousness." Throughout the rest of his life, the Isles of Shoals provided a respite for him.

John's earliest years were difficult because so much attention was focused on his two brothers. Yet he, too, had problems, particularly in the area of academics. In a letter to his mother in April 1863, when he was nine years old, he tried to print neatly, but his difficulty with spelling and writing was already apparent: "Dear mama papa has got a new saddle and bridel [sic], and he is going to ta-ke [sic] us all to ride horse back . . . polly has gone home to her sisters today and wont [sic] be back till next saterday [sic]. your affectionate son."[4] Like his brothers, he was home-schooled and later attended a school in town, but there seemed to be no thought of his going to college.

Roland, nicknamed Lony, was his parents' favorite. When he was four, Celia wrote to her friend Sarah Weiss:

How is Roland, you asked. . . . Roland is heavenly, Roland is bewitching, Roland is the joy and pride and delight of our lives. I tell Levi I am afraid it's a sin to dote on anything as we do on Lony . . . especially as Levi does. I never did see such a weak minded Pater Familias. If Lony has a mind to call sixteen times from his crib . . . while we are at tea, "Papa I want to kiss you," sixteen times will Levi rise up in a rapture and go and kiss him. . . . Every morning I take the little fellow out for his and my airing, and he has such superb color and looks so lovely in his little shaggy coat and dark blue cap. . . . When there is coasting, we coast, but today we went into the quiet pine woods and . . . filled his little basket.[5]

Still, many of Celia's earliest worries were about Lony's health; he was always a delicate child, with more than his share of sickness. When he was only three, he almost died of what the doctor called "diphtherial croup."[6] Throughout his life he continued to be plagued with a variety of other illnesses: an unexplained fever in Florida, knee surgery after college, gastric ulcers as an adult.

Levi worked hard to provide the boys with a thorough education in science; however, his enthusiasm sometimes backfired, as Celia explained to her friend Lizzie:

> Roland reverently gathered a skunk cabbage flower and carried it up to school in West Newton, to the teacher of botany in whose class he was a pupil, and she hove it out of the window with speed, and said she never saw it before and never wished to see it again. . . . Imagine Levi's extreme disgust! . . .[7]

In the same letter, Celia also voiced her objection to some of Levi's methods:

> The boys and Levi have guns and go murdering round the country in the name of science till my heart is broken into shreds. They are horribly learned, but that doesn't compensate for one little life destroyed, in my woman's way of viewing it.[8]

Thaxter's description of her objection to hunting in terms of a woman's point of view is what today would be called ecofeminism.

A further problem Celia faced during these years was the realization that her marriage was deteriorating. This was caused by many factors, beginning with the dramatic event in the fall of 1855 when Levi and Oscar almost drowned and Levi sold Thomas his remaining fifty acres on the island and the little cottage where he and Celia had lived since their marriage. There can be no doubt that Celia was distressed at the loss of their first home on Appledore, but she was powerless to stop him since she owned neither the land nor the cottage. When they moved into their Newtonville home, Levi, who had vowed not to return to Appledore, found the perfect excuse for his family to stay on the mainland. For more than a year, Celia was unable to visit Appledore, because their large house and yard required constant work. Over the years, Levi changed his mind about not going to the islands, but he went only rarely, preferring to vacation in Maine or Canada. By 1863, Roland and John were old enough to accompany him, setting the stage for the separate lives he and Celia were beginning to live.

There were financial issues as well. Initially, Celia did not seem to mind that Levi did not have an occupation. They subsisted on gifts from Levi's father and, after 1861, on money Celia earned from her writing. But as the years went by, the stress caused by their irregular income began to take its toll. A hundred years after Celia's birth, Jean Stafford wrote: "Being a writer and being married is a back-breaking job and my back is now broken. I've now decided that writers shouldn't be married and certainly women writers shouldn't be unless they are married to rich, responsible husbands who fill their house with servants."[9] While Celia would not have articulated her feelings quite this way, she certainly would have been happier with a wealthier and more dependable husband—or at least one who made some regular financial contribution to his family.

These years were difficult for the children as well as for the parents. That the boys were home-schooled for the most part was not unusual, but that the younger ones endured long separations from their mother must have been disturbing. Despite her constant expressions of love and concern, Celia committed only a limited amount of her time to John and Roland. One reason was that she was simply overwhelmed by her responsibilities. She had three children by the time she was twenty-three; her husband seemed unable to find an occupation; she was frightened by the financial burdens she constantly faced; and she assumed that she would be Karl's caretaker for his entire life. Therefore, it became imperative that she pursue her writing career with dogged determination, which she did. Encouraged by the reception she received from Annie and James Fields and the readers of the *Atlantic*, she worked endlessly during the years following the publication of "Land-locked."

Considering all the demands upon her time, the quality of Thaxter's poetry during the early 1860s is impressive. Drawing upon her childhood experiences, her poems were original and imaginative. Annie Fields praised her enthusiastically, and James was eager to publish her work. Yet Jane Vallier, who has analyzed Celia's poetry, believes that the Fieldses' influence eventually led to stagnation in her poetic imagination and hindered rather than helped her professional growth:

> Thaxter's earliest poems were remarkable for their freedom from moralizing and sensuality, but as the influence of James and Annie Fields grew, so did the didacticism of Celia's poems. Before she was drawn into the Fields' social and literary life, Celia had only Levi Thaxter and his tastes for Browning and the Pre-Raphaelites to guide her. If Celia's first poem "Land-locked" had marked the beginning, not the height which her poetry might reach, one can only speculate where her talent might have taken her.[10]

However, all the blame cannot be placed on Annie and James. Thaxter instinctively espoused the ideas of the Fireside Poets—John Greenleaf Whittier, Henry Wadsworth Longfellow, and Oliver Wendell Holmes—whose writing celebrated the virtues of home and hearth. Like Annie, they embodied those traits synonymous with gentility that Celia so admired. She shared their optimism, didacticism, and preference for a conventional style of writing. She also agreed with their female counterparts: Lucy Larcom, Elizabeth Stuart Phelps, and Mary Mapes Dodge. Where she parted company with these women was in her relationship to Christianity; she never embraced their traditional viewpoint, but instead developed a nontraditional religion, grounded in nature, spiritualism, and Eastern beliefs.

The Fireside Poets envisioned their poems being read at family gatherings by the fireside. What better venue for Longfellow's "Paul Revere's Ride," Holmes's "The Deacon's Masterpiece," and Whittier's "Snow-Bound"? Influenced by Browning's dramatic monologues, which Levi read, and by the Fireside Poets, Thaxter also wrote with the idea of performing her poetry. Her daily readings were one of the highlights of her summer salon. Unfortunately, her fondness for performing sometimes served to hinder her poetic development. As Vallier writes: "She read her own poetry first and foremost, and this is perhaps one reason why she did not polish the written versions of all of her poems, especially the later ones. They came to life in oral performance, not on the written page."[11]

In her earliest poems, Thaxter dwelled on her sadness and loneliness. By 1865, she had begun to turn to the wealth of inspiration she derived from the Isles of

Shoals. "The Spaniards' Graves" is one of her most engaging poems. Standing at the graves of shipwrecked sailors (probably from the wreck of the *Sagunto* in 1813),[12] the female narrator reaches across the boundaries of time and space to empathize with the grieving women:

> Wives, mothers, maidens, wistfully, in vain
> > Questioned the distance for the yearning sail,
> That, leaning landward, should have stretched again
> > White arms wide on the gale,
> To bring back their beloved. Year by year,
> > Weary they watched, till youth and beauty passed,
> And lustrous eyes grew dim and age drew near,
> > And hope was dead at last. . . .

In the final verse, she assures them that she is watching over the graves of their loved ones:

> Dear dark-eyed sisters, you remember yet
> > These you have lost, but you can never know
> One stands at their bleak graves whose eyes are wet
> > With thinking of your woe![13]

"The Wreck of the Pocahontas" (1867) was another popular early poem. As in "Watching," the child narrator is lighting lamps, but this time a storm appears, which is so violent that the islanders are isolated for weeks and a ship, the *Pocahontas*, is destroyed on the rocks. In *Among the Isles of Shoals*, Thaxter describes how she actually witnessed this storm in 1839 when she was living on White Island.[14] The child in the poem—like Thaxter herself—struggles to find meaning in the dichotomy between nature's beauty and nature's destructiveness, until she hears "a voice eternal" telling her to accept "Life's rapture and life's ill."[15]

In 1863, Levi, pursuing his interest in ornithology, decided to explore Grand Manan Island in Canada. Thus, Celia was able to return for an extended visit to Appledore. By this time, however, her role had changed, as this letter to Kate Field[16] makes clear:

> Thank you for your letter, you were good to write. I wish I were having such a lazy time as you're having! Dear me, what fun it must be to do just what one likes and nothing, if one chooses. But in the first

place I have three ruffians to take care of in the shape of my dear and innocent offspring. In the next place I am staying with mama and papa and the latter has had a paralytic stroke which renders him very nearly helpless, so that it is my duty and my pleasure to be ready at his call. Then we keep house and have only one small Irish handmaiden, so that the greater part of the work falls on me. Then there are 300 souls, I was going to say bodies, I mean, to be fed at the hotel and one kitchen establishment hardly sufficient so that mother and I vary the scene by making a bushel or two of doughnuts and several stacks of sponge cakes. The fact is I seldom if ever get one free hour during the day.[17]

The original hotel had grown to accommodate over 250 guests, and Celia's responsibilities had expanded as well. In addition to nursing her father, she cared for her three young children and assisted her mother with the cooking. Day after day they baked wonderful pies, cakes, and other sweets in addition to the doughnuts and sponge cakes.[18] Celia's recipe for "Graham Pies," which "can be eaten by any dyspeptic," appeared in *The Appledore Cook Book*.[19]

By now, word of the hotel had spread to musicians, artists, and writers. Among the guests was pianist William Mason (1829–1908), who described how the hotel appealed to those who sought peace and quiet, rather than sociability:

My first visit to Appledore was in August 1863, two of my brothers having discovered the island, so to speak, the year before. We were enthusiastic fishermen, and during our summer vacation almost lived on the ocean. Furthermore, during almost the entire year I was engaged in teaching or in public appearances as a concert-player, so that in my vacation I detested the very sight or even thought of a pianoforte. Appledore afforded an ideal retreat where retirement verging almost on oblivion was possible, and thus it happened that I had spent many summers there before my musical vocation was brought to light.[20]

While the presence of visitors like William Mason must have been exciting, by the end of this summer Thaxter was exhausted. Levi offered to take Roland and John home while Celia and Karl remained for a week. This respite provided a much needed return to her childhood; she and her brother Cedric rowed and sailed each day, even visiting White Island. The islands still enchanted her:

We spread our little spritsail and flitted across—it was so beautiful, the water so cool and clear, the faint wind so perfectly delicious with its sea-scents. Every sail on the horizon filled me with a kind of inexpressible joy. I'm sure I don't know why, but they always do. We stayed there all morning and went to all our dear old haunts and I wished I could go back and live there forever.[21]

With Thomas Laighton's death in 1866, Oscar, then twenty-seven, and Cedric, twenty-six, inherited Appledore House. In his will, their father left Eliza the house they had built in 1863 and "$800 a year to be paid by sons Oscar and Cedric out of the devise." To Celia, he left "$5,200.00 to be paid by Oscar and Cedric out of the property bequeathed them to be paid in five equal payments. . . . All the rest and residue to Oscar and Cedric, subject only to payment of above legacies and subject to life estate of mother in house and land."[22] The probable (and thoughtful) reason Thomas did not bequeath land to Celia was that an outright gift of money was shielded from the laws of dower, inheritance laws that in the nineteenth century placed legal limitations on married women owning real property alone.[23]

Although the brothers appeared naive and unaccustomed to the outside world, the resort prospered. With their parents' Yankee trader instincts, their charm, and the unqualified support (and free labor) of their mother and sister, they were successful for many years. While they always depended on Celia's help in managing their ever growing hotel, she also never refused—not only because Appledore was a refuge but because she enjoyed the daily challenges, the opportunities to meet exciting guests, the freedom from the restrictions of life on land.

Throughout her adult life, Thaxter returned to the Isles of Shoals whenever she could. Some siren sang to her from these islands, luring her to those rocky shores year after year. While she needed the solace of home and family, there was something else as well. On this barren soil, a magnificent garden filled with flowers of every hue flourished. In this same isolated spot, where she had spent her happy childhood, a summer resort now thrived, a watering spot for many of the nineteenth century's most prominent citizens. The garden, the memories, the guests at Appledore House, the opportunity to leave the demands of the mainland behind, despite the other demands she faced on the island, enticed Celia. Above all else, she was a poet and an artist who needed not just a room of her own but an island of her own.

In the summer of 1866, Annie and James Fields sailed to the Isles of Shoals for the first time, joining the long list of enthusiastic visitors to Appledore House. During the winter, Thaxter's visits to 148 Charles Street continued, and her friendship with the Fieldses grew as she responded to the empathy that dwelled beneath their air of sophistication.

When the first signs of her dissatisfaction with her married life began to appear, Celia was able to disclose them to James: "The rhymes in my head are all that keep me alive, I do believe, lifting me in a half unconscious condition over the ashes heap, so that I don't half realize how dry and dusty it is! . . . I wish you'd tell Annie that I have had infinite satisfaction and refreshment out of her tickets already, and forget all weariness and perplexity on the crest of a breaker of earthly bliss while Emerson discourses."[24]

Thaxter's friendship with James was based on mutual admiration: hers for his position in the literary and social world of Boston, his for her skill, charm, and devotion to his wife. Moreover, he must have admired her self-confidence when she displayed enough self-assurance to challenge his editorial decisions. Just a year after "Land-locked" was published, she wrote:

> I thank you very much for the kind things you have said about my lit-
> tle poem and am grateful for the trouble you took in looking it over
> and making suggestions. I am sorry I could not act upon them all. I am
> not good at making alterations. The only merit of my small produc-
> tions lies in their straight forward simplicity, and when that bloom is
> rubbed off by the effort to better them, they lose what little good they
> originally possessed.[25]

Recognizing Thaxter's appeal for his nineteenth-century readers, Fields acqui-esced to most of her suggestions. During his ten years as publisher of the *Atlantic*, he published fifteen of her poems; much to his delight, she became one of the *Atlantic*'s most popular woman poets.

One of the most exciting times in Thaxter's new life began in November 1866, when Charles Dickens arrived in Boston to begin his American reading tour, which James had arranged. For the next five months, Dickens and his needs dominated the Fieldses' lives. Annie was attracted by both the charm and the dependency of the man she called "the Great Enchanter." Motivated originally by business interests, James experienced an unusual bonding with Dickens, who could be as warm, outgoing, and fun-loving as himself. Celia and Levi

were overjoyed when they received an invitation to attend a dinner party with
the distinguished visitor in January. Annie described the occasion in her diary:
"Sunday night dinner went off brilliantly. Longfellow, Appleton [artist John
Appleton Brown], and Mr. and Mrs. Thaxter came to meet 'the chief' and ourselves. . . . Mrs. Thaxter's stories took strong hold on Dickens's fancy, and he
told me afterward that when he awakened in the night he thought of her."[26]
Although she must have been awed by Dickens's presence, Thaxter apparently
displayed the same self-confidence in her conversations with him as she did
when she first met Hawthorne.

In April they attended another party, where guests again included John
Appleton Brown and Henry Wadsworth Longfellow and his daughter Alice, as
well as William Morris Hunt and his wife, Louisa, Ralph Waldo Emerson and
his daughter Ellen, and Dr. Oliver Wendell Holmes.[27] As Thaxter reported to
a friend:

> We have been into town rather oftener than usual, there has been so
> much going on. One evening we dined with Mr. Dickens at Mr.
> Fields' house and sat down to dinner at six o'clock and didn't rise from
> the table till eleven at night! I stayed in town, but Mr. Thaxter missed
> his last train, as did Mr. Longfellow, and they walked out to Cam-
> bridge together, and then Mr. Thaxter walked on to Newtonville and
> got home about two o'clock in the morning. We had a splendid time,
> and he doesn't mind walking, you know.[28]

Whatever jealousy Levi endured because of Celia's success was tempered by
opportunities to spend evenings such as these.

James Fields was just one of Celia's close male friends. John Greenleaf Whittier
(1807–1892) played an important role in her life, too. Both men were consid-
erably older than she and undoubtedly served as father figures. Her own father,
who had been a strong, positive influence upon her, died in 1866, the year
Thaxter renewed her friendship with Whittier and began to strengthen her ties
with Fields. Even more important, she felt a genuine affection for them, which
each reciprocated.

Celia met Whittier when she and Levi lived at Artichoke Mills. Their earlier
acquaintance blossomed again in the summers of 1863 and 1866 when he was
a guest at Appledore House, and they were able to spend many hours together.
Despite the disparity in their ages (he was sixty and already in frail health and

she was thirty-two), their friendship developed quickly and continued until his death in 1892, just two years before her own.

The best description of this quiet, charming man occurs in his own poem "The Tent on the Beach":

> And one there was, a dreamer born,
> > Who, with a mission to fulfil,
> Had left the Muses' haunts to turn
> > The crank of an opinion-mill,
> Making his rustic reed of song
> A weapon in the war with wrong,
> Yoking his fancy to the breaking-plough
> That beam-deep turned the soil for truth
> > to spring and grow. . . .[29]

Whittier's transformation from poet to warrior developed from his deep commitment to the Quaker religion. His religious beliefs provided the foundation for his dedication to social justice for American Indians and African slaves, his support of equal rights for women, his commitment to nonviolence, and his objection to capital punishment.[30]

Despite his professed shyness ("A silent, shy, peace-loving man")[31] and his sometimes delicate physical and mental health, Whittier was clearly a political activist, speaking out against the repeal of the Missouri Compromise, the Fugitive Slave Law, and the Dred Scott decision. His poem "Ichabod" was a scathing indictment of Daniel Webster's support for the Fugitive Slave Law:

> So fallen! So lost! The light withdrawn
> > Which once he wore!
> The glory from his gray hairs gone
> > Forevermore![32]

Whittier wrote poetry throughout his life. By 1843, he had attracted the attention of James Fields, who subsequently published all his work, including his contributions to the newly founded *Atlantic Monthly*. His association with James led to fame, fortune, and a lifelong friendship with Annie. It was in the October 1863 *Atlantic* that his most famous Civil War poem, "Barbara Frietchie," appeared. Thaxter, who eagerly read the *Atlantic* each month, wrote him: "Barbara Frietchie made a great enthusiasm in this family. Our oldest boy copied it into his book of poetry along with 'The Charge of the Light Brigade.' . . ."[33]

After the Civil War ended, Whittier helped former slaves find jobs and became one of the supporters of the Hampton Institute in Virginia, which educated black and Native American youths. He also became an activist in the suffrage movement, advocating for a woman's right to vote and working for higher education for women. In 1875 he helped found Wellesley College, and in 1881 he was appointed a trustee of Brown University, where Pembroke College for Women opened ten years later.

There has been a great deal of speculation about Whittier's decision to remain a bachelor. His biographer John Pollard commented that "Whittier probably thought more and did less about marriage than about anything else in life."[34] Described by his contemporaries as handsome, shy, and charming, he had many female friends, yet he decided early in life to remain single. He accepted his bachelorhood with good humor, encouraged his friends to marry, and seemed to enjoy a fulfilling social life. What went on within his mind, no one will ever know, although—as Robert Penn Warren points out—"there was some deep inner conflict in Whittier, with fits of self-pity and depression, breakdowns and withdrawals from the world, violent chronic headaches and insomnia."[35] Perhaps this needy side of his nature added to his appeal to the women to whom he endeared himself. Women writers in particular were among his closest friends; Gail Hamilton, Lucy Larcom, Harriet Beecher Stowe, Lydia Maria Child, Sarah Orne Jewett—and, of course, Celia Thaxter—were the lucky recipients of his friendship and caring advice.

Thaxter could not help being flattered by the attention of one of America's foremost poets. Each of his many letters concluded with "Thy Friend," and each of her letters was filled with concern for his well-being. A few of his letters to Thaxter contained suggestions for improving her poems: "There are verses in thy poem in the Atlantic which are the best and strongest thee ever wrote. Thy "Discontent" is liable to the fault of being too good, too preachy, like some of my sermons. "For Thoughts" is not so good and yet a great deal better, full of grace and passion and beauty. . . ."[36] But most were filled with compliments: "I know of no one who so well describes the sea and sky and the wild island scenery. Thy pictures glow with life and color. I am only afraid that I shall be tempted to appropriate them some time, they so exactly express what I feel but cannot say. . . . As a Quaker, thee knows, I cannot have anything to do with the old heathen Nine, and so I have made thee serve my purpose as a sort of tenth Muse. I could not have a better."[37]

After the publication of "The Wreck of the Pocahontas," which received much acclaim, Thaxter received this letter from Whittier:

> My dear friend,
>
> I suspect thee are in the predicament of the man who says he "woked up one morning and found himself famous." But, I hope thee will still recognize thy old friends when thee meet them. . . . Don't set up for

a strong-minded woman. But surely, the poem in the Atlantic is liked
by everybody, and all the more that its author is not a writer by profession. It is so pleasant to know that such things can be done by a
woman who looks to her own household, and makes her fireside circle happy, and knows how to render lighter her daily cares and
labors by throwing over them the charm of her free idealization.
I think men are inclined to deprecate the idea of a literary woman.
But when the charm of true womanliness is preserved, when the
heart's warmth is not absorbed by the intellect, and to this is added
the power to move the public heart and satisfy the demands of the
highest taste and culture, what can we do but admire and say God-
speed!

Indeed, I don't believe in anybody's making literature the great
aim of life. Greater than all books is man or woman. . . .[38]

How should we interpret this letter? Surely Whittier meant to compliment
Thaxter; surely she saw it as a compliment. For modern feminists, the phrase
"true womanliness" may seem to be unflattering, but taken in the context of its
time, this letter was a remarkable statement of support. Whittier criticized men
who "deprecate the idea of a literary woman." He asked only that the heart not
be sacrificed to the "head." In fact, he went one step further and said that he did
not believe in *anybody* "making literature the great aim of life" and insisted that
humankind is greater than all books. For a young woman beginning her career,
pleased by her initial success, yet in need of male approval to make up for her
husband's grudging praise, this letter was indeed a godsend.

One way Thaxter reciprocated Whittier's kindness was by commemorating
his birthdays with poems, the most charming of which she wrote for his eight-
ieth birthday in 1887:

> Old friend, dear friend, in summer days gone by
> > You brought me roses delicate and fair.
> > That blossomed wild in our New England air.
> And they are fragrant still, though dead and dry.
> Now, when for us comes winter on apace,
> > Within the garden of my thought there grows
> > For you a fadeless flower, as sweet a rose
> As ever summer wore with youthful grace. . . .[39]

Annie and James were the friends Thaxter visited most often; Whittier she saw
as frequently as possible. However, as her family responsibilities grew and as
the necessity for earning money increased, other friendships became largely
epistolary. In her correspondence, Thaxter expressed her distress at not seeing
these friends more frequently, shared everyday events in her life, and revealed
a compassionate concern for the lives of these women that transcended the
miles that separated them. Helen Heineman, author of *Restless Angels: The Friendship of Six Victorian Women*, describes the importance of epistolary friendships to
Victorian women:

> Their commitment to a mutual correspondence kept them sensitive to
> the quality of one another's experience and made them friends for life,
> though their futures were widely divergent. . . . These familiar letters
> unlock the inner lives of women, moving the reader beyond the evi-
> dence of statistics or cultural artifacts in tracing the dawning con-
> sciousness of a shared female condition.[40]

For nineteenth-century women, corresponding was more than a commitment; it was a substitute for a visit. Most women enjoyed writing letters, mail
service was frequent (often a letter written in the morning was delivered by the
afternoon), and letters were eagerly anticipated. Thanks to their correspondence, friends felt less isolated, because they were able to share their joys and
sorrows without the necessity of being face to face.

Thaxter's letters provide insights into many of her private thoughts. To Sarah
Weiss, her confidante from her earliest days as a wife and mother, Celia often
wrote of her longing to return to her beloved islands. Year after year, she
shared her worries about her children, described her own illnesses, and wrote
of day-to-day happenings. One very early letter is compelling; Rosamond
Thaxter discovered it and marked it "too personal to copy." Written from the
Shoals, the letter has several pages that are not in sequence but were placed
together in the file. It begins: "Sarah darling—was ever anybody so stupid
before! How *horrid*. I wonder if I ever did such a thing before. I always thought
I was a fool, now I know it. I don't owe you a note, but I wished to express my
disgust at myself & also to tell you that everything was tranquil & peaceful—
and that L. was going to put poor Karly in some safe good place right off, but
I begged him to wait a couple of months or so, for I feared the effect so terrible a (   )." The next page appears to be out of order, but it begins with "sadly
afraid he will never come back."[41] It is intriguing to speculate about what
Thaxter might have said or done to evoke such a letter—perhaps she herself,
in a moment of desperation, suggested placing Karl in a home, as she says Levi

had done. The stress this difficult child placed on his young mother must have been enormous!

Other letters were more upbeat; one to Mary Lawson, a neighbor who apparently moved away, is fun to read. Thaxter was still happy in her marriage; she was excited by her friendship with James and Annie; she was enjoying her children. This letter reflects Celia as a young wife and mother, up-and-coming author, and caring friend:

> . . . We were all delighted with the baby's picture. What a dear little thing she must be! . . . And Jenny, too, and pretty little Florence. I suppose they have grown ever so much. Mr. Thaxter sent two books for them a week ago. . . . I haven't seen a soul in the village all winter except poor Mrs. Lane, whose husband committed the forgery, you know, and left her almost heartbroken. But we have been into town rather oftener than usual, there has been so much going on. . . .
>
> Roland has got a gun as well as John, tell Jenny, and the other day he went out the lane and shot a cat nearly as big as himself and came in with it by the tail, as old as Methuselah and calm as a clock. Not a bit excited by the performance. He goes out shooting with his father and they scour the country for game. It breaks my heart to have them kill the birds, but they don't shoot a great many. . . . Mr. Thaxter sends much love to you and the children. . . . With much love to yourself and kind remembrances to your mother and father.[42]

Thaxter's letters to her friends reveal her need to be connected to a caring group of women. In the tradition of self-reliance that dominated nineteenth-century life, Ralph Waldo Emerson wrote: "It is simpler to be self-dependent. The height, the deity of man is to be self-sustained, to need no gift, no foreign force. Society is good when it does not violate me, but best when it is likest to solitude."[43] An admiring Whitman echoed the sentiment: "One's Self I sing, a simple separate person."[44] In contrast with Emerson, Whitman, Thoreau, and other male writers of this time, Thaxter and her friends found fulfillment in their lives through their gift of sympathy, their ability to empathize with others.[45] It is important to view the nineteenth century from this standpoint of human connection, as well from the traditional belief in self-reliance. This perspective adds a new dimension to our appreciation of the lives of the gifted authors, talented artists, and loving wives and mothers who were part of Thaxter's ever widening circle.

Current theories of the psychodynamics of female friendship provide an understanding of the role of connection in women's lives. New hypotheses about women's development emerged in the 1970s as a result of studies indicating that there are substantial differences between men's and women's psychological experiences and their development of self. These guidelines for analyzing women's emotional growth are in opposition to Freudian and other male-oriented theories. Carol Gilligan, author of *In a Different Voice* (1982), presented valuable insights into this approach. For her, the "different voice" can be discovered by observing the emotional development in women: "In the different voice of women lies the truth of an ethic of care, the tie between relationship and responsibility, and the origins of aggression in the failure of connection."[46] In contrast with the emphasis men place on individuality, she believes that women evolve through connection, and she emphasizes its centrality as a woman matures.

For Thaxter, these bonds were particularly important. Like many traditional nineteenth-century women, she began life with the expectation that she would be dependent upon men most of her life, first as a daughter, then as a wife. This perception began to change when her success as a poet led to new feelings of self-esteem. As she came to recognize Levi's shortcomings, she began to seek other close relationships in which she was empowered rather than dependent. As part of Annie's inner circle of friends and as hostess of her own salon, Thaxter gained power—not the traditional notion of power but the kind described by the modern feminist writer Carolyn Heilbrun: "The true representation of power is not of a big man beating a smaller man or a woman. Power is the ability to take one's place in whatever discourse is essential to action and the right to have one's part matter. This is true in the Pentagon, in marriage, in friendship, and in politics."[47]

Being in a position of power had not been part of the conventional role for women: cooperation, not competition, was the feminine paradigm. But the need for empowerment was beginning to grow among women writers. James Fields and his male friends, particularly Hawthorne, Emerson, Holmes, Whittier, and Dickens, had an abundance of political, literary, and social power. It was different for female authors. As social and literary critic Ann Douglas wrote in *The Feminization of American Culture*:

> . . . both women and ministers had special reasons for being attracted
> to a literary career, yet it is nonetheless true that such a career gave
> the women, as it did not the ministers, a first glimpse of the privileges
> that professional life could bestow: an independent income, a group

of friends outside the family circle, and self-sufficient creative activity beyond the procreation of children.[48]

In other words, these women gained a feeling of empowerment through their newly earned money, independence, and, most important, friendships. Under nineteenth-century laws, women had no legal identity separate from their husbands and fathers. Having her own income enabled Thaxter not only to feel independent; it actually gave her a degree of independence. In addition, her friendships fostered self-confidence and provided a connection with women who shared her goals and valued her ideas. Striving for recognition in nineteenth-century America was a difficult and undesirable task for a woman alone; the empowerment gained through female connectedness helped to pave the way for a talented woman like Celia Thaxter. Annie Fields acknowledged this when she wrote of "the power that lies in friendship to sustain the giver as well as the receiver."[49] Through the gift of sympathy, Thaxter's life and the lives of her friends were enhanced.

6 *The Difficult Years, 1868–1877*

You would never know now that she had been a spray sprite,
and danced among the breakers, and talked and laughed with
the loons, for she is like everybody else, except that, sleeping
or waking, year after year, she keeps in her ears the sad, mysterious murmur of the sea, just like a hollow shell.[1]

—CELIA THAXTER, *Stories and Poems for Children*

As THE YEAR 1868 BEGAN, THAXTER SUMMARIZED HER FAMILY LIFE TO HER FRIEND MARY
Lawson:

> . . . Mr. Thaxter has not been well this winter, has suffered from rheu-
> matism, and rheumatism in the chest, which isn't a good place to have
> it. He declares he never will spend another winter in this climate. I
> have an addition to my family in the shape of a young Hungarian by
> the name of Ignatius Grossman, about fifteen years old. We have taken
> him for good. He is a lovely boy and a great comfort. . . . The Thaxter
> boys are as rampageous as usual. Karl and Ignatius go to grammar
> school together. Mr. Thaxter teaches John and Lony and is fitting
> John for High School. . . .[2]

This letter foretold the path of their lives for the years to come. Levi's decision
never to spend another winter in Newtonville was not a surprise; both physically and emotionally he needed to distance himself from Celia. By assuming
even more care of the two younger boys and their education, he found another
justification for his long scientific trips with them.

The reference to Ignatius Grossman was a positive note. It is a mystery as to
where Levi and Celia might have found this young Hungarian boy, but possibly he was among the immigrant orphans who came to America and were
allowed to be adopted upon their arrival. Eventually Ignatius went to college,
married Edwina Booth, daughter of actor Edwin Booth, and moved to New

York. But he continued to keep in touch with Celia. In 1891 she wrote to Annie: "Ignatius and Edwina were coming to Portsmouth from Jackson Oct. 12th to see me, but alas I fear I shall not get there in time. . . ."[3]

During the winter of 1868, Thaxter made her first long winter visit to the Shoals, leaving a young girl to help Levi care for the children. In the summer, she returned again because there was an "emergency" in the kitchen; the emergency was that the Laightons needed another cook! As a result of her intense attachment to her mother, Celia was willing to go to the islands for almost any reason. Although she constantly complained about the rigors of life during the long winter months—it was lonely, dreary, boring, and frightening—she spent an inordinate amount of time there. The shipwrecks continued to traumatize her, as they had done ever since her childhood; she wrote Annie: "there is such a roaring gale this morning that a vessel has gone ashore before our eyes on Londoners Island and the hurricane is such that no boat can put off to her relief. . . . I can't describe to you how distressing this wreck is! We see the poor fellows walking to and fro on the rock trying to keep themselves from freezing, and we cannot get across the terrible raging sea to help them. There were eight to be counted on board before she struck, now we only see one or two walking up and down."[4] Yet she returned year after year.

Throughout the winter of 1868, Levi suffered from rheumatism; his doctor said that the next year he must go to a warmer climate—a perfect reason for his first trip to Florida with his sons. Unfortunately, Roland became seriously ill when they were in Saint Augustine, and his father and brother nursed him anxiously for days. A poignant entry in Levi's journal expresses his fears at that time:

> My imagination worked so amid the dismal realms of disease and death. To have a dear child sick at home with friends and sympathy at hand is bad enough but far away among strangers to have one sick with an unfamiliar and mysterious disease was to me terrible. I supposed I should bear even the worst but how could I? I felt myself getting excited and unnerved. I had staid in the house and in one room too long for I had hardly been out of it for nearly a week. John was a great comfort. I could talk with him. He could do a thousand things for me and we could sympathize together.[5]

While Levi was in Florida with John, who was now thirteen, and Roland, who was nine, Celia and fifteen-year-old Karl once again went to Appledore for the winter; there she continued to write poetry and care for her mother and brothers. In 1869, she accepted James Fields and John Greenleaf Whittier's suggestions that she describe her island home in prose as well as poetry and began writing articles about the islands for the *Atlantic*. The readers were enchanted with her descriptions, which appeared in serial form between 1869 and 1870; as a result, business at the family hotel increased by leaps and bounds. The articles were then gathered into a book and published as *Among the Isles of Shoals* in 1873. In addition to a hardcover edition, it was printed in a fifty-cent version as a guidebook and was sold in railroad stations. Thaxter wrote Fields: "I shall be so glad to have it done, not that I care to be in people's vest pockets, heaven save the mark! but I should be so deeply thankful to have Osgood's check in my pocket!"[6] While "Osgood's check" helped with her immediate financial problems, she continued to be plagued by a lack of money.[7]

By 1869, the pattern of separate lives had begun, with Levi taking one or both of the younger boys south each winter while Celia went to Appledore. In addition, he and his sons usually went away again in the summer because Levi could stand neither heat nor cold. In a letter to her friend Lizzie Hoxie, Thaxter wrote of Levi's winter camping trip in Florida with Lony and John, where the three of them hunted for birds, followed by a summer journey to Nova Scotia. She and Karl remained on the Isles of Shoals for seven months: "Our house is let and we're houseless and homeless,"[8] she concluded. Again in 1870, Thaxter sadly described their lives to her friend: "I don't see but we have become a kind of human shuttlecocks and battledores, for Levi must go south in the winter and fly north in the summer, from rheumatism in winter and from fever and ague in summer. . . . 'Come home' I say—there won't be any more home, which makes me feel forlorn."[9]

Unfortunately, Thaxter's description of their life as a kind of badminton game was only too accurate. They bounced aimlessly from place to place with no discernible plan. Both she and Levi were unable to live in their own home together: his physical condition seemed to necessitate his avoiding New England's extremes of temperature; her attachment to her family and the Isles of Shoals eventually drew her to the islands in both winter and summer. Despite Celia's sadness, there seemed to be no way for them to stay together, and eventually they drew apart emotionally as well as physically.

The next few years passed quietly. In the winter of 1871, Levi and Roland traveled south, and Karl and Celia went to Appledore. John, whose volatility was beginning to surface, was now in high school, staying with friends in Dedham. "John is learning to play on the piano to my great joy. It is such a kind of safety valve and such a source of enjoyment," wrote Thaxter to her friend Lizzie Hoxie.[10] In 1872, *Poems*, Thaxter's first collection of poetry, was published. In addition to those that had been published previously in the *Atlantic*, the book contained five new poems, including "Sandpiper." Over the years, "Sandpiper" has appeared in countless anthologies, children's books, and school texts. The reader can almost see Thaxter and the bird "flitting" along the island beaches, the lighthouse protecting them, the threatening clouds overhead, the boats in the distance. The innocence of the child narrator, her love of nature, and her faith in God have given this poem universal and lasting appeal:

Across the narrow beach we flit,
    One little sandpiper and I,
And fast I gather, bit by bit,
    The scattered driftwood bleached and dry.
The wild waves reach their hands for it,
    The wild wind raves, the tide runs high,
As up and down the beach we flit, —
    One little sandpiper and I.

Above our heads the sullen clouds
    Scud black and swift across the sky;
Like silent ghosts in misty shrouds
    Stand out the white lighthouses high.
Almost as far as eye can reach,
    I see the close-reefed vessels fly,
As fast we flit along the beach, —
    One little sandpiper and I.

I watch him as he skims along,
    Uttering his sweet and mournful cry.
He starts not at my fitful song,
    Or flash of fluttering drapery.
He has no thought of any wrong;
    He scans me with a fearless eye,
Staunch friends are we, well tried and strong,
    The little sandpiper and I.

Comrade, where wilt thou be to-night,
     When the loosed storm breaks furiously?
My driftwood fire will burn so bright!
     To what warm shelter canst thou fly?
I do not fear for thee, though wroth
     The tempest rushes through the sky:
For are we not God's children both?
     Thou, little sandpiper and I?[11]

When Thaxter and her friends invented pet names for one another, Sarah Orne Jewett became "Owl" and Celia, of course, was "Sandpiper."

In 1874, Thaxter's second book, also titled *Poems* and containing twenty-eight new works, was published. James Fields's words of praise must have overjoyed her:

> This morning I rose up at 5 o'clock and sat over against the bay and read your poems one and all, straight through. Of course I know nearly all the poems well, but now I know them as a book of lyrics. Just what this little note is written for is to express what I feel to be an unchallengeable fact: that you can now take your place among the Singers high up in the beautiful ranks. It seems to be that no collection of modern poems can be considered excellent, either in England or at home, without some of your perfect pieces. I am rejoiced at your success and proud of your assured fame. You too are a bringer of consolation and beauty into a world which sorely needs all good things. With Annie's love and mine to you and your dear Mother.[12]

Jane Vallier believes that *"Poems,* 1874, marks the beginning of the second stage [of Thaxter's literary life] with its growing commitment to female experience, and thus to the female literary imagination."[13] "In Kittery Churchyard," which appeared in this volume, is a dramatic monologue inspired by the speaker's thoughts as she kneels at the grave of a young woman who died at the age of twenty-four in 1758. It is one of the few poems in which Celia is sympathetic to the plight of the husband: "And yet from out the vanished past I hear / His cry of anguish sounding deep and clear / And all my heart with pity melts, as though / To-day's bright sun were looking on his woe." Although she writes, "Doubtless he found another mate before / He followed Mary to the happy shore," she still empathizes with the grief-stricken husband: "And in my eyes I feel the foolish tears / For buried sorrow, dead a hundred years!"[14]

Among the Isles of Shoals, Thaxter's first book of prose, appeared in 1873. Recently, it has received renewed attention as contemporary critics have praised it as an example of women's regional writing and of ecofeminist writing. Although *Among the Isles of Shoals* is not a work of fiction in the tradition of Sarah Orne Jewett and Mary Wilkins Freeman, critic Judith Fetterley believes that in this book, Thaxter provides an important example of regionalism that explores "the connection between person, place, and writing."[15] For Fetterley, it is Thaxter's devotion "to the particular, to the poetics of detail"[16] that makes her work memorable. The personalization of her writing and her gift for descriptions make *Among the Isles of Shoals* so appealing that readers are literally drawn into her childhood, into the recesses of the island, and into the memories that crowd her imagination. Thaxter creates a window through which to explore the complexity of her relationship to her island home; as Fetterley concludes, "On the islands, Thaxter entered an environment that nourished her sense of singularity, provided a balance against inexorable sadness, and made it possible for her to be defiantly creative."[17]

In another recent study, "From Transcendentalism to Ecofeminism: Celia Thaxter and Sarah Orne Jewett's Island Views Revisited," Marcia Littenberg defines ecofeminism:

> For ecofeminism in essence is the reclaiming of our ancient connection to the natural world and to each other, a "reweaving" of old stories with new perspectives that acknowledge and value the interconnectedness of all living systems. These themes are central to Jewett's as well as Thaxter's portraits of their region.[18]

While transcendental ideals were an important component of the education and thinking of both women, each of them reevaluated transcendentalism and gave it a feminine perspective through her use of the first-person narrative. Within what was ostensibly a travel manual, Thaxter included her family history, oral tradition, detailed descriptions of birds and flowers, and astute observations of seasonal changes. In comparing passages from Thoreau's *Cape Cod* with the description of the sea that occurs at the beginning of *Among the Isles of Shoals*, Littenberg makes a critical observation about one difference between Thaxter and Henry David Thoreau. She explains that "Thaxter invites the onlooker to relinquish self-consciousness, to view the familiar sea and islands 'islandly,' as she does. In contrast to Thoreau's sense of alienation, Thaxter invites a sympathetic identification with both land and sea that transfigures the scene. . . . She urges readers of *Among the Isles of Shoals* to learn to see with native eyes, to appreciate the connections between all things in this place."[19]

These newer interpretations are also reflected in the introductory paragraphs of *Among the Isles of Shoals* when Thaxter invites her readers to compare her islands with Melville's Galapagos Islands. This comparison is misleading, because Melville saw them from afar, while Thaxter knows the shoals intimately. Affirming the connection between Fetterley's "person, place, and writing,"[20] she takes the visitor on a tour of all the islands, describing them meticulously: the pebbles on the beach, the driftwood, the varieties of wildflowers, ferns, grasses, and plants. She welcomes the newly arrived visitor, who will find that this "world is like a new-blown rose, and in the heart of it he stands, with only the caressing music of the water to break the utter silence, unless perhaps, a song-sparrow pours out its blissful warble like an embodied joy."[21]

Thaxter immerses the reader in the human aspect of the islands as well, from the known inhabitants, like early settler Samuel Haley, to the unnamed sailors who died in the terrible shipwrecks and who became subjects for so many of her poems. Her own family history, as well as that of the "Shoalers," is woven into the book, skillfully combining autobiography and journalism. In addition, Thaxter describes how the seasons shaped life on the Isles of Shoals. In painstaking detail, she pictures the late-arriving summer, followed by "the loveliness of her lingering into autumn; for when the pride of trees and flowers is despoiled by frost on shore, the little gardens here are glowing at their brightest, and day after day of mellow splendor drops like a benediction from the hand of God."[22] The air in September is so "transparent" that "the peaks of Mounts Madison, Washington and Jefferson are seen distinctly at a distance of one hundred miles. In the early light, even the green color of the trees is perceptible on the Rye shore."[23] Again and again, Thaxter turns to color to emphasize the delights of the islands; her descriptions of the fall flowers, the goldenrod, seaside roses, iris, and berries, evoke images of masses of color beckoning the visitor. As the glorious colors of autumn's sky and sea fade, the lack of color becomes a symbol for the hardships of winter:

> In December the colors seem to fade out of the world, and utter ungraciousness prevails. The great, cool, whispering, delicious sea, that encircled us with a thousand caresses the beautiful summer through, turns slowly our sullen and inveterate enemy; leaden it lies beneath a sky like tip, and rolls its "white, cold, heavy-plunging foam" against a shore of iron. Each island wears its chalk-white girdle of ice between the rising and falling tides . . . making the stern bare rocks above more

forbidding by their contrast with its stark whiteness,—and the whiteness of salt-water ice is ghastly.[24]

Thaxter's description of the cruelty of winter, with that "leaden" enemy, the sea, reflects the fears, loneliness, and dread that permeated her winters on Appledore. Her description recalls not so much Melville's "Encantadas" but his introduction to "Benito Cereno": "The sky seemed a gray surtout. Flights of troubled gray fowl, kith and kin with flights of troubled gray vapors among which they were, skimmed low and fitfully over the waters, as swallows over meadows before storms. Shadows present, foreshadowing deeper shadows to come."[25]

With her description of spring, "The rainy days in May at the Isles of Shoals have seemed to me more lovely than the sunshine in Paradise could be," Thaxter returns to the gentle, welcoming islands of her favorite memories. She celebrates the clear call of the sandpipers, "cheerful music" of the song sparrows, and the "neutral tints" of the sea and sky, "gentle and refreshing."[26] By summer, "The world is at the high tide of delight":[27] the hummingbirds have arrived; the butterflies are everywhere; the wild roses are blossoming once again. The satisfied reader, who has followed the seasons on the Isles of Shoals, has found a new appreciation for nature and its endless possibilities for renewal of the heart and spirit.

In addition to her books and her contributions to the *Atlantic*, Thaxter's children's stories were beginning to be published in the leading juvenile magazines: *Youth's Companion*, *Our Young Folks*, and *St. Nicholas*. This was the "Golden Age" for children's literature. While the earliest periodicals contained only religious and inspirational poems and stories, by midcentury the emphasis had shifted, and the magazines became livelier and more interesting. Thaxter realized that these magazines could be an outlet for her work so she contacted new friends she had met at Annie's home. In 1867 she wrote to Gail Hamilton,[28] who, with Whittier's friend Lucy Larcom (1824–1893) and juvenile author J. T. Trowbridge (1827–1916), edited *Our Young Folks*:

> My dear friend,
>
> Do you want this very minute literary effort for the young folks? Or are you over-run with things of the sort? I have many little stories of this sort to tell of various birds and beasts, and if you like, I will send them. Please let me know and will you not do me the favor to point

out any great imperfections which may affect my production, for I don't know how to use the King's English. . . .[29]

Later, she approached Mary Mapes Dodge (1831–1905), who had become the editor of *St. Nicholas*. Dodge, who was well known as the author of *Hans Brinker*, once said that a children's magazine "must not be a milk-and-water variety of the periodical for adults. In fact, it needs to be stronger, truer, bolder, more uncompromising than the other . . . it must mean freshness and heartiness, life and joy."[30] Her approach succeeded—*St. Nicholas* became one of the country's most popular children's magazines. It was published for almost thirty years, from 1873 until her death in 1905. Its contributors, in addition to Thaxter, included Louisa May Alcott, Rudyard Kipling, and Sarah Orne Jewett.

Youth's Companion first appeared in 1827 as an overtly didactic and religious publication. By midcentury, it had altered its format and became one of the longest-lived and most popular magazines ever; it had a circulation of 480,000 by the mid-1890s, when some of Emily Dickinson's poems were printed. It was published until 1929.[31]

Thaxter's children's poems and stories are delightful; in them she reveals her remarkable ability to relate to young people. Her writing is neither preachy nor sentimental; it is the work of a skillful storyteller, who writes with humor and understanding. Using the literary techniques of the first-person narrator and direct address, she personalizes the relationship between the reader and the author. In addition, she draws upon her own experiences as a child growing up on an island, where nature was an intimate part of her life.

"The Spray Sprite" is clearly autobiographical, a child's version of "Landlocked." It begins:

> Once upon a time, a thousand years ago, there dwelt by the sea a little maid. . . . It was bliss to her to watch that great sea, to hear its sweet or awful voices, to feel the salt wind lift her thick brown hair and kiss her cheek; to wade, bare footed into the singing, sparkling brine. Above all things, she hated to sew patchwork. Oh, but she was a naughty child,—not at all like the good, decorous little girls who will perhaps read this story. She didn't like to sweep and dust, and keep all things bright and tidy. She wished to splash in the water the whole day long, and dance, and sing, and string shells, and be idle like the lovely white kittiwakes that flew to and fro above her. . . .[32]

As much as she enjoyed this idyllic life, the young girl was also curious about what lay beyond the horizon. Eventually a fairy prince came to her: "He came near and took her hand, and as he did so all the sandpipers cried aloud in their dreams, and made their playmate tremble with mournful foreboding."[33] "Without knowing how," the girl found herself "sitting in the beautiful boat by his side," with the fairies singing happily and the sandpipers crying "more disconsolately."[34] They sailed and sailed until they reached the land she had seen from the distance. But there she discovered that everyone was doing patchwork; all the children had work to do, work they had learned while she was dancing next to the sea. The story ends on a sad note: "You would never know now that she had been a spray sprite, and danced among the breakers, and talked and laughed with the loons, for she is like everybody else, except that, sleeping or waking, year after year, she keeps in her ears the sad, mysterious murmur of the sea, just like a hollow shell."[35]

"The Spray Sprite" was included in *Stories and Poems for Children*, a collection of works that had appeared in *St. Nicholas*. Other entertaining stories in this book are "Madame Arachne," a lively anthropomorphic tale of the adventures of a spider whose children are massacred by a nuthatch,[36] and "Bergetta's Misfortunes," a whimsical account of the adventures of a cat and a lobster: "Dear children, those among you who never have seen a living lobster would be quite as astonished as the cats were at its unpleasant aspect."[37]

Thaxter's juvenile poetry is also charming. Written mostly in quatrains, it appeals to young readers through its sprightly language and musical rhymes. "Spring" is reminiscent of Helen Hunt Jackson's (1830–1885) more famous poem "September," which begins: "The goldenrod is yellow / The corn is turning brown / The trees in apple orchards / With fruit are bending down. . . ."[38] In Celia's poem, she writes: "The alder by the river / Shakes out her powdery curls / The willow buds in silver / For little boys and girls.[39]

Other poems mirror the realities of nature, such as "The Butcher Bird," in which a canary is murdered by a butcher-bird. But the poem is not overly dark, for it ends: "And would you like, O children / His final fate to know? / To Agassiz's Museum / That pirate bird did go!"[40] "Jack Frost" is a wonderfully written poem, depicting the beauty of nature: ". . . Jack Frost came down last night; He slid to the earth on a starbeam, keen and sparkling bright /" as well as the cruelty: "He sought in the grass for the crickets with delicate icy spear / So sharp and fine and fatal, and he stabbed them far and near."[41]

In her introduction to this children's book, Sarah Orne Jewett wrote of Thaxter's "gift of teaching young eyes to see the flowers and birds; to know her island of Appledore and its sea and sky."[42] She also had the gift of entertaining and delighting her readers.

Appledore House grew impressively during the early 1870s, partly in response to the new business generated by Thaxter's Isles of Shoals articles in the *Atlantic*. In 1870 the brothers decided to enlarge the hotel again. The following summer, she lent them twenty-three hundred dollars (at 7 percent interest) for another addition. Despite her continual complaints of poverty, she appeared to have money for this enterprise.

In 1871, John Poor, a former guest at Appledore House, purchased Star Island and the next winter built the Oceanic Hotel, the Laightons' first rival. Taking advantage of the harbor at Star Island, Poor advertised among the yacht clubs along the New England coast. He gained a great deal of publicity for his Grand Regatta, held in August 1873. However, as only Rosamond Thaxter could declare, "so many noisy and objectionable people came to the new Oceanic Hotel, the more discriminating guests moved to the Appledore House where the atmosphere continued one of refinement and culture."[43] Nevertheless, even she admitted that the hotel provided competition for Appledore House, forcing Oscar and Cedric to build a landing pier. In 1874, the Oceanic Hotel burned to the ground; John Poor had the resources to rebuild it but eventually became discouraged and offered to sell it to the Laightons.

Although the Laighton brothers were still in debt as the result of all the improvements they had been making, their cousin Christopher Rymes agreed to invest in the venture, and they made a deal with Poor for one hundred thousand dollars. The Oceanic was purchased in 1875, a year before Eliza's death and at a time when she could not be of much help. Celia, of course, remained their mainstay. Not only did she handle the reservations during the summer, but her responsibilities continued throughout the year. Because she lived near a city, special shopping chores were delegated to her: finding wallpaper, carpeting, home furnishings, and curtains and then arranging for them to be shipped to the islands. Her mother even sent her one hundred dollars and asked her to go to Boston and buy her two and a half yards of lace for her cap and "the largest corset available."[44] Notwithstanding these obligations, her summers invigorated her; the pleasures of entertaining her ever growing circle of literary, artistic, and musical friends gave her a raison d'être and compensated for the hours of hard work at Appledore and the conflicted life in Newtonville.

The presence of a growing number of musicians was particularly satisfying. In the mid-1860s, John Paine (1839–1906), Harvard professor and America's first symphonic composer, became a frequent visitor. It was he who arranged for a piano to be delivered to Thaxter's parlor. By then, William Mason, who was staying for the entire summer, decided "that in the nature of things I could not fish all the time and gradually formed a habit of playing in Mrs. Thaxter's cottage every day from eleven in the morning until the arrival of the boat, about an hour and a half later."[45] Eventually Julius Eichberg, founder of the Boston Conservatory of Music, and Norwegian violinist Ole Bull joined the resident musicians.

In March 1873, an horrific event occurred on the Isles of Shoals: the infamous murder at Smuttynose, when two young Norwegian women were bludgeoned to death by a heartless drifter. For Thaxter, it was one of the most disturbing and incomprehensible events of her life.

Thaxter had always been intrigued by the Norwegians, who began settling the islands after the Civil War. The Census of 1870 listed Edward Ingebretson, a mariner, age forty-four, and Andrina, "keep of the house," also forty-four, and eight children, all born in Norway. It also listed one other couple and two single mariners from Norway.[46] The next arrivals were the family of Ben Berntsen, a Norwegian sailor who worked at Appledore; the Laightons advanced money for their passage and allowed them to use the Haley cottage on Smuttynose Island. The family was described by Oscar as "a dear old mother, four nice girls and two boys."[47] The oldest girls, Mina and Ovidia, went to work for Eliza; Mina stayed with the family until after Celia's death.

Unfortunately, the Norwegians, whom Thaxter described as "a fine, self-respecting race . . . thrifty, cleanly, well-mannered, and generally excellent,"[48] were plagued by problems in their new land. They had trouble providing food and shelter for themselves during the bitter winters; help from the Laightons was often thwarted by the heavy snowstorms. Several family members suffered nervous breakdowns, and Annie Berntsen committed suicide.

But by far the greatest tragedy that confronted them was the murder on the island of Smuttynose, which was owned by the Laighton family. At the time of the killing, there were only fifty people on all the Isles of Shoals: a few on Star and White Islands; Eliza, Oscar, Cedric, and Celia on Appledore; and a family of six Norwegians, the Hontvets, on Smuttynose. Five years before the murders, John and Maren Hontvet had come to America and settled in one of the tiny cottages facing Appledore Island. John earned a living as a fisherman. A few years later, Maren's sister Karen came and worked at the hotel on Appledore until two weeks before her death. Next, Ivan Christensen and his young bride, Anethe Mathea, came and shared John and Maren's home. Finally, John's brother Mathew also joined the family. Celia described life in this household as idyllic:

They abode in peace and quiet, with not an evil thought in their minds, kind and considerate toward each other, the men devoted to their women and the women repaying them with interest, till out of the perfectly cloudless sky one day a blot descended, without a whisper of warning, and brought ruin and desolation into that peaceful home.[49]

The murderer was a twenty-eight-year-old Prussian immigrant, Louis Wagner, who had found his way to the Isles of Shoals, occasionally working as a fisherman. Thaxter described him in sinister tones: "He was always lurking in corners, lingering, looking, listening, and he would look no man straight in the eyes."[50] Nevertheless, the Hontvet family often invited him for dinner when he seemed destitute and even allowed him to stay with them one summer when he was ill with rheumatism. For a while he worked with the Hontvet fishing business, but then left to join another fishing schooner. This one was wrecked, and Wagner returned to Portsmouth, unemployed and desperate for money.

On March 5, John Hontvet, his brother Mathew, and Ivan Christensen went to sea with their trawler. They intended to return by dinner, but the wind was blowing toward Portsmouth, so they decided to go there directly with their fish, planning to return that night. Unfortunately, they were delayed waiting for bait to arrive from Boston, and for the first time, the women were alone on the island. Expecting the men to return later, the women went to bed around ten—Karen slept in the kitchen, Maren and Anethe in a room close by. The unsuspecting fishermen met Louis Wagner in town and mentioned to him that they would not be able to return to the islands until the morning; John also told Wagner that he had cleared about six hundred dollars from his fishing business.

What happened next was recorded in all its gory detail by Thaxter in an article for the *Atlantic Monthly*. Using her extensive knowledge of the sea and the islands, together with her gift for melodrama, she painted a vivid picture of the terrible event. For hours, Louis Wagner was not seen in Portsmouth; during this time Thaxter (and eventually the jury that convicted him) believed that he rowed out to the islands: "Unchallenged by anything in earth or heaven, he kept on his way and gained the great outer ocean. . . . That little toy of a boat with its one occupant in the midst of the awful, black, heaving sea! . . ."[51] Because he had been in the Hontvet home so often, Wagner was able to land his boat on rocks nearby, walk stealthily into the house, and begin a frenzied murder spree. First he attacked Karen in the kitchen; when the dog began to bark, Maren came to her bedroom door. Realizing that something terrible was happening, she screamed, but young Anethe lay paralyzed with fear. Somehow, Maren made Anethe jump from their bedroom window, but Louis saw her. Grabbing an ax that was lying in the snow, he hit Anethe over and over again. Miraculously, Maren was able to escape from another window and hide outside. However, Karen, who was already half dead, was unable to escape; Wagner returned to murder her—first with the ax, finally by strangling her with a handkerchief. By now it was almost morning, and Wagner realized he must find the money he had come for before daybreak. Despite his frantic searching, he discovered only fifteen dollars. Calling him a monster, Thaxter described what happened next:

> After all this hard work he must have refreshment to support him in the long row back to the land; knife and fork, cup and plate, were found next morning on the table near where Anethe lay. . . . The handle of the tea-pot which she had left on the stove was stained and smeared with blood. Can the human mind conceive of such hideous *nonchalance?*[52]

Meanwhile, the panic-stricken Maren made her way to the edge of Malaga Island, which is connected to Smuttynose, where the Ingebretsons were living. After Jorge, the father of the family, learned what had happened, he went to Appledore to gather the men who were working at the hotel. They rushed to Smuttynose, hoping to find the murderer, but instead found only the two dead women. By this time Thaxter, who was seated at her desk in front of a window in Appledore, realized something was wrong. In a letter to a friend, she wrote:

> I run out into the servants' quarters; there are all the men assembled, an awe-stricken crowd. Old Ingebretson comes forward and tells me the bare facts and how Maren lies at his house, half crazy, suffering with her torn and frozen feet. . . . I go over to Maren to see if I can do anything for her. . . . as I go into the room where Maren lies, she catches my hands crying, "Oh, I so glad to see you! I so glad I save my life!" and with her dry lips she tells me all the story as I have told it here. . . . Upon her cheek is yet the blood-stain from the blow he struck her with a chair, and she shows me two more upon her shoulder, and her torn feet. I go back for arnica[53] with which to bathe them. What a mockery seems to me the "jocund day" as I emerge into the sunshine, and looking across the space of blue, sparkling water, see the house wherein all the horror lies!"[54]

In her account of the tragedy, Thaxter spared no detail of Maren's reaction to the fearful events of that night, the anguish of Ivan for his dead bride, the distress John felt for his injured wife.

Meanwhile, Louis Wagner, who had rowed back to Portsmouth, tried to invent alibis for the night he had spent away from his boardinghouse; no one believed him, and, realizing that he was about to be caught, he fled to Boston, where he was quickly captured. Although he was convicted at his trial, he somehow managed to gain some sympathy while in jail. Even after an aborted escape attempt, there were those who felt that he displayed no characteristics of a killer—he was fair-haired, God-fearing, the victim of circumstantial evidence. Nevertheless, after several delays, Louis Wagner—along with another murderer—was executed on June 25, 1875.

In addition to the horror of the murders at Smuttynose, Thaxter must have been shaken by the intrusion of the outside world upon her safe haven. Characteristically, she turned to writing to restore her equilibrium. She spent hours obsessively reading all the newspaper files on the subject and then wrote "A Memorable Murder," her version of what had happened.

After it was completed, she told Annie Fields: "I am only waiting for Wagner to be hung or not (next Friday is the day appointed for his execution) to rush to your threshold with my manuscript and read it to you and J. T. F. that you may tell me if I offend against good taste or the proprieties of existence. For it is a delicate subject to handle, so notorious, so ghastly and dreadful—and I would not dare to send it to Howells without asking Mr. Fields first."[55] Both Mr. Fields and the *Atlantic's* next editor, William Dean Howells, approved of her account of the story, although some Boston Brahmins were said to be offended by such violence on the pages of their favorite magazine.[56]

That Thaxter would turn to Annie and James before submitting "A Memorable Murder" for publication is indicative of her continuing dependency upon their advice. It is not clear, however, if she realized that James faced business and personal problems in the years after Charles Dickens's 1867 visit. He was still the most respected editor and publisher in Boston, surrounded by many admiring friends; however, the economic uncertainties of post–Civil War America led to instability in the book trade. In addition, he was experiencing other problems at the *Atlantic Monthly*. Although the circulation of the *Atlantic* dropped only slightly, there was increasing criticism of its editor by younger authors whose work was not being accepted. James was accused of provincialism, of favoritism toward his New England authors (including Thaxter), of being heavy-handed in his editing, and of holding articles too long before printing them. For someone for whom good public relations were paramount, this criticism was unsettling. To add to his problems, he had an unpleasant falling-out with his partners. After stormy negotiations, Ticknor was bought out. Much to Fields's relief, a new partnership, Fields, Osgood and Company, was formed in November 1868.

Even more disturbing than these problems with his magazines and his partners were Fields's disputes with a number of his authors engendered by accusations made by Gail Hamilton.[57] She claimed that she had been unfairly reimbursed for her writing. Soon Lucy Larcom and Sophia Hawthorne were drawn into the argument. Ultimately the dispute was settled, but it had a disquieting effect on both Annie and James. As a result of the strain of business and physical problems (he suffered from migraine headaches and a lame wrist), James left Fields, Osgood and Company in 1870, and in 1871 retired from the *Atlantic*. Although he was only fifty-three at the time, he had become sick and depressed and welcomed the opportunity to turn to writing and the lecture circuit. Despite a variety of illnesses, he began traveling to New York, Philadelphia, and throughout New England.

James's retirement signaled a change in Annie and James's relationship. As Rita Gollin observes: "In many ways, Annie and James grew closer after he retired. Their age difference diminished as Annie moved into middle age, and they could as easily discuss financial issues, housing reforms, guest lists, and each other's manuscripts."[58] In 1873 they built a summer home in Manchester-by-the-Sea, which became a comforting retreat for them for the rest of both their lives.

With the pressure of entertaining James's clients relieved, Annie began to look for another outlet for her talents—and that became a commitment to philanthropy. Thaxter, with all the burdens of her family life, had little time for charitable work. But for Fields, helping others was a predictable result of her background, her education, and her gift of sympathy. Her mother's family, the Mays, were noted social reformers and abolitionists. Her old "schoolmaster," George Emerson, had urged his graduates to prepare themselves for a life of dispensing charity and helping the poor: "[A charitable woman] visits the poor, feels for them, becomes acquainted with them, ministers to their wants, is a friend and advisor . . . teaches them to respect themselves and resist evil."[59] Annie's sense of empathy increased her devotion to the causes she espoused: the care of the elderly, the young, and the disenfranchised.

Beginning in the early 1870s, Fields volunteered once or twice a week at "missions" in the North End of Boston, which had been established by the Protestant churches to help working girls (usually Irish immigrants) gain an education. She taught French and enlisted the help of James, Oliver Wendell Holmes, and John Greenleaf Whittier for Friday night lectures to larger audiences of men and women. Another of her concerns was the drinking problems among immigrant Irish men. From 1870 to 1872 she worked to establish coffee-houses to replace the pubs that many of them frequented. She continued to support these coffeehouses throughout her career with the Associated Charities.

Fields's most lasting philanthropic contribution was her determination to change the existing welfare polices. She objected to the established program called "out-door relief." Under this system, money was given to needy people without regard for how the recipients spent it. In a letter to the *Boston Herald*, which she signed "A Friend of the Poor," she asked: "Who wants to throw away $60,000 if he can help it—the sum that Boston raises by taxation every year to be given away to the poor in sums ranging from $2 to $3 at a time to $10 per month?" She suggested that private societies investigate individual cases and offer help rather than simply handing out small sums of money or admitting indigent people to poorhouses.[60] In 1875 she joined with her friend and co-worker Mary Greenwood Lodge to establish a new group called the Cooperative Society of Visitors, which lasted from 1875 to 1879 and then was absorbed into the Associated Charities of Boston, a clearinghouse for all the public and private charitable organizations in Boston. Fields served on the board of directors from its founding until her death.

That Thaxter was wary of Fields's activities was evident when she wrote: "Do you go down to Chardon Street, Tuesdays? . . . I hope you're not doing it—upon my word, I think a stronger, more tough and brawny creature should undertake that work."[61] She was happier when Fields wrote *The Return of Persephone: A Dramatic Sketch* in 1877. After receiving a copy, Thaxter responded: "Lovely Persephone came, indeed it is altogether lovely, dear Annie, melodious and beautiful all the way through . . ."[62]

While no one ever replaced Annie Fields, Thaxter began developing other close female friendships. Many visitors who flocked to Appledore Island became devoted to their charismatic hostess (although she was very particular about whom she invited into her parlor). Among those she particularly enjoyed were Mary Hemenway (1820–1894), a Boston philanthropist to whom she dedicated *An Island Garden*, and Rose Lamb, an artist who had a studio at Appledore and who, with Annie, edited Thaxter's letters after her death. She welcomed author Harriet Prescott Spofford (1835–1921), journalist Kate Field, and Lucy Larcom into her circle as well. Celia visited with these women when she was on the mainland in the winter and again in the summer when they came to the Isles of Shoals. She also continued her epistolary friendships with Lizzie Curzon Hoxie, Mary Lawson, and Sarah Weiss.

The years 1876 and 1877 were the most difficult in Thaxter's life. Not only was her mother becoming weaker and more demanding, but Celia was increasingly aware that she and Levi were incompatible. Her letters to Annie chronicle her anxiety and despair, particularly a letter in 1876 describing her reaction to a letter from Levi, who was once again in Florida. With poignancy and honesty she revealed her conflicting emotions:

> I thank you so much for your letter. . . . One also came from Florida. And when I get one from Florida I feel like saying as I stand before its threshold, "Leave hope behind all ye who enter here." Yet it is one of the best of men who writes. O Annie, if it were only possible to go back and pick up the thread of one's life anew! I am wild to think of it. . . . How threads entangle themselves in this extraordinary existence of ours, how inexorably sadness grasps us, how the waters of bitterness almost close over our desperate endurance. I fight to keep my head above water, to find something to thank heaven for—and I am grateful for food and shelter, for any kindness that falls to my lot, for my mother's freedom from pain—I hold on to these things with all my might. O Annie, pardon me.[63]

Even allowing for Thaxter's dramatic style, this letter is disturbing. Written four years before she and Levi separated, it portrays the feelings of hopelessness that pervaded her life. While acknowledging that Levi was good person, she also recognized that she had made a tragic mistake by marrying him. Her allusions to drowning in "the waters of bitterness" reveal her desperation.

In April, Thaxter wrote to Fields about her son Karl, her other great sorrow: "Were you disgusted at me because I said the springs of cheerfulness were broken forever and aye within my mental and moral machinery? It was only in fun! But I die twenty thousand deaths of anguish and anxiety over my unfortunate boy in Ipswich, from whom I have not heard one syllable since I came home. Always he makes an under current of misery in my life deep down in the sources of my being. But I never mean to talk. . . ."[64]

In another letter, Thaxter clearly revealed where her family loyalties lay: "You heard how a telegram summoned me from the cooking stove in Newton to my Mother's sick bed here, how my brother and I came out in a steamer at midnight a week ago today. . . . Mr. T. writes me that Roland's illness caused their sudden return [from Florida]. I am sorry to have been obliged to be away from N'ville now. Mother will not hear of my going away again, "make everyone come here," she says, poor thing."[65] Her choice to be with her mother rather than her son, to think of her mother as "poor thing," with very little regard for her worried husband and ill son, is telling. That she felt *obliged* to be away from Newtonville and that Eliza said that she should "make everyone come here" exposes the collusion between mother and daughter; their unhealthy mutual dependency overrode the needs of her immediate family.

In January 1877, Celia was once again at Appledore with her mother: "Dear and beautiful Annie Adams Fields . . . I'm so sick of the rage of the elements . . . it has made poor mother sick. . . . Such days and nights we have gone through. . . . O, thank all your fortunate stars you are not on a desolate island . . . but are in the centre of civilization with friends at hand, and help . . . and advice and sympathy and no end of apothecary shops to comfort and assist you! I sent an order in longing haste to a druggist in Portsmouth days ago, by that infrequent fishing boat 'on which our hopes of Heaven depend,' namely communication with the continent, and we might all die seven times before we shall see the fishing boat again or the anodynes I sent for. . . . Do write to my forlornness, you charitable angel!"[66] Throughout the winter, Thaxter sat at her mother's side; eventually the strain took its toll: "Yes, I was ill for weeks, coughed at night and in the morning, was so tired all the time, had a series of chills and feverishness—spent too much vital force through the summer the Doctor said. . . . Dr. Adams and Dr. Bowditch pummeled my chest to find out what was the matter, ordered me quinine. . . . Annie, dear, we have had a dreadful fortnight, mother and I—since New Year's day she has not left her room. . . ."[67]

Fortunately Thaxter had begun drawing landscapes and painting on china, which provided a welcome diversion from her writing and helped to relieve the boredom of her vigil: "Am I writing? Nothing—hardly have done enough to provide myself with shoes and gloves for the winter. I haven't got an idea in my stupid head. Gibbering idiocy would set in if it weren't for my china painting—which is an everlasting delight. I sent some china to Mrs. Reed in Montpelier the other day . . . I enclose her note of delight. . . ."[68]

By August, both Eliza's physical condition and Celia's emotional state had deteriorated:

My dear mother has been so miserable all the time! And we've been fighting opium, but now the doctor says it's of no use—we must make her comfortable. . . . I am too blue to live and wish I could die out of the sunshine off the earth, into oblivion. . . . Appleton Brown is here and I am having some lessons. I will have my revenge on the hoary winter world and paint it in all its gristliness, I will render its desolation and its lonely sorrow after a fashion most assuredly. I have begun this morning and painted a lonesome schooner in a grey sky and sea—so sad and quiet a little picture. Mr. Brown has given me a glorious painting of sea and sky, it glorifies the room truly. . . . I am too sad, too sad to write, my darling. The winter terror draws so near and I am full of dread.[69]

By early fall, the family brought Eliza to Portsmouth, where she would be closer to medical care and to the family's dear friends, the Reverend James De Normandie and his wife. They hired a nurse, which gave Celia time to paint and ride horseback for two hours each day. By mid-November, the end was near; Thaxter's grief was overwhelming:

Annie darling,

My eyes are stiff with weeping and watching, but I want to send you a word. My beautiful, dear mother is sinking away, and we are heartbroken beyond bearing. It seems as if I *must* go, too; I cannot let her go alone. She lies looking like an angel, talking and babbling of green fields, and clinging to us, and whispering blessings, and smiling as no one else can smile for us in the wide world! Almost I perish in the grasp of this grief. What do I care for this world without her? If I could but go, too! I know you will be sorry for us. My brothers are utterly overpowered. . . ."[70]

And finally, on November 19:

This morning, at half past seven, the sweetest mother in the world went, God alone knows where, away from us! There is no comfort for us anywhere except by the gradual hand of time. The "consolations of religion" I cannot bear. I can bear my anguish better than their emptiness, though I am crushed breathless by sorrow. It seems as if I could never fill my lungs with air again, as if I never wished to look upon the light of the day. . . . She lies close by me . . . her pillow strewn with the brightest flowers that bloom. . . . "Don't bring me your sick tints," I cried, ". . . Flowers with life in them and warmth and gladness, those are what belong here." . . . It seems as if the whole range of the Himalayas lay upon my heart. Shall I ever breathe again freely, I wonder?[71]

In retrospect, Thaxter's extreme reaction to her mother's death is frightening. It brings to mind Emily Dickinson's words: ". . . We hated Death and hated Life / And nowhere was to go— / Than Sea and continent there is / A larger—it is Woe—."[72] Although she was forty-two years old, with a family of her own and a successful career in both writing and painting, her whole identity was so intertwined with her mother that she was completely overwhelmed when her mother died. It took years for her to go beyond their relationship, to put it in perspective, and become her own person.

The most immediate reason for Thaxter's despair was that, with her mother's death, she was forced to acknowledge her own situation vis-à-vis her family. While still in Portsmouth after the funeral, she wrote another telling letter to Annie:

> I wish I could go to you . . . but you know I have to go to Newtonville, where it is drear and sad and hard and not half so comfortable as any other place, but where my children are and where it is my duty to be also, I suppose. I only have lingered here to make my brothers comfortable . . . I wish I could stay here. I love the town and would fain try to comfort and cheer my brothers who are desperately forlorn, having nothing in the shape of a woman to look to but me. . . . Ah me, when I think of Newtonville. . . . I think I shall go back to Newtonville Wednesday and come back here again, after a while, and then go back there and so divide my unimportant personality between the two. I feel so colorless, it does not seem as if I could be of use to anybody but I try. Goodbye, you kind, dear angel. Love to James Field.[73]

For her, Newtonville was the most uncomfortable place she could be; she went back out of a sense of duty and would have much preferred to stay in Portsmouth, her first home, or on Appledore with her brothers. That she felt useless and "colorless" is heartbreaking because it implies that, without her mother, she felt like a nonentity.

Sadly, Celia never mentioned that Levi provided her comfort at this, the lowest point of her life. But she was able to take consolation in her sons and returned to Newtonville to spend Thanksgiving with them: "My only hope of comfort is in my boys at home. To them I am dear, to them I am welcome and I can cheer them and make them comfortable."[74]

During the endless months that Thaxter nursed her mother before her death, Karl usually stayed with her at Appledore. Levi, preoccupied with John and Roland, remained home in Newtonville or traveled on one of his scientific trips. A series of letters that Levi wrote to John during these years reveal not only his eccentricities but also his sense of responsibility and his love for his son. At the time they were written, John was twenty-two and jobless. Levi, sounding very much like his own father, urged John to choose a career. Writing from Apalachicola, Florida, where he was traveling with Roland in March 1876, Levi said:

> You must try to think ahead as far as possible and do for the present what will help you most in the future. . . . If worst came to the worst, one might grub out a living, even in Appalachicola [*sic*]. But that would be somewhere near the superlative degree of bad. . . . I cannot bear to think of you giving up at your age all New England advantages of possible improvement, companionship, and the thousand good things that belong there, for the mere living in a pleasanter climate which you must content yourself with almost anywhere in Florida. . . ."[75]

John finally decided to go to Glencoe in Greenbriar County, West Virginia, to work for a Mr. Lawrence, who had a cattle business in which Levi had invested. As he made abundantly clear, Levi hoped to make a profit from this venture in addition to providing John with an occupation: "Think this well over and always keep in mind that I have *purchased* this opportunity, and at what is very likely to prove a dear rate, by lending Mr. Lawrence & Co. a considerable sum of money *without security*—or what amounts to the same thing. I hope to get back my principal and do not count on interest or profits—Perhaps I shall if you look out sharply for me. . . ."[76]

John went south in March, and by May it was obvious that Mr. Lawrence was a fraud. Levi had invested twenty-five hundred dollars in a cattle-raising scheme that turned out to be a hoax. John stayed on, trying to recoup his father's money. During the next year, Levi sent John many letters filled with advice on such diverse subjects as John's health, his inability to spell, and how he should approach Mr. Lawrence to recover his investment.

Unfortunately John's letters were not saved; it would be wonderful to know how he reacted, particularly to the spelling improvement correspondence:

> I am sorry to say a word about spelling—but it does seem absolutely necessary to call your attention to the mistakes in your last letter: You wrote sueing it should be suing—the e is omitted in the participle— *Apparently* which was rightly spelt—you altered to aparently. For *bites* off his own nose you wrote *bights*!!!! Meloncoly!—phew! *melancholy* is right. For *whatever*—you wrote watever.
>
> The lower classes in England drop their h's in speaking—but you should not in speaking or writing.[77]

Occasionally, however, John succeeded in winning some praise: "Your letter from White Sulphur Springs written in pink ink came yesterday, much to the gratification of Lony and myself. Let me say it was very creditable in appearance and a great improvement over the last. Do persevere and keep at it til you have entirely reformed your writing and spelling."[78]

Levi in the role of the Yankee trader was an unfamiliar one, but he assumed it now in earnest: "I hope you took a *receipt* when you handed over the check to Mr. Lawrence. Please let me know about it and if you did, keep it carefully in a safe place, locked up. It may be very necessary and useful. You must keep yourself as fully informed as possible about the whole cattle operation. Take pains to understand all particulars, precisely how many are bought for the twenty-five hundred dollars—and at what price per head. Set down everything you can find out about them and let me know at some convenient time. . . . You must calculate to a fraction of a cent what they cost and what they are likely to come to."[79]

Alone in Newtonville, Levi grew more and more unhappy. He complained to John: "Your letters will be more to me than ever as I am compelled to stay at home so entirely where save for dear Lony it is really quiet. It pains me, though, to think of him so tied to me, and losing so much of other companionship and of the thousand and one delights that, at his age, ought to come to him free as air. Perhaps there will be some compensation in the future. I can only hope." This long letter also contained one of his rare mentions of Celia: "I shall forward today a book from your mother. She has lost your address and I shall insert in it a little list of words for you to correct. Do have a little book and jot them all down, your wrong spelling on the side and the correct spelling on the other. You have your dictionary I believe with you."[80] Celia lost his address? Perhaps it is unwise to read too much into this, but it seems curious that the ever-worrying mother lost her son's address.

After one of his rare visits to Appledore that same year, Levi mentioned Celia again: "There was an endless succession of people coming and going through your mother's little parlor. Some of them were most agreeable and pleasant, but I should think she would weary to death of so many. The piazza is like a street in a city, so I did not pass much of my time there. To me the pleasantest occupation was to sit on the rocks looking East in the afternoon, with the light behind making the great sea before more beautiful than it is at any other time."[81] This letter, one of the very few in which Levi is critical of Celia, gives insight into his disapproval—and jealousy—of her popularity and suggests that he, too, was an unhappy partner in their marriage.

By September, there were indications that John's patience, never his strong point, was beginning to wear thin. Levi admonished him: "I hope you withheld your tongue when you last saw Mr. Lawrence. When it does no good and cannot possibly help matters to call a man "a swindler" and "a pauper" it is the part of wisdom not to fashion such epithets. You only make a sacrifice of your own dignity."[82]

Apparently this was the last straw. In October, John left the employ of Mr. Lawrence for good and was on his way home, sincerely welcomed by his father: "I know of no words to express my sympathy with you in the troubles you have to endure or to tell you how glad I shall be to see you once again at home. If I am drastically weary of the very thought of Glencoe and West Virginia, what must be the state of your exhaustion—I shall go to town tomorrow and make the arrangement you desire."[83] And so ended John's sojourn to the south; his attempt to find a career away from New England had failed, and he did not resume farming until the family purchased the Kittery farm in 1880.

At this same time, although he continued to worry about Roland, Levi was finally tired of maintaining the Newtonville house. Writing to John, he said:

> I think there is no doubt that we shall quit this house for the winter by the middle of November or a little later. Perhaps I may see the way to stay part of the winter in Boston—as I should like to do—but it is not clear at present. Lony is working very hard and if he should break down, it would materially alter the aspect of my affairs. Of course we shall sell the horse (and at what sacrifice!)—a horse being a useless expense—and inexpressible trouble in winter. Watertown will be much nearer Cambridge for Lony (he can go almost from door to door in bad weather in horsecart) and for me Boston will be more accessible than it is here. I detest Watertown and personally should

prefer to remain in my own garret here, but on the whole it will meet the convenience of collective family much better than Newtonville.[84]

Clearly the time was drawing near when both Levi and Celia would admit that their lives would be better if they no longer maintained even a pretense of living together.

7 New Beginnings, 1878–1886

By the way,
The works of women are symbolical.
We sew, sew, prick our fingers, dull our sight,
Producing what? A pair of slippers sir . . .[1]

—ELIZABETH BARRETT BROWNING,
Aurora Leigh

AFTER HER MOTHER'S DEATH, THAXTER WAS FORCED TO TURN HER FULL ATTENTION TO her own family. She could no longer use her mother's illness as an excuse to escape to the islands and had to face the realities of her own life.

One of these realities was her ongoing responsibility for Karl. Celia continued to fear that Levi would institutionalize him, although there is no evidence that he ever attempted to do so. In fact, Levi always appeared to be concerned about him. In a letter to John, when Karl was twenty-five, Levi said:

> Karly was off to the Island yesterday morning bag and baggage and I miss him already. He is very kind and obliging and pleasant if you deal with him in the right way and use a little tact and patience. He is much liked too, for all his eccentricities, by others—sensitive people. I have heard lately of a lady—so intelligent and well accomplished that she is going to try for the Harvard examinations—who said half the pleasure would be gone for her if she did not find K at the Island where she is about to go."[2]

Naturally, since Levi was not with Karl for an extended period of time after 1869, it was easier for him to "use a little tact and patience" than it was for Celia, who was with him most of the time.

Although Karl had been unable to hold a steady job, he attempted to develop a printing business. "Karl is having a new printing press," Celia wrote to John, "& hopes to get the bills to print for both houses [both hotels]. Uncles

Oscar & Cedric have promised to let him have a chance at it & if he only does it he will really earn something, which I will give him credit for being very eager & anxious to do."[3] Later, he became interested in photography and took pictures of guests at Appledore. Nevertheless, his erratic behavior was an unending source of anxiety. In a heartbreaking letter to John, Celia wrote: "I had a very sorrowful Xmas, for there came again another bill that had been ruining us all summer which my poor daft boy had contracted & a kind of despair came over me, a hopelessness of any end after all. And when I spoke to him about it he fell into such a dreadful mood of wrath & despair that I knew not what to do. Alas—I can not think of what may, what must be the end of all this."[4] Another time, Celia wrote her friend Sarah Weiss about Karl's erratic and bizarre behavior: "If I had you here I should tell you of the week before, which was a sad one for Karly & I. A great part of his clothes disappeared & I made him lead me to a far off pile of rocks wherein he had hidden them all & fastened them down with stones—& we both sat down & bitterly cried together."[5] In a letter to her friend Charlotte Dana, Celia apologized for becoming separated from her at the train station: "What must you think of me to have lost you so completely! When the cars came in I had all I could do to engineer Karl & his bundles, he gets perfectly daft under such circumstances—his poor head won't work quickly enough you see. Dennis, one of our men, took me by the elbow & hurried me into a car with him."[6] Celia also described him falling into deep depressions and sitting and weeping for hours.

There was never any indication that the Thaxters sought medical help for Karl; instead Celia assumed the burden of his care and did as well as she could. She tried several short-term solutions, such as letting him live with John in Kittery or having him stay on the islands with his uncles, but, ultimately, the most satisfactory arrangement was having him with her either in Boston or at Appledore.

While not as dramatic as Karl's difficulties, John, too, continued to present problems. His formal education was spotty, and he had difficulty finding a suitable occupation. He was hotheaded and argumentative, the bane of both his parents' existence because of his bad spelling and refusal to answer their letters. This letter is typical of Celia's correspondence with him as he grew older: "I have been grieved to think you could let all this time go by and never say one word to me. . . . Don't let it be so long again that you do not write. . . . 'You have had so much writing to do'? Have you any friend who cares so much to hear from you as I? I think not, and you might have put off some of that 'writing' for an hour or two at least, till you could send me a word. But I don't want to scold you—only I am grieved."[7] Guilt and grief did not work, however, and John never became a good correspondent.

There was also conflict between John and his brothers; in particular, his reaction to Karl provoked Celia:

> No, I do not think you ungrateful or unfaithful, but your letter makes me feel anything but pleasantly. I know you have a trial to your patience, but you often make so much of little things, mountains out of molehills, so to speak . . . & I do think that sometimes you are not wise or kind in the way you speak to Karl, considering that you are blessed with reason & superior intelligence. To tell him, when the sun shines so that it pains his poor wretched eyes that "it's no matter" is neither wise nor kind. . . . Yes, I do call him poor Karly & so might you—you might have been in his place & then it would have been poor John, poor, wretched, unfortunate fellow who has no chance in his life. . . . For sure I give you credit for all the patience & forbearance you exercise toward him to the furthest limit. But it will not hurt you.[8]

In another letter Celia rebuked John again: "I think your attitude toward Lony is unkind & unpleasant, if he is inclined to throw cold water it is because you are inclined to spend too freely. . . . Do try to be good to him & pleasant to him. . . . Do be nice at meals; don't bring your grievances & scold over them at meals—if you only knew how dreadful it was for people who listen, you would never do it. . . ."[9]

Celia's letters to John provide a window into their relationship. On the one hand, she often found fault with him, but on the other, she confided in him, particularly during Levi's final illness and when she was under extreme stress with Karl. Her detailed and loving letters to him when she and Oscar went abroad in 1880 were typical; while she admonished him for not writing, she also said: "Dear John, I think of you every day. I wish you could see this beautiful county of Italy and the things therein so beautiful and wonderful."[10] In the final analysis, he was the son with whom she had the most honest relationship; she chastised him or confided in him as the spirit moved her without the mixed emotions that characterized her involvement with Karl and Roland. It was a great relief to her that John did not have the health problems that plagued her other sons and her husband, and she was able to enjoy him without the sense of foreboding that existed with the others.

As Roland was growing up, he spent most of his time with his father. While Celia was in Appledore with her mother, Roland accompanied Levi to Florida, to Maine, and on several sea voyages. That he might have occasionally questioned his father's ideas is revealed in a letter to his brother John, written in

Levi Thaxter. PHOTOGRAPH, COURTESY JONATHAN HUBBARD.

1878: "P. is reading me Goethe's Waldmeister now which is very interesting, and instructive, and awfully immoral; at least it seems to me, though the simple heretic German may think otherwise."[11] However, under Levi's tutelage, he gained a fine, if unorthodox, education. In addition, he attended several "real" schools for short periods of time, enough to assure his admittance to Harvard, alma mater of his father and paternal grandfather. Although Celia was proud of his achievements, she worried about his delicate health. First, there was the stress of the Harvard entrance exams, then surgery on his knee. After the operation, he came to Appledore, where, she told a friend, "I sit at my painting table at work and he lies outside on a couch with pillows, within reach of my hand, and he hears all the lovely music, for Mr. Eichberg and Paine and Van Raalte

Roland Thaxter, age 14. PHOTOGRAPH, COURTESY JONATHAN HUBBARD.

and William Mason and Frank Johnson's tenor voice all combine and give wonderful mornings and evenings of delight."[12]

Four years later, when he was about to enter medical school, both she and Levi were again concerned. Celia wrote John: "Lony I expect to see today. I told you that papa wants him to take a year to rest before entering the Med. School. I trust to heaven he will—if he doesn't I'm afraid he'll have lost the little chance he has left to gain some strength & health—his bright eyes & pale face make me anxious—but he declares he is all entirely right now."[13] She finally breathed a sigh of relief in 1883 when she related to friends: "I have been made very grateful however, by his [Roland's] having left the medical school &

John Thaxter. PHOTOGRAPH, COURTESY JONATHAN HUBBARD.

taken the Harris Fellowship in Cambridge, because, devoting his life to science, if he is spared, will be so much easier than a career as a physician for
which his mind is filled, but not his body=it is too frail for the wear & tear of
such exposure to anxiety."[14]

Despite her concern for him, Roland, of all the children, most resented the
time Celia spent away from her family caring for her mother and pursuing her
career. Rosamond Thaxter wrote that, although he was twenty at the time, he
begged Celia to come home after her mother's death, saying, "everyone has
had more of you than I, who feel as if I had never had a mother."[15] She com-
plied and returned to Newtonville for the winter to be with her family.

For the next two years, 1878 and 1879, Thaxter spent most of her winters at
home in Newtonville. She devoted hours to painting and writing. *Driftwood*, her

next book of poems, was published in 1878. She also found time to ride regularly at the Cambridge Riding School, thanks to the generosity of her friend the philanthropist Mary Hemenway. In the evenings she often went to the opera or to concerts; she even had a gown made of black cashmere, silk, and satin with a sweeping train. When Levi could not accompany her, she spent the night in town with friends.

During this time, Celia's relationship with Levi continued to deteriorate. Once more, the contrast between her life as wife and mother and her life as a respected author tormented her. In one of her most desperate letters, written from Appledore, she confided to Annie:

> O Annie, burn up this note straight way and do not breathe the madness to anybody, but do you know Mr. Thaxter refuses to have any servant at Newtonville, no, not if I pay her wages and her board besides, and if I go home into the turmoil of the kitchen eternally, I shall go under in despair. I had all my family here last week, and I did beg so hard to be allowed to have one person to help do the work, but this poor man said no—and Annie, I don't want to go home. . . .
>
> Mrs. Reed is very anxious I should go to Montpelier. . . . The Eichbergs want me to come and stay with them. . . . And my new friends in Cambridge urge me to them. Ah the world is good to me. But my place is in that dear, despairing Newtonville, where I am not wanted, where they would like to keep me away. What shall I do? I have but one thought, to go there and live in sufferance, as I did last winter. Take my place in the kitchen if I must. But my work! And useless waste of time and strength when I can earn enough to pay a servant and live decently! Dear Annie, I am poor, perplexed but loving, Celia Thaxter[16]

This letter discloses a vindictive side of Levi that Celia had never acknowledged. Perhaps he had been equally cruel at some other time, but Celia never mentioned it until this letter. That he should deny her household help, even when she begged him and offered to pay, expresses the depth of his anger toward her. It was caused by a variety of reasons: jealousy of her popularity, pain at his own lack of success, resentment for the months she spent at Appledore while he was alone in a home that he, too, was beginning to hate. Her plight was intensified by what might have been—she could have been entertained by admiring friends but instead bowed to his demands and returned to her unhappy home.

In the summer of 1879, in an effort to help his dear friend William Morris Hunt (1824–1879), Levi overcame his aversion to the Isles of Shoals and went to Appledore. As described by Van Wyck Brooks, Hunt was one of the more unusual members of Celia and Levi's circle of friends:

> A rangy, spare, muscular man, with a bony nose and flashing eyes, Hunt looked like Don Quixote or an Arab. He had kept his own horses in Paris, tall hunters and fast trotters, and every day at Newport he had galloped on the sands, with the air of a Moorish sheik . . . or one saw him spinning along in a racing-buggy, with velvet jacket and scarlet sash, and a beard like a fountain in the wind. In Boston, with his art-classes, he stirred up a rage for charcoal-drawing . . . and he liked nothing better than to tease the Boston people, whose niggling conscientiousness annoyed him. . . . An actor, a mimic, a fiddler, whose violin had belonged to Balzac, he would meet an organ-grinder on the street, seize the organ and play it and collect the money, while the forlorn Italian stood by astonished. . . .[17]

No wonder Celia enjoyed his frequent visits to her home!

Hunt and Levi had met at Harvard and remained friends. According to Rosamond Thaxter, when Celia was away, it was James Russell Lowell, John Weiss, and "most of all William Morris Hunt [who] were the ones to whom Levi turned in his loneliness. Hunt was his oldest friend. They spent many hours together in the Newtonville house . . . and it was on one of these occasions that Thaxter, with difficulty, restrained Hunt from destroying the manuscript of his later-famous *Talks on Art*.[18] Levi's influence can be found in Hunt's marginalia, which include several quotations from Browning, who was a major topic of discussion among the friends. A charcoal sketch, *The Bathers*, drawn at Appledore, and extraordinary portraits of Levi and Roland are other reminders of the relationship between the two men.

Although Hunt was born in Brattleboro, Vermont, he was most often associated with Europe, Newport, Rhode Island, and Boston. In Europe, he fell under the influence of Millet and the Barbizon school; in Newport, he established his first art school; and in Boston, he opened another school, which catered to aspiring women artists. Rose Lamb and Sarah Wyman Whitman, who designed the lovely cover for *An Island Garden*, were among his students. He was married to Louisa Perkins, a member of a wealthy and socially prominent Boston family. Helped by his social connections, as well as his talent, Hunt was invited to show his work in the city's most prestigious galleries.

In 1876, Hunt was asked to design two murals for the Albany State Capitol Building. When the new building opened in January 1879, everyone praised his work. According to biographer Sally Webster, even today these murals "remain among the most important paintings in late nineteenth-century art."[19] For years a study for his frescoes hung in Celia's parlor.

Unfortunately, there was a dark side to Hunt's life. On November 6, 1872, a fire destroyed large areas of central Boston, including the studio that housed many of Hunt's own works as well as his extensive collection of paintings by the Barbizon masters Millet, Corot, and Diaz. In addition, over the years his marriage began to fail, and in 1874 he and Louisa separated. Finally, the experience of painting the Albany murals exhausted him, and when he returned to Boston, Hunt was physically and emotionally drained. Frightened by what was then called "melancholia" and "nervous prostration," his friends tried to help him by encouraging a visit to Appledore. Levi took the room next to him. Celia welcomed her old friend with open arms: "I told him I wished he would consider my little den, my nook, my bower this fresh and fragrant little parlor as his own particular property, and he said, 'You dear child! You don't know what a miserable, sick, weak, good-for-nothing I am, fit only for my bed.'"[20]

At first his spirits appeared to revive, but on September 8 Hunt disappeared. It was a rainy morning, and he had gone for a walk, begging his friends not to follow him. When they realized how long he had been away, the search began. It was Celia who discovered his body in a tiny pond:

> *I* found him. It was reserved for me, who loved him truly, that bitterness. . . . Up on that bright, sunny piazza of mine, where he had watched the flowers and heard the music all summer long, they laid his beautiful, dripping length, his gold watch-chain glittering, swinging. They tried to find some life; there was none. We took him in, put in blankets, rubbed and rubbed. It was mockery; he had been dead for hours.[21]

Both Celia and Levi mourned his death and were deeply affected by their inability to prevent it.

After these tragic events at Appledore, Levi returned to Newtonville alone. It was apparent that neither he nor Celia could be happy there; it also was time to help John find land that he might use to begin a career as a dairy farmer. The farm would also (hopefully) provide a future home for Karl. In the winter of 1879, Levi purchased a 186-acre farm on Cutts Island in Kittery Point, Maine. It had originally been owned by Robert and Richard Cutts, whose father had come there from the Isles of Shoals. Later it was bought by an Englishman, Captain Francis Champernowne. In the spring of 1880, the house in Newtonville was sold, and the family moved into their new home. In all directions, the views were beautiful: pastures, pine woods, and a beach, from which Appledore could be seen on a clear day.

The property, known as Champernowne Farm, was given jointly to John and Roland. After their father's death, the sons divided the property, with John keeping the house, barn, pasture, and tillable land, and Roland the beach, the oak grove, and half the ocean shorefront. In later years, Roland built a house there for his aunt Lucy, his father's devoted sister, which he and his family shared during their summer vacations. Little could anyone imagine that a small portion of the land that Levi paid $9,000 for in 1879 would be on the market for $1.75 million in 1998![22]

After Levi purchased the land, he demolished the existing house and built a large new one on the same site. In the fall, Celia (still trying to be a good mother and caretaker) came with a helper to put the house in order since John and Karl were planning to spend the winter there. Roland also could live there comfortably when he was not at Harvard; the third floor was his, with shelves to hold his butterfly and moth collections.

Although she was still spending most of the year at Appledore, Celia bombarded John with anxious letters: "I hope to see Karl today. I tried to flash the light over, as he asked, Friday afternoon, but suppose it was too stormy for anyone to see, if anyone looked. I long to hear a word from Lony & papa, I feel so anxious, but hope no news is good news, in your case too. I know you are so busy, but I wish you could put a word on a postal & send me, just how you are & if you got a horse yet & if papa is there . . ."[23] Two days later: "I just have a note from Lony which makes me feel very anxious—he has had to come home from Cambridge with his sore throat—it was written four days ago. . . . Tell K. I have flashed the light every afternoon at five o'clock & for ten minutes after. . . . Do for mercy's sake drop me a line & tell me how you are & what is the news! Your loving Mum."[24] The following week, after Karl's return to the islands, she wrote again: "I wish I *could* have just a word from you saying what the state of things is at Cutts. *Have* you got a horse? You can't live without one. . . . Please send me one word & tell me if you have the horse, how the house gets on, if anybody has turned up in place of that idiot—oh, what a *fool!*[25] I have no patience when I think of her. I wish I could get your meals for you, dear; wish I were near enough to get them & send them over. It is *too* bad for you to have that bother. . . . If papa is with you, please ask him if he got my note & say that K's overalls & trousers came. I have never seen poor K so daft. I think he is going to lose what little mind he has, poor, unfortunate fellow. It is too dreadful. Thank the Lord that you have got your wits & Cutts farm, dear John, & have your chance in the world, which poor K. never can have. I pity him so I don't know what to do.[26] Her concerns seem genuine, but—even after her mother's death—she was still unable to leave Appledore.

Although there is no written evidence, it is clear that by 1880 Celia and Levi had reached their decision to live apart. For Celia, this was an act of courage, particularly when seen in the light of the nineteenth century's "Cult of True Womanhood." The Cult of True Womanhood was the belief that a woman should devote herself to the private sphere of the home, while her husband, working in the outside world, remained the head of the family. These views played an important role in domestic relations during the Victorian era. One of its chief spokespersons was Catharine Beecher, who wrote her best-selling *Treatise on Domestic Economy* in 1841. Dedicated to "American Mothers," her book dictated the rules for middle-class white households, where a woman's role was to make a man's home his castle. Her views were echoed in leading women's publications, such as *Ladies Magazine* and *Godey's Lady's Book*.

Not everyone agreed, however. Elizabeth Barrett Browning gave voice to the conflict that this attitude engendered in some women. In her poem *Aurora Leigh*, which Levi and Celia had so enjoyed in the early years of their marriage, she wrote:

> By the way,
> The works of women are symbolical.
> We sew, sew, prick our fingers, dull our sight,
> Producing what? A pair of slippers sir . . .
> Or else at best, a cushion, where you lean

And sleep, and dream of something we are not
But would be for your sake. . . .[27]

Celia was caught in the ambivalence created by this movement. As historian Barbara Welter has pointed out, the standards for defining women were set not only by men but by women themselves:

> The attributes of True Womanhood, by which a woman judged herself and was judged by her husband, her neighbors and society, could be divided into four cardinal virtues — piety, purity, submissiveness and domesticity. Put them all together and they spelled mother, daughter, sister, wife — woman. Without them, no matter whether there was fame, achievement or wealth, all was ashes. With them she was promised happiness and power.[28]

Looking at Welter's definition of the true woman, the angel in the house, do we see Celia Thaxter? "Piety, purity, submissiveness and domesticity" do not accurately describe her. Yes, she was "pure," which was a code for implying that a woman did not have lovers. But her "submissiveness" was complex; while she would not openly defy Levi, she clearly became more and more independent of him, even before they separated.

Thaxter was not pious; she questioned traditional Christianity, dabbled in spiritualism and Hinduism, looked forward to an afterlife more than a life on earth, read the Bhagavad Gita as often as she read the Bible. Domestic? Although she complained of her bondage to her home, she in fact spent much time away while Levi cared for the children. For all his faults, he was her ticket out of a large part of her duties as a parent. Although Celia enjoyed their home life when she was very young, her real "domestic" happiness came in later years at her cottage on Appledore, without Levi, surrounded by her flowers, her art, and her many ardent admirers.

Celia's decision to live separately from Levi was not only courageous but wise. With her mother gone, the family finances always in a turmoil, and her relationship with her husband being uncertain, this was the most pragmatic solution to her predicament. It seems doubtful that Levi objected. In all the many letters he wrote during his lifetime, there is seldom any criticism of Celia. However, there is no praise either; in fact, he rarely mentioned her. Gradually, each of them reached the decision that their lives would be happier if they lived apart. As Alfred Lord Tennyson, Celia's favorite poet, wrote, "It is the little rift within the lute / That by and by will make the music mute / And ever widening slowly silence all."[29]

Evidently, Levi's separation from Celia provided the impetus he needed to choose a profession. After selling the house in Newtonville in the spring of 1880, he began giving public readings of the works of Robert Browning. He lived with his sister Lucy in Boston and paid occasional visits to the farm at Kittery.

Celia's immediate response to the situation was to set sail for Europe with her brother Oscar. The ostensible reason was that Oscar had suffered a nervous breakdown when "the love of his life" turned him down, but it was also a good time for Thaxter to begin her new life. Although she had never traveled farther than Boston, she was ready for a trip abroad. When she returned, Levi found rooms for her and Karl in Boston; they remained there in the winter and lived on Appledore during the rest of the year. This arrangement continued even after Levi's death.

Thaxter was not brave enough to go to Europe alone, so she compromised by making the trip with Oscar. The best account of this memorable journey can be found in Oscar's whimsical autobiography, *Ninety Years at the Isles of Shoals*.

Year after year, Oscar fell in love with young women who visited Appledore, and year after year they left, leaving Oscar feeling lonely and bereft. In September 1880, he was recovering from yet another thwarted summer love affair with a young woman whose parents had written to her cautioning: "Beware of entanglement at the Isles of Shoals. We have other plans for you. Shall expect you home at once."[30] Once again Oscar was heartbroken, so his friend J. Ingersoll Bowditch, scion of a noted Portsmouth family, urged him to spend the winter abroad with his sister; Bowditch even provided much of the money for the journey.

The day of their departure on the *Batavia* was so beautiful that Oscar wondered "if we should find anything across the water more delightful than Boston Harbour."[31] Unfortunately, just as the ship was pulling out of its berth, Oscar spotted his latest love, waving her shawl to him: "'Stop the ship!' I cried, too late. 'Goodbye, sweetheart!' My sister tried to calm me as I was about to spring over the taffrail in my intense excitement."[32] This was an inauspicious beginning to their journey, but luckily they were befriended by the boat's captain and by an Englishwoman and her daughter Emily, who were returning home. Oscar recovered from his despair at the dock by falling in love with his new acquaintance.

England was the first stop on their grand tour. Thaxter, who had been given a letter of introduction to Robert Browning, eagerly went to visit him. While she was gone, Oscar found a tailor on Oxford Street who made him a "dress suit" for their next destination, Paris. After describing his visit to London, he quickly passed over the remainder of their trip:

> I had planned to write our adventures on the Continent but I find that there is not room in this modest journal. . . . I must defer telling about the lady, like a creation of Tintoretto, I met in Venice, and another one at Nice. . . . I look back with pleasure to our Grand Tour, remembering the enjoyment of my dear sister in our travels. Suffice it to say that we spent six months in Europe, visiting the cities made famous by the magic brush, or chisel, of the Old Masters, and finally finished up our tour in England. We sailed from here April 15, 1881, on the "S.S. Malta," of the Cunard Line.[33]

Thaxter's description of the trip was less genial. In Italy she had a wonderful time at Villa Novella, the home of authors Mary and Charles Cowden-Clarke. The Clarkes, who were friends of Annie and James, were living in a villa in Genoa overlooking the Mediterranean. However, Celia disliked Naples intensely. To Annie she wrote: "Have you been here? God made it the devinest [sic] place—men have converted it into a pigsty of unspeakable squalor—the best thing that could happen to it would be to have Vesuvius roll a league or so of red hot lava over it."[34] Milan, too, offended her New England sensibility: "I saw a priest the living image of John G. Whittier, and a younger one who looked like my Roland. But a great many of them were very piggy indeed. Oh, their laces, their silks, their gold and silver and precious stones, their bowing and courtseying [sic], how tedious! how like the dancing of the common Lancers of our country!"[35]

England seemed to be her favorite spot, highlighted by two visits with Browning during which, despite their estrangement, she was able to tout Levi's passion for his work. She also loved Cannes and the Mediterranean: "the whole Riviera is a wilderness of flowers. . . . I have nearly gone frantic with the strange wild blooms I have seen from the car windows & I couldn't stop the train to get out & gather them! But I've painted as many as I could."[36]

However, Oscar was not the ideal traveling companion. By the end of December, Thaxter's patience was clearly wearing thin; complaining to Fields, she wrote:

> My brother is just crazy to get home. . . . You say "Do let Oscar keep as quiet as he wishes!" Bella Madonna! Quiet! He can't keep quiet a

minute as he rushes over the face of the globe like a lunatic comet. . . .
It is he who won't be still & I who love to stay in quiet somewhere long
enough to gather my wits together & collect so many distracting impressions into some shape. . . . I wrote to you from Genoa. I had been
once to Villa Novella . . . the 2nd day I took my brother by the hair of
his reluctant head, so to speak, & made him go, the only time I have
tried to make him do anything. O how he hated it! said he'd rather
die, but I took no notice & was inexorable & didn't he rejoice he went!
The moment he got inside the doors he was in heaven, of *course*, as I
knew he would be, & instead of moping in his room in the hotel over
a nasty (I beg pardon I mean stupid) book, he had an evening he never
will forget in his life & never wished to leave the place he hated so to
enter . . . sweet Mrs. Clarke put on her most wonderful Point d'Agnille
to please Oscar who has a passion for lace . . . he was in heaven & they
praised his verses & petted him generally.[37]

Clearly it was time to come home! But, unfortunately, the return trip was not
pleasant; describing it to John Field, a wealthy American expatriate she had
met in Europe, Thaxter wrote: "Our voyage of 13 days was rough & stormy—
going from Marseilles to Lyons in 7 hours from summer heat to winter cold, we
both felt it intensely, both took cold & still kept coughing—I was not able to
speak a loud word for weeks and even now I cannot laugh, & have not got control over my voice when I can make an audible sound."[38]

Despite her complaints, Thaxter's European trip was a significant event in
her life. Even with Oscar as her companion, the trip allowed her to be self-
reliant, free of her obligations to her family. It also introduced her to art and to
landscapes that were completely different from those of New England; her
sketches and her memories enriched her own paintings for the rest of her life.

While Celia was on her European trip, Levi was happily pursuing his new
career. Reciting Browning's poetry at public lectures was the perfect choice for
him. As a Harvard undergraduate, he had discovered *Bells and Pomegranates*, a
series of Browning's plays, and immediately became enamored of the poet.
When he was tutoring Celia, he introduced her to Browning as well; she told a
friend that she and Levi found an infinite source of pleasure and consolation
reading Browning's "Men and Women" together.[39] Browning was also a favorite
subject at Levi's club, the Brothers and Sisters. Throughout his lifetime, even as
his health deteriorated, Levi delighted in Browning.

Public readings were a popular form of entertainment among culture-conscious Bostonians. As Levi became known as an interpreter of Browning's works, he received invitations to women's clubs, atheneums, and private homes. In an essay about her grandfather Levi, Rosamond wrote admiringly of his success:

> Thaxter's Diary of 1881 lists one series in "Tremont" and goes on to mention other engagements at the houses of Mrs. Bowditch of Worcester, Miss Bedford, Mrs. Hall, and Mrs. Hemenway . . . which he noted as bringing in from $300 an evening to one at Mrs. Wells when only $15.00 was given or collected. . . . But another critic wrote: "One feels at once how sacrilegious it would be to think that the desire for money was the main motive of the Thaxter readings! It is rather as if the reader were counting his treasures in the hope of sharing them with his listeners. Mr. Thaxter's quick modulation of voice from firm fine appeal to the tenderness of eternity is a perfect bit of nature. Each poem read has been a faultless gem set in a few explanatory words."[40]

At age fifty-six, Levi settled upon an occupation at last! Undoubtedly he needed money to sustain the Kittery farm, but he had needed money before. What appealed to him was that he had found a career in which he could combine his old love of acting with his scholarly bent. Like Celia, he wanted to pick up the threads of his life anew. Living with her had not been easy; now he had his sister as his housekeeper, his sons nearby, and an opportunity to do what he had always enjoyed. In addition, his appearances at women's clubs provided him with admiration from women as intelligent as Celia but certainly less threatening.

Not surprisingly, Levi chose a subject for his lectures who was not popular. In a letter to the *Literary World* in 1882 he wrote: "For forty years I have been an enthusiastic admirer of Robert Browning's poems, watchful of and interested in everything relating to him and his works. I must confess, however, to a plentiful lack of sympathy from others in this matter, during these many years. . . . I do not think the American public 'love' him any better than the 'British public.' . . . The fact that the American publishers ceased some time to reprint his annual volumes speaks for itself."[41] Yet, despite this perceived lack of interest, Levi managed to establish a reputation for himself. In fact, Van Wyck Brooks wrote, "the immense and early American vogue of Browning . . . was largely the result of Thaxter's readings."[42] Levi gained praise from contemporary critics as well. According to one newspaper clipping:

A series of readings were commenced on Tuesday last by Mr. Levi L. Thaxter at the Women's Club, 3 Park Street—the first being selections from the works of Robert Browning. . . . It is seldom that so rare an enjoyment is offered to the public, as Mr. Thaxter makes his selections with taste and discrimination, and renders them with all the power or pathos, the verve or tenderness which each requires. His finely modulated voice enables him to give picturesque contrasts— the alternations of pleasure and pain, of light and shade, being given with true dramatic effect.[43]

It probably also pleased Levi when one irate Bostonian wrote to the *Boston Daily Advertiser* that "Pippa Passes" should not be read in its entirety to a mixed audience: "Mr. T. is catering to a taste which he should be the last to foster. . . . The shrub house scene is more indecent than books suppressed at the Public Library! Mr. T. should be forced to omit these lines by outraged public opinion! It would be impossible for a mother to take her son to such a reading! There are things intended to be done and not to be spoken of. . . ."[44]

Why was Levi so attracted to Browning and so anxious to advance Browning's reputation? Perhaps because there were similarities in their lives that Levi recognized: both men depended upon their parents for financial support during most of their adult lives; both were married to women with more successful careers than their own. Both eventually lived with their sisters: Levi, when he and Celia separated; Browning, after his wife's death. Each was attracted to the theater. Biographer Clyde Ryals wrote that after Browning saw Edmund Kean play Richard III in October 1832, he thought, "What if, like Shakespeare, he were to create a theatrical world and, moreover, be, like Kean, its actor-manager?"[45] Shortly after his graduation from college, Levi spent time in New York studying with Charles Kean, also hoping to become an actor. Levi was unable to achieve his goal as an actor, and Browning's plays were unsuccessful; this common bond of unfulfilled ambition must have intrigued Levi, particularly when he was a young man.

However, the most important reason Browning appealed to Levi was simply that he loved Browning's poetry. Celia, writing to Browning on Levi's behalf, said: "He has for you and all your work an enthusiastic appreciation such is seldom found on this planet. . . . He knows every line you have ever written; long ago your Sordello was an open book to him from the title page to closing line and *all* you have written since has been as eagerly and studiously devoured. He reads you aloud (and his reading is a fine art) to crowds of astonished people. . . . You are the great enthusiasm of his life . . ."[46] *Sordello*, which in the next century was much admired by T. S. Eliot and Ezra Pound, has been described as ". . . a wonderful zany poem. Carefully ordered but appearing unstructured, announcedly historical but deeply personal, constantly reflecting both itself and its author, generically indeterminate, stylistically complex, it is without counterpart in literary history. . . ."[47] Undoubtedly, the eccentricities of *Sordello* made it one of Levi's favorites.

As Levi pursued his readings, it became apparent that Browning's works stimulated him both from a literary and from an intellectual point of view. As a Boston reviewer wrote:

> Mr. Thaxter's reading of Browning is remarkable, his style is perfectly simple and straightforward, intelligent and self-controlled. His voice is sweet, firm and of considerable range, his elocution clear, his pronunciation correct, and exquisitely cultivated! The source of Mr. Thaxter's peculiar power was his quick penetrating sympathy with the poet and the poems and his perfect grasp and comprehension of their meaning. To read "Pippa Passes" in such a way as to convey its sense and comprehensibility to an audience in a hall, he performed a real feat! No single shade was lost or blurred. Mr. Thaxter has neither been equaled or approached as a great interpreter of a great master![48]

The reviewer's observation of Levi's sympathy with Browning reveals the heart of their relationship. Robert Browning gave voice to emotions and ideas that Levi harbored but was otherwise unable to express; Levi, in turn, presented an interpretation that reached his listeners and introduced Browning to an American audience.

As Levi became better known through his public readings, his and Celia's "separation" came under scrutiny. What seemed to them to be a reasonable solution to their incompatibility—separate living arrangements but continued communication and sharing of family responsibilities—was criticized by acquaintances. There is no indication of what had been said to provoke so strong a reaction, but in a letter to John, Celia vigorously expressed her anger and angst at criticism that had been leveled against Levi:

> If you had taken a sledge hammer & dealt me a blow full between the eyes, I could not have been more shocked & distressed than I was at your letter. I did not notice how Mrs. Waldo spoke of the farm. I

happened to see her at the Eichbergs when I was there in the spring. She asked about you, having met you the winter you lived in town & I told her you had a farm in Kittery & were very happy there. Send me the letter & let me see what she said. My most ardent wish is to put an end to any kind of talk to your father's disparagement, if any such exists. *I* never hear of a breath or a whisper of anything of the sort & I only wish I could get hold of the person or person who spread such reports. I only wish I knew who does it, who keeps filling his ears with such wretched folly, such lies, such hateful nonsense. Do you suppose I would neglect a chance of "correcting" with all my powers any thing "disparaging" to him or to any of you? If you do, you wrong me beyond expression.

I cannot but think the whole thing absolutely exaggerated, but at any rate I have a right to know how & whence & from whom you hear such injurious slander. I am perfectly willing to go round the world with a placard before & behind indignantly denying the whole thing, willing to give my whole energies to it, to destroying any such idea. *I shall think of nothing else.* It makes me so miserable I had much rather be dead than alive. I was not "mad" at your letter but cried all night & I only wish to heaven I could get out of the whole wretched business, into the earth, under the sod, where nobody could accuse me of things so mean & monstrous.[49]

Unfortunately, there is no other reference to this incident, but it is clear that Celia, with her high emotions and ready pen, would always defend Levi, maintain their mutually respectful arrangement—and protect herself as well.

Despite whatever gossip occurred, their unconventional arrangement continued. Levi spent the winters in Boston with his sister Lucy Titcomb; Celia and Karl lived in rooms that he had found for them in a nearby hotel. Levi stopped traveling and concentrated on his readings. With the pressure of sharing a home relieved, Celia and Levi seemed to be on the best of terms, communicating frequently, seeing each other often in Boston, at Kittery Point, and even at the Shoals. In October 1882, Celia wrote Julius Eichberg, the composer: "This morning, at four o'clock, Mr. Thaxter knocked at my door and asked me if I did not wish to look at the comet. I went to the window, and such a supremely beautiful and wonderful sight met my eyes. . . ."[50] A month later, she described their Thanksgiving Day at the farm to Annie Fields: "Mr. Thaxter came in the afternoon, wishing to get here by daylight. I was surprised to see him—the boys did not get here till nearly eight o'clock. I had a nice dinner ready and everything bright and comfortable. . . . I am very thankful they all got here safely and things are pleasant but somebody came in the same train whose name is Care.[51] What emotions or problems "Care" refers to is unclear, but at least the family was able to celebrate happily with one another.

Celia and Levi's life continued in this way until December 1883, when Levi was taken sick with his final illness. The cause of death is unclear, but in letters to John describing her observations, Celia mentioned problems with his kidneys, pains in his legs, and continual weight loss. Roland, who had graduated from Harvard with plans to attend medical school, assumed responsibility for his father's care. Roland had been unhappy with his parents' estrangement and blamed Celia for it. As a result, while his father was dying, he took charge of the sickroom and limited his mother's visits. Celia complained to John: "I went to see papa yesterday—indeed I go every aft. & would stay if they would say the word. . . ."[52]

Levi died on May 31, 1884, and was buried in the old First Congregational Church cemetery at Kittery Point. His obituary reported that "Mr. Thaxter's wife was the poetess Celia Thaxter, so closely identified with the Isles of Shoals, but he was a little restless and eccentric by nature, and has not always been content to spend even his summers at that favorite mid-ocean resort. . . ."[53] Fortunately the family seemed not to have noticed this unflattering portrayal of Levi. Instead, they were very proud that Robert Browning composed an epitaph for his gravestone. This is the only known Browning epitaph in the world. It begins: "Thou, whom these eyes saw never,—say friends true / who say my soul, helped onward by my song / Though all unwittingly, has helped thee too?"[54]

Ultimately Levi played several roles in Celia Thaxter's life. As her tutor, he brought a world of life and literature to Celia, who, using Hawthorne's words, often referred to herself as "an island Miranda." In particular, Levi's love of Browning influenced her. After his death, Celia wrote to a friend: "I am intensely interested in the fact that you've discovered Browning—was there ever anything so wonderful as his insight, his prophetic power, his subtle wisdom? . . . My husband who made of him a life study, early taught me all these things about him."[55] However, Browning was not their only literary delight. In an earlier letter to Lizzie Hoxie, Celia described the pleasure she and Levi derived from reading together Elizabeth Barrett Browning's *Aurora Leigh*, Harriet Beecher Stowe's *Dred*, and two volumes of Elisha Kane's description of his Arctic expeditions.[56] These years of reading inspired Celia, sparked her vivid imagination, and led her to acquire a sophistication and breadth of knowledge that enhanced her writing and her life.

Unfortunately, this dependent relationship with Levi had another side. Despite the praise she received from the world at large, Celia never felt confident of his approval. When she was in England in 1880, she wrote to Anne Ritchie (Thackeray's daughter and herself an author) about her preparation for a visit with Robert Browning: "all the while I was thinking of my husband & his joy if I really should behold his idol, the questions he would ask & I should delight to answer, & the feeling of value I should gain in his eyes. . . . The first thing he did when he found me, a little savage (on my island)—only eight years old, was to read Browning to me, beginning with Pied Piper and going on, as I grew older, with all the rest. . . ."[57] Despite success as an artist, author, and hostess, gaining value in Levi's eyes was still important for Celia.

Their marriage did not succeed for many reasons. Some are obvious: the disparity in age and backgrounds, the stress of raising Karl, the constant lack of money, Levi's refusal to get a job. Both were strong willed and reluctant to compromise. Other reasons are more subtle, such as Levi's jealousy of Celia's success and his perception that she was more powerful and self-assured than he. After all, she was the one to write Browning and eventually visit him. Perhaps Levi never made the effort to meet the man he so admired because he believed that Celia surpassed him in both confidence and achievement.

On Celia's part, although she needed Levi's approval, eventually she did not love him, and her life with him was not fulfilling. In comparison with the artists, writers, and musicians whom she came to know, he must have seemed pale and ineffectual.

We will never know the whole story of their relationship. What we do know is that, as time went by, they simply shut each other out from important areas of their lives. While Celia was more forthcoming in expressing her feelings than many of her contemporaries, she still guarded her most personal thoughts. Her relationship with her husband remains part of the paradox of her life.

8 Annie and Sarah

She was not only Annie's darling, she was everybody's darling; in Boston as well as Berwick she was "our dear Sarah."[1]

—PAULA BLANCHARD, *Sarah Orne Jewett*

THAXTER'S LIFE IN 1881 WAS NEVER DULL. SHE CELEBRATED HER BROTHER CEDRIC'S MARriage to Julia Stowell; she continued to spend time in Kittery helping to organize the household; and, most important, she consoled Annie when James Fields died.

Despite his poor health, James had enthusiastically pursued his lecturing career after his retirement. However, in May 1879, while lecturing at Wellesley College, he experienced a brain hemorrhage and collapsed. During the next two years, two more hemorrhages and a massive heart attack occurred. Finally, on April 23, 1881, at home with his wife, he suffered a fatal attack. Thaxter happened to be visiting the Fieldses at the time and was able to support and comfort Annie in the days after James's death and then in the weeks and months that followed. In a letter written a few months later, Celia pleaded with Annie:

> Of all things, on earth don't shut yourself away; throw bridges over your moat and let love come to you or you will die a thousand deaths of silence, and sorrow and despair. . . . Do not give up your work— what will become of you without it?[2]

Perhaps as a result of this letter, Annie invited Sarah Orne Jewett (1849–1909) to 148 Charles Street. The two originally met in August 1880 when both Jewett and the Fields were vacationing at Appledore. When Sarah came to Boston the following year, she consoled her bereaved hostess, and Annie comforted

Sarah, who was suffering from rheumatoid arthritis. After spending the winter together, they decided to go abroad. For Fields, it would be a distraction from her mourning; for Jewett, it would be a search for relief from her illness.

The trip proved successful, and the next year Fields and Jewett began a twenty-eight-year relationship, which ended with Sarah's death.[3] Their friendship was a Boston Marriage, a common and socially acceptable relationship in the nineteenth century, particularly among upper-class women. Thaxter described their friendship to the naturalist Bradford Torrey, her epistolary friend, in very simple terms: "Miss Jewett and Mrs. Fields are housemates, you know, a great part of the time, all Miss Jewett can spare from her mother and sisters at Berwick, for Mrs. Fields is quite alone. They are very fond of each other."[4]

Sarah Orne Jewett was born in South Berwick, Maine, in 1849, the second of three daughters; she grew up in a happy, closely knit, upper-middle-class family. Her maternal grandfather was a sea captain, who left his children and grandchildren independently wealthy; her paternal grandfather was a country doctor, as was her father. Although as an adult she traveled extensively, most of her writing was set in Maine. One reason for this enduring connection with her home was her attachment to her father, Theodore, who was one of the most important influences on her life. He has been described as her "father, teacher, comrade and model;"[5] she accompanied him on his country rounds, admiring his devotion to his patients and absorbing his love of reading and knowledge of human nature. Sarah also had a close relationship with her mother, Caroline Jewett, who loved reading and, in the manner of small-town New Englanders, enjoyed entertaining her friends and relatives at home. It was a tradition Sarah and her sisters continued after their mother's death and which appears as a symbol for human interdependence in much of Sarah's writing.

Jewett's first published story, "Jenny Garrow's Lovers," appeared when she was eighteen. However, she regarded the publication of "Mr. Bruce" in the *Atlantic Monthly* in 1873 as the beginning of her career. Several significant events occurred in the years after "Mr. Bruce" appeared. After the death of her maternal grandmother in 1870, she suffered from a depression that lasted almost eight years. She was plagued with uncertainty about her self-worth, questioning—in terms evocative of many women today—what her role in life should be: "Above all, she was tormented by doubts about what her 'work' really was. Certainly writing stories was work, but she did not know whether writing letters, running errands, visiting the aunts, and so on was not equally her 'work' as a woman. Trying to do everything, she accomplished very little."[6] Jewett turned to the religious commitment of her friend Phillips Brooks, Boston's charismatic Episcopal minister, for support. By immersing herself in the doctrines and activities of the church, she found a way to assuage her anxieties through the help of what she perceived as a loving and caring God.

In this spirit of religious devotion, Jewett expanded her reading to include exemplary Christian writers, especially Theophilus Parsons, a Harvard law professor and Swedenborgian, with whom she developed a friendship. Because Swedenborgian philosophy emphasized individual responsibility, her relationship with Parsons helped her achieve a calmer and more cosmic view of life. He strengthened her commitment to her career and urged her to reach out to others. Through his encouragement, she regained her self-confidence and began to write seriously.

In 1877, *Deephaven*, her first novel, was published. The book is a series of sketches about a pair of wealthy young city women who spend a summer together in the small fishing village of Deephaven. Elements of plot, theme, and character in *Deephaven* foreshadow Jewett's later stories and novels. Young women from the city learning from a generation of men and women who have faced the vicissitudes of seafaring life became a favorite subject, culminating in *The Country of the Pointed Firs* in 1896.[7] *Deephaven* not only anticipates her later works but also expresses Jewett's long-standing concern with friendship. Describing their final days in Deephaven, the narrator, Helen, says:

> We both grew so well and brown and strong, and Kate and I did not get tired of each other at all, which I think was wonderful, for few friendships could bear such a test. We were together always, and alone together a great deal: and we became wonderfully well acquainted.[8]

This passage was written four years before Fields and Jewett began living together, but it describes the spirit of empathy, which was their relationship's predominant feature.

Upon their return from Europe in 1881, Annie and Sarah settled into a routine they would follow for many years: winters in Boston, followed by a spring visit to Maine, and summers in Manchester-by-the-Sea. During their years together, Fields maintained her role as a charming hostess, as well as developing her new reputation as a dedicated social worker, and Jewett wrote her best books and short stories. Her themes changed and matured, from girls' friendships to questions of career versus marriage in *A Country Doctor* (1884) and the problems of the intrusion of urban life upon the countryside in "The White Heron" (1886). She also wrote rural sketches, classic spinster tales including "The Dulham Ladies" (1886), and stories focusing on father-child relationships, such as "The King of Folly Island" (1886).

All Fieldses' friends, including Thaxter, were delighted with Sarah Jewett. According to biographer Paula Blanchard, "She was not only Annie's darling, she was everybody's darling; in Boston as well as Berwick she was 'our dear Sarah.'"[9] As early as December 1881, Celia wrote to Annie: "I am glad the dear Owl[10] is with you and I wish she would stay forever, happy is the creature who has her near."[11]

Thaxter and Jewett had a great deal in common. Both were writers, although Jewett's literary reputation today far exceeds Thaxter's. Each had a father who devoted a great deal of time to her, provided the basis for her education, and nurtured her independence. Blanchard observed many other similarities:

> Celia Thaxter's tendency to rapidly fall in and out of love with ideas was one of many traits she shared with Sarah Orne Jewett. Another was an understanding of the natural world that surpassed Jewett's own. . . . Her small garden, always brilliant with color, expressed her love for all growing things but also made a kind of statement, like Jewett's, that here a minute symbol of womanly tradition and order made its stand. Like Jewett, too, she felt an immediate link with history, and she had grown up listening to the rough, quirky talk of the island natives and their tales of pirate ghosts. . . .[12]

Falling "in and out of love with ideas" is a compelling image. Thaxter's fascination with spiritualism and Eastern religions after her mother's death was matched by Jewett's early preoccupation with Swedenborg. Both women became devoted to these philosophical ideas when they first encountered them and were influenced by them throughout the rest of their lives. However, each eventually moved beyond them and found fulfillment elsewhere: Jewett, through her writing; Thaxter, through her gardening and painting.

Both Thaxter's and Jewett's connection to the natural world was extraordinary. They wrote "not only about nature but about men and women who live close to nature, who accept not only its power and beauty but its rhythms and cycles."[13] In *Among the Isles of Shoals*, Thaxter describes the early inhabitants of Appledore: "I love to people these solitudes again, and think that those who lived here centuries ago were decent, God-fearing folk. . . . And all the pictures over which I dream are set in this framework of the sea, that sparkled and sang, or frowned and threatened, in the ages that are gone as it does today. . . ."[14] She wanted to share with her readers her connection to these

Annie Adams Fields. DAGUERREOTYPE, COURTESY OF THE
MASSACHUSETTS HISTORICAL SOCIETY.

men and women whose lives were shaped by their relationship to the constantly changing sea.

Jewett's stories also celebrate the men and women who not only lived in
environments dependent upon the vicissitudes of nature but rejoiced in their
connection to it. In her description of the Bowden family reunion in *The Country of the Pointed Firs*, she writes lovingly of the generations of New Englanders
who had participated in this yearly celebration:

> There was a wide path mowed for us across the field, and, as we
> moved along, the birds flew up out of the thick second crop of clover,
> and the bees hummed as if it still were June. There was a flashing of
> white gulls over the water where the fleet of boats rode the low waves

Sarah Orne Jewett. PHOTOGRAPH, COURTESY PORTSMOUTH
ATHENÆUM.

together in the cove, swaying their small masts as if they kept time
to our steps. The plash of water could be heard faintly, yet still be
heard. . . . It was strangely moving to see this and to make part of it.
The sky, the sea, have watched poor humanity at its rites so long; we
were no more a New England family celebrating its own existence and
simple progress; we carried the tokens and inheritance of all such
households from which this had descended, and were only the latest
of our line. . . .[15]

Like Thaxter, Jewett is able to bring her readers into her world, to create a bond with the inhabitants of that world, a community with them not only through nature but through a shared humanity.

Sarah and Celia's love of gardens and the traditions they represented formed another important link between them. In an article titled "By Pen and Spade," Patrice Todisco writes:

> The gardens they [Jewett and Thaxter] created were an integral part of their daily lives and surfaced in their writings as part of the intimate landscape which was celebrated in their work. In this world of household chores and endless rounds of social duties, to be alone and to be creative was an incredible act of freedom. . . . To claim nature within a personal space was the joy the garden provided, enabling them to construct an intimate environment from which to observe and record the universe beyond the garden gate.[16]

For both women, gardening established a circumscribed sphere of activity in which they could find respite from their cares, time to think and plan, peace and quiet in the sometimes hectic world in which they lived. Each enjoyed the actual physical work of gardening, although it was sometimes difficult for Jewett, who suffered from rheumatoid arthritis. Tellingly, their gardens reflected their personalities: when Sarah and her sister moved into their grandfather's house, they created a proper New England front yard garden with its lilacs, roses, and old-fashioned perennials.[17] On the more exposed soil of the Isles of Shoals, Thaxter planted a cutting bed, small but with a magnificent display of poppies and smaller groupings of pansies, nasturtiums, sweet peas, hollyhocks, and many other flowers carefully cultivated to adorn her parlor.

Thaxter's garden was also a medium through which she communicated with her friends, giving them gardening advice and sending actual plant specimens. Once, her friend Rose Lamb asked for suggestions on planning a garden; after many paragraphs describing plants she recommended, including their Latin names, Celia concluded: "I haven't begun to talk about the flowers as I wish, but I might take all day and not have done. You will have splendid pansies, I know, they want *shade*, moisture (they must never get dry) & the richest stable manure."[18]

Yet another similarity between Thaxter and Jewett was their childhood. While Sarah's early years in a village on the seacoast, surrounded by an extended family, was different from Celia's isolated life on the Isles of Shoals, their acquaintance with men and women who lived at the mercy of nature provided a unique worldview that few other women writers have shared. Thaxter's

Among the Isles of Shoals and Jewett's books and stories display a fascinating knowledge of the lives and the language of these people. Sarah Orne Jewett is at her best in *Country of the Pointed Firs*. In one scene, Mrs. Todd comments to the narrator, who has been talking to old Captain Littlepage: "I see you sleevin' the old gentleman down the hill . . . I expect he got tellin' of you some o' his great narratives."[19] In *Among the Isles of Shoals* Thaxter repeats a story told to her by "a lean, brown, hollow-eyed old woman from Star Island," whose daughter-in-law, Mary Hannah, saw ghosts as she lay dying:

> Ma'y Hahner, she said to me, a whisperin, says she, "Who's that scratching, tearing the house down underneath the window?" "No, it ain't nothin'," says I; "Ma'y Hahner, there ain't nobody a tearin' the house down underneath the winder." "Yes, yes, there is, says she . . . I hear 'em scratching, scratching, tearing the house down underneath the winder!" And then I kno'd Ma'y Hahner was goin' to die, and so she did afore mornin'."[20]

The ability of both writers to use nuances of language to suggest understanding and empathy for their fellow New Englanders is remarkable.

As with any relationship based on a gift of sympathy, the friendship between Jewett and Thaxter benefited both women: Thaxter gained a supportive friend and strengthened her ties to Fields; Jewett used material provided by Celia for some of her most thoughtful work. For example, in her short story "The Foreigner" (1900), Sarah describes how the pathetic Mrs. Tolland saw her mother on her deathbed, just as Thaxter described seeing her mother during a seance.[21] In addition, many have recognized a resemblance to Thaxter in the character of Mrs. Blackett in *The Country of the Pointed Firs*. Mrs. Blackett's warmth as a hostess and her independent life on Green Island reminds us of Thaxter on Appledore.

But it is in Jewett's short story "The White Heron" and Thaxter's poem "The Great Blue Heron" that the connection is most obvious. "The White Heron" is the story of a little girl living on a farm with her grandmother. Wandering home with her cow, she encounters a "tall young man, who carried a gun over his shoulder."[22] He informs the child that he is hunting for birds and needs a place to stay. She brings him to her grandmother, who welcomes him to her home and tells him of "Sylvy's" knowledge of birds: "There ain't a foot o' ground she don't know her way over, and the wild creatures counts her one o' themselves."[23] Their guest is thrilled because he has come to the islands to find a rare white heron, which he once saw there. He plans to kill it and add it to his collection of stuffed birds. Realizing that Sylvia must have seen the heron, he tries to entice the child into revealing its whereabouts. He offers her ten dollars to show it to him; he gives her a jackknife; he speaks to her kindly and sympathetically: "She had never seen anybody so charming and delightful; the woman's heart, asleep in the child, was vaguely thrilled by a dream of love."[24] The next morning, Sylvia creeps out of bed before dawn and goes to the edge of the woods, where she climbs a huge old pine tree. As the sun comes up, she sees the heron and hears him calling to his mate in their nest. When she returns home, she will not speak to her grandmother or the young man: "The murmur of the pine's green branches is in her ears, she remembers how the white heron came flying through the golden air and how they watched the sea and the morning together, and Sylvia cannot speak; she cannot tell the heron's secret and give its life away."[25]

"A White Heron" can be read on several levels. Above all, it is a charming story of a young girl's loss of innocence. Sylvia is confronted with a choice she has never anticipated: protecting the heron or pleasing the hunter. Her decision reflects Jewett's own valuing of nature. The child protecting the bird is portrayed as the heroine; the adults, as the betrayers. The story is also evocative of Thaxter's life; like Levi, who loved to hunt and stuff birds, a young man has come into a peaceful environment and has tried to subvert an innocent child. After clearly agonizing over her decision, she remains loyal to the natural world. "A White Heron" is a lasting tribute to Celia from her dear friend.

"The Great Blue Heron," included in Thaxter's *Stories and Poems for Children* (1883), can also be read on several levels. The female narrator describes seeing a blue heron:

> The great blue heron stood all alone
>   By the edge of the solemn sea
> On a broken boulder of gray trap stone;
>   He was lost in a reverie . . .

As she climbs up the wall, she breathes a warning to him:

> "You cannot know of the being called Man . . .
> "He's not a hospitable friend! If he sees
>   Some wonderful, beautiful thing
> That runs in the woodland, or floats in the breeze
>   On the bannerlike breadth of its wing,

"Straight he goes for his gun, its sweet life to destroy
　　For mere pleasure of killing alone
He will ruin its beauty and quench all its joy
　　Though 'tis useless to him as a stone . . ."

She continues to urge the bird to fly away until:

　. . . he rose and soared high, and swept eastward at last,
　　Trailing long legs and wings in the air.
　"Now perhaps you may live and be happy," I said,
　　"Sail away, Beauty, fast as you can!
　Put the width of the earth and the breadth of the sea
　　Betwixt you and the Being called Man."[26]

Like "A White Heron," this poem exemplifies sympathy for a creature in the wild that is being threatened by a human. On another level, there is an echo of Thaxter's plaintive remark to Fields: "Could I but be ten years old again! I believe I would climb to my lighthouse top and set at defiance anything in the shape of man!"[27] In "The Great Blue Heron," this warning against "Man" appears again, but here the bird is cautioned about the danger and escapes—perhaps as the poet wishes she had been able to do.

Thaxter and Jewett's friendship grew steadily over the years. During the summer Sarah and Annie vacationed at Appledore. In the winter Celia visited Sarah not only in Boston but also at the Jewett family home in Berwick. Jewett was heartbroken when Thaxter died. Writing to their mutual friend, the artist Sarah Wyman Whitman, she described their unique friendship:

> I must write you out of loneliness and pretty deep-down sadness to-night. I had a telegram Monday morning that Celia Thaxter had died, dear old Sandpiper, as was my foolish and fond name, these many years. We were more neighbours and compatriots than most people. I knew the island, the Portsmouth side of her life, better than did others, and those days we spent together last month brought me to know better than ever a truly generous and noble heart. When her old mother lay dying, she called her boys, and said, "Be good to sister, she has had a very hard time"; and it was all true. She was past it all when I was with her in July. Life had come to be quite heavenly with her . . .[28]

In tribute to Celia, Sarah edited the Appledore edition of her poems as well as *Stories and Poems for Children*, assuring that Thaxter's writing would be enjoyed by future generations.

When Jewett and Thaxter first met, Celia was still grieving over her mother's death. Almira Todd, the crusty protagonist of *The Country of the Pointed Firs*, said: "You never get over bein' a child long's you have a mother to go to."[29] Without her mother, Thaxter was indeed like a lost child. In desperation, she turned to the Spiritualist movement to regain contact with her.

The Spiritualism in which Thaxter believed was not new in America; the first "rappings" were heard in Rochester, New York, in March 1848 by the young Fox sisters. The movement reached its height after the Civil War. As author Barbara Goldsmith observes, "The rise of Spiritualism coincided with Samuel B. Morse's invention of the telegraph, an invisible means of communication, and expanded at a time when a devastating war had imposed the unbearable loss of husbands, sons, and lovers."[30] Because women had always been involved with death, Spiritualism became primarily their movement. At last there was a means to discover the fate of loved ones: the survivors "could now see these dear souls safely nestled in the hand of God."[31]

For Thaxter, who always had difficulty accepting traditional Christianity, Spiritualism was the perfect solution for coping with the loss of her mother. She became devoted to a clever medium, Rose Darrah, who contacted her in 1882 to say that she had received a message from William Morris Hunt. Mrs. Darrah claimed that he had asked her to tell Thaxter that Celia was going to have a communication from her mother. Of course, this was all that Thaxter had to hear; she immediately invited her to Appledore and prepared a room in her cottage where the two could wait for messages from Eliza. Thaxter convinced Sarah and Annie to consult her too, because the cunning Mrs. Darrah had announced that she was also in contact with James Fields and Theodore Jewett, Sarah's father. In a letter to John Greenleaf Whittier, whom she knew to be sympathetic, Thaxter described an experience she had shared with Fields and Jewett:

> Last week we went to Annie Fields. I tell *this to no one but you*, guard it safely—I know you will—After dinner we sat before the fire in the room we know & love, upstairs Roger [Sarah's dog] lay on the rug, Sarah J. on one side the fire, Annie on the other, we opposite by the

sofa. . . . As we sat there presently I saw by the expression of Mrs. D's beautiful face that she began to see something, I looked at her enquiringly. She said: "Do you wish me to tell you what I see?" We cried, "O, *yes!*" Then she said, "I see a misty something, have seen it for some minutes, moving slowly about over the rug"—presently she said: "It lengthens & takes shapes: it is a young man, a blond young man, he walks about, now he stoops & touches the dog." *Roger* lifted his head & growled . . . "& now two shapes come from the little room & down slowly past the piano, one a tall, slender, graceful lady with light reddish hair, the other a man, I think it is Longfellow"—after a minute— "No, it is a larger, fuller, younger man, with a firm presence," she described him—she had never seen James [Fields], nor any picture of him. She said, "he has straight dark hair, darker than his beard & *tumbled at the parting.* (You remember how he always did that?) his eyes are dark, his beard is large & seems rather square, it is curly, wavy, & has streaks of gray down the front." In short she described him perfectly & he spoke so that she could hear & repeated what you would expect from him. She spoke of the arch, merry, *human* expressions. She described in her exquisite way all that passed before her, till we were all sobbing . . . while I was eagerly leaning forward by Mrs. D's side to catch everything that passed, trying for Annie to be comforted, suddenly something blew softly in my ear & touched my cheek—I clasped my head with my hands & cried out so sudden, & Mrs. D. turning to me, exclaimed, "your mother is standing just behind your chair trying to attract your attention!" Think of it![32]

While Jewett and Fields shared Thaxter's enthusiasm for these séances for several years, they eventually became convinced that Mrs. Darrah was a fraud and ceased to believe in her powers. Even when Thaxter finally realized that her medium had been deceiving her, she never entirely gave up her belief in Spiritualism. As she was dying, she saw a vision of her mother standing at the foot of her bed.

After her disillusionment with Rose Darrah, Thaxter turned to religion, not a traditional New England Christianity, of course, but to Theosophy, an ancient faith that was revived in modern form in the nineteenth century. Helen Blavatsky, the founder of the movement, was born Helena von Hahn in the Ukraine in 1831. In 1849, she married Nikifor Blavatsky, an older man, whom she soon left as she began her travels around the world. In 1874, on a trip to the United States, she met Colonel Henry Steel Olcott, who became her companion; together they founded the Theosophical Society in 1875. However, Mme. Blavatsky never believed in Spiritualism, saying that "believers in such communication are simply dishonoring the dead and performing sacrilege. It was called 'necromancy' in days of old."[33]

Theosophists believe that there are ways to answer questions about our existence. As Robert Ellwood, author of *Theosophy: A Modern Expression of the Wisdom of the Ages*, explains: "In the nature of things, the answers can never be absolute, but they can illumine basic principles which help one understand—and joyously live in—this very confusing, buzzing, imperfect world."[34]

Although Thaxter never met Mme. Blavatsky, she fell under the influence of one of her followers, a questionable character named Mohini Chattergi, who encouraged her to read both the Bhagavad Gita and the New Testament. Celia described the effects of his teaching to John Greenleaf Whittier:

> There are two elements which Mohini brings which make clear the scheme of things; one is the law of incarnation, the rebirths upon this earth, in which all the Eastern nations believe as a matter of course, and to which our Christ refers in one or two of the gospels; and the other, the law of cause and effect, called Karma, the results of lives in the past. When salvation is spoken of, it always means the being saved from further earthly lives. . . .[35]

Whittier had always been perplexed by Thaxter's untraditional approach to religion. In fact, once when she told him that she never prayed, he replied, "I am sure thee does without knowing it."[36] For such a devout Quaker, her new enthusiasm for Theosophy must have been particularly hard to accept.

Thaxter, still seeking to reconcile herself to her mother's death, became as enthralled with Mohini as she had been with Mrs. Darrah. She wrote to her friend Mrs. Ward:

> I am going to send you a photo of the young Hindu, the Brahmin Mohini whom we have had in Boston this winter, the most wonderful being ever dreamed of, I assure you! He is hardly to be described, but he speaks the words of Angels and has been expounding the *New Testament!* to eager listeners all winter. His long soft hair, which looks blond, is really black as midnight, but being lustrous with youth gives back the light as you see. He is younger than my youngest boy, not

20, I think. He is all spirit, as impersonal as light, himself. When you come in the summer . . . you can bring me the picture unless you care to keep it. . . .[37]

The main attraction of Theosophy was that it offered Thaxter a comforting philosophy of a life after death. "Pardon me, dear friend," she wrote to Feroline Fox, "if I weary you with this talk, but my heart is so full of it, death seems such a different thing from what it used, such joy, such comfort, it is so sweet to look forward to; and for those who have gone on I have only rejoicing, and the consciousness of their well-being makes it easier for me to bear the loneliness without them."[38]

Through her exploration of Theosophy, Thaxter found the inner peace she was so desperately seeking and gradually evolved religious views of her own that incorporated a belief in reincarnation, in life after death, and, not unlike the Unitarians and Transcendentalists, the conviction that God is love. Her perseverance and courage in searching for a path to inner peace was finally successful.

9 The Aesthetic Movement: Finding a Voice

> But perhaps the glory of the room was her arrangement of
> flowers at one end—the "Altar," as we called it—where she
> had banked masses of flowers in dozens of vases of all sizes. I
> remember one day counting one hundred and ten. . . . It was
> not by chance that she had accomplished this glorious color
> scheme, for she worked over it for hours each day, putting a
> touch here and another there, almost as one would paint a
> picture or compose a sonata.[1]
>
> —MAUDE APPLETON MCDOWELL,
> "Childhood Memories of Celia Thaxter"

THE AESTHETIC MOVEMENT, WHICH BEGAN WITH THE PHILADELPHIA CENTENNIAL EXHIBI-
tion of 1876 and Oscar Wilde's 1882 American tour, inspired Thaxter and
other women throughout the country to experiment with the latest fashions in
art and aesthetics in their homes—particularly their parlors. Although short-
lived (it ended with Wilde's imprisonment in 1895), it affected the thousands of
Americans who took seriously Wilde's dictum that "Art is not something which
you can take or leave. It is a necessity of human life."[2] With her magical, mys-
tical parlor, artistic friends, and lush gardens, Celia Thaxter personified the
Aesthetic Movement in New England.

The Philadelphia Centennial Exhibition, celebrating the hundredth anni-
versary of the signing of the Declaration of Independence, was the first inter-
national trade fair ever held in the United States. Covering more than 450
acres of Philadelphia's Fairmont Park, it took ten years to plan and cost more
than eleven million dollars. Ulysses S. Grant opened the Exhibition on May 10,
1876, and in six months ten million people viewed the works of thirty thousand
exhibitors.[3] Many of the visitors, particularly women, flocked to the home design and ceramics exhibits, returning home to experiment with the new ideas
they had encountered. As a result, the Exhibition exerted a lasting influence on
households across America.

Sarah Orne Jewett celebrated the Exhibition in her wonderful short story
"The Flight of Miss Betsey Lane," in which Miss Betsey Lane, a resident of the
poorhouse in Byfleet, Maine, used an unexpected gift to fulfill her ambition to

go to "Pheladelphy." Once there she spent her days exploring the fairgrounds: "She saw the wonders of the West and the splendors of the East with equal calmness and satisfaction; she had always known that there was an amazing world outside the boundaries of Byfleet."[4] Upon her return, she informed her friends where she had been: "All ought to go that can; why, you feel's if you'd be'n all around the world. I guess I've got enough to think of and tell ye for the rest o' my days."[5]

"The splendors of the East" that Betsey Lane saw were largely from Japan. The opening of trade between Japan and the Western world began in 1853 when Commodore Perry arrived in Tokyo to establish diplomatic relations. However, there was little popular awareness of Japanese art until London's Great Exhibition of 1862; then the ceramic industry adopted every possible Japanese theme: sprays of cherry blossoms, sparrows, bamboos, and fan shapes were reproduced endlessly. Victorian watercolors of primroses and violets, nosegays of roses, and bunches of bluebells were abandoned in favor of lilies, sunflowers, chrysanthemums, and peonies.

By the early 1870s, enthusiasm for things Japanese had spread throughout America and was reflected in all the decorative arts of the Aesthetic period: Tiffany silver, porcelain, furniture—and china painting. Thaxter's first attempts as an artist were as a painter of china, the most popular home art form of the day. The craze began with the Philadelphia Exhibition and continued until well after World War I, engaging more than twenty-five thousand women artists by 1893.[6] While most of the china painters lived in New York, Boston, and Philadelphia, many of these domestic artists were also in Chicago, Cincinnati, and all across the country. In Willa Cather's *My Antonia*, the wife of the evil Wick Cutter "painted china so assiduously that even her washbowls and pitchers, and her husband's shaving mug were covered with violets and lilies."[7]

Betsey Lane went to Philadelphia for a glimpse of the world outside Maine, for a once-in-a-lifetime adventure; in real life, the philosophy of aesthetics introduced in Philadelphia proved equally rewarding. In their quest to enrich their aesthetic life, particularly in their enthusiasm for china painting, middle-class nineteenth-century women found an escape from the bonds of convention, a refuge from their traditional roles, and a well-needed outlet for their creativity. They were able, at least during their leisure time, to escape the constraints of domesticity by embellishing their Victorian homes with the latest styles in decorated china, pastel paintings, exotic fabrics, and every conceivable knickknack, all in a variety of shapes, designs, and colors. An outpouring of instruction manuals for china painting appeared: approximately fifty were published between 1870 and 1920. In addition, writes art historian Cynthia Brandimarte: "By the 1880s special-interest periodicals such as *China Decorator, Ceramic Monthly, Art Amateur,* and *Brush and Pencil* provided instructions, color studies for copying at home and hints on firing. *Keramic Studio* carried a nation-wide directory of teachers, and, locally, instructors advertised in newspapers and in city and business directories."[8]

Of course, the Victorian housewife's artistic output was always within the prescribed realm of women's work: men created fine art; women painted choco-late pots and teacups. Nevertheless, some of these goods created at home and for the home were sold in the "real" world. Increasingly china painting was pro-moted as a way to make money. Brandimarte says that "one author blandly stated that china painters 'received a handsome sum annually from orders for work, from sales and from lessons to pupils' and described china painting as 'a solution, to some extent, of the problem of self-support and independence for women.'"[9] While this may have been an exaggeration, surely Thaxter, along with many women all across America, benefited from this domestic occupa-tion. And, as they started to earn money, women also began to envision new possibilities for establishing control over their own lives.

While many feel that the Aesthetic Movement was born in Philadelphia, oth-ers see Boston as its birthplace. As the preeminent observer of the era, Van Wyck Brooks, wrote:

> Meanwhile, in Boston the interest grew in things aesthetic. The Mu-seum of Fine Arts was founded in 1870, the symbol and crystallization of this movement of feeling. . . . Lounges appeared in houses that were studies in colour, hung with purple curtains, and with rooms that were harmonies in green or melodies in blue. . . . On all sides, the question rose, What place was art to have in the satisfactory human life that Boston was trying to realize? Already a species of art-cant, as sharp observers called it, was displacing the commoner cant of religion and culture, and one heard on every hand the phrase, "He is a true artist," or "She has not the feeling of an artist." Everything was "artistic" or "inartistic." The great question "Love or Art?" filled many a youthful imagination that had fed upon Mrs. Browning's *Aurora Leigh*.[10]

Influenced by her early introduction to *Aurora Leigh* and by the "art-cant" Brooks described, Thaxter joined other women who flocked to classes and public lectures to learn about the current trends in the decorative arts. Her artistic friends provided the right connections to the best teachers. In 1877, she studied china painting with John Appleton Brown and drawing with Ross Turner and Childe Hassam. Other Appledore artists encouraged her extravagantly. Levi's friend William Morris Hunt was especially supportive. "Mr. Hunt said to me once," she confided to Annie Fields, "'You are not afraid; therefore you will be able to do anything,' and I never forgot it."[11]

The earliest evidence we have of Thaxter's interest in painting was recorded by her faithful brother Cedric in January 1864: "Your elegantly illuminated letter of the thirteenth arrived last Thursday."[12] However, her artistic career began in earnest in 1874, as she wrote to her friend Feroline Fox:

> Did Carry tell you I have taken to painting, — "wrestling with art," I call it, in the wildest manner? This woodbine leaf at the top of the first page I copied from nature. Of course it isn't very good, but it shows hope of better things, don't you think so? Do say you do! I can scarcely think of anything else. I want to paint everything I see: every leaf, stem, seed vessel, grass blade, rush, and reed and flower has new charms, and I thought I knew them all before. Such a new world opens, for I feel it in me; I know I can do it, and I am going to do it! What a resource for the dreary winter days to come![13]

Thaxter became amazingly productive, not only because she needed money desperately, but because writing no longer satisfied her. It had become a means to an end, a relatively easy source of income. Her aesthetic sense had been stifled during the course of her life thus far: her domestic duties and financial problems had left no time to pursue another career. But now, the time was ripe; art was in the air; she was ready to fulfill her artistic dreams.

The Aesthetic Movement also had a more subtle effect on Thaxter's life; it provided an opportunity to bend (but not break) some of the bonds of home and motherhood. She was able to earn extra money for herself and her family while remaining within the bounds of propriety and without violating any of the rules of domesticity. However, she never became an authentic New Woman, the type historian Nancy Woloch says was exemplified by the well-known social worker and suffragette Jane Addams. Addams "discarded an old persona, that of the dutiful daughter and neurasthenic invalid, and transformed herself into a public figure of national repute, admired and emulated."[14] While Thaxter declared her independence from Levi, reaped financial and artistic benefits from the Aesthetic Movement, and encouraged further development of her summer salon, she did not become a public figure outside her sheltered New England world. By choosing a way of life that was both conforming and non-traditional, Thaxter showed that she recognized her limitations.

At first, armed only with her natural talent and her unique empathy with nature, Thaxter began illustrating greeting cards and children's books and painting landscapes and china. Lithographer Louis Prang welcomed her drawings for his greeting cards, which he produced as works of art, not mere illustrations. His company offered facsimiles of oil and watercolor paintings ranging in price from ten cents to fifteen dollars.[15] The guests at Appledore House and her wide circle of friends provided a market for Thaxter's decorative art: one friend reports, "she was always busy with her sketching, illustrating her books printed on water color paper, which were often sold for fifty dollars before she could finish them."[16]

Following John Ruskin's advice to artists, Thaxter began with her knowledge of nature, carefully reproducing her favorite poppies, scarlet pimpernels, and other garden flowers. As she became more skillful, she used Japanese motifs in her painting: "I have done one of the coffee and milk colored tiles with two spangling sprawling storks in mid sky, working their way toward an enormous sun in the Zenith, copied from a Japanese book."[17] Later, during her trip to Europe in 1880, she illustrated her sketchbooks with the plants she enjoyed, recording them in detail and painting them in vivid colors. Her visit to Italy inspired designs of olives and olive branches, deep purple for the fruit and varying tones of green for the leaves and often accompanied by a painted inscription in ancient Greek. "Yesterday I was able to paint an olive pitcher for Mr. Ware," she wrote Fields, "and he sent me such a beautiful inscription in Greek to put on it, and that made me think of you. . . . Mr Thaxter and Roland hunted up the ancient Greek letters for me (the quotation came from Oedipus Colonos)."[18] She often used this olive and inscription pattern on her china and on the Prang greeting cards.

During her long winter confinements caring for her mother, Thaxter was the most creative and productive. In another letter to Fields, she describes how rewarding her aesthetic interests had become despite the hardships of life at Appledore:

Stoneware jug with olive branch painted by Celia in 1881.
COURTESY PORTSMOUTH ATHENÆUM.

This afternoon, while mother slept, I sat with her, and laid on my only tile, first, a warm summer sky of delicate flushed rose melting into softest pearly gray high up (the sky which faces the west at sunset); and far off I made the low hills melt in the distance; and nearer, quiet green fields and bits of wood with groups of poplar and thicker masses of green. . . . I live in these little landscapes I fashion; I love the flowers, and the living things, and quaint Japanese I work among, with a perfect passion. It is all my entertainment, all the amusement I have. I am up at six o'clock in the morning, often before, laying my plans for dinner for the family of eleven . . . that I may paint every minute of daylight that I can steal. . . . I have painted this winter one hundred and fourteen pieces for different people—cups, saucers, plates of all kinds, a great deal of immensely careful and elaborate work.[19]

Landscape painted in watercolor by Celia in 1884: *Champernowne Farm and Elm.*
COURTESY JONATHAN HUBBARD.

Thaxter's obsession with her work—"I live in these little landscapes I fashion"—reflected her need to discover an escape from her troubles and find a new focus for her life. As Sharon Stephan, curator of *One Woman's Work: The Visual Art of Celia Laighton Thaxter*, wrote, "it was her work with the visual arts, rather than her writing that became the greatest source of personal pleasure and fulfillment."[20] Writing, painting, caring for her mother, managing her brothers and their hotel, were tasks that would have overwhelmed many women, but Thaxter responded to her situation with her customary blend of self-sacrifice and determination. She not only increased her income but also developed artistically, enriching her life in the years after her mother's death and her estrangement from Levi.

Drawing and painting were one aspect of the Aesthetic Movement; experimenting in the realms of the occult, the evocative, and the fantastic was another. Oscar Wilde's words "the real life is the life we do not lead"[21] echoed in

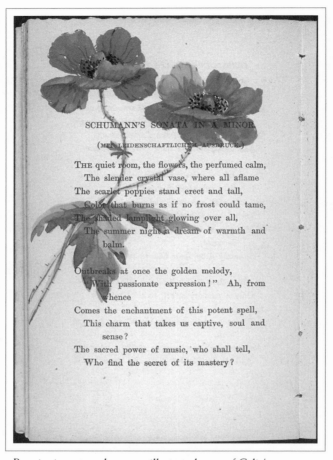

Poppies in watercolor on an illustrated page of Celia's poem "Schumann's Sonata in A Minor." POPPY: WATERCOLOR OVER SET TYPE, HAND-ILLUSTRATED PAGE FROM *THE CRUISE OF THE MYSTERY AND OTHER POEMS* BY CELIA THAXTER, 1866, FROM THE COLLECTION OF DONNA MARION TITUS.

the Aesthetic parlor, which was designed not only as a temple to art but as a seductive stage. Writers and speakers on home decor "suggested that the boundaries of the Victorian home could encompass the Moorish boudoirs, Turkish anterooms, and Japanese sitting rooms."[22] That Thaxter responded to their suggestions is evident in her description of her Appledore parlor, her island salon:

Porcelain teacup and saucer with a pimpernel design painted by Celia in 1878.
COURTESY SANDRA SMITH.

> Enchanting days, and evenings still more so, if that were possible!
> With the music still thrilling within the lighted room where the flow-
> ers glow under the lamplight, while floods of moonlight make more
> mystic the charmed night without. The thick curtain of the green vine
> that drapes the piazza is hung over its whole surface with the long
> drooping clusters of its starry flowers that lose all their sweetness
> upon the air, and show from the garden beneath like an immense veil
> of delicate white lace in the moonlight. . . . Through the windows cut
> in this living curtain of leaves and flowers we look out over the sea
> beneath the moon—is anything more mysteriously beautiful? . . .
> Lilies gleam, and the white stars of the Nicotiana, the white Poppies,
> the white Asters . . . nothing disturbs their slumber save perhaps the
> wheeling of the rosy-winged Sphinx moth that flutters like the spirit
> of the night above them as they dream.[23]

Enchanting days and more enchanting evenings; the scent of flowers indoors
and out; moonlight flooding the piazza and the parlor; the sea, mysterious and
beautiful; the poppies and lilies dreaming in the shadow of the sphinx moth—
clearly Celia Thaxter had found her place in the Aesthetic Movement.

Safe in her Appledore parlor during the final years of her life, Thaxter
assumed a new persona reflecting the mature woman she had become. She was
no longer the young bride, the "pretty little Miranda" who had so charmed

Hawthorne, nor the exhausted thirty-year-old housewife she had described to James Fields.[24] The death of her parents and her husband, her forays into Spiritualism, and the appeal of the Aesthetic Movement freed her from many of her past troubles. At last she developed a role that she thoroughly enjoyed: she became an actor in her own home. Within the dark green parlor with its long sofas, easy chairs, and walls covered with paintings, surrounded by artfully arranged flowers, she was transformed into the goddess at the altar, complete with a coterie of admirers: artists, writers, musicians, Boston Brahmins. On her walls hung original works of art supplied by her artistic friends as well as reproductions of works by European painters including Millet, William Morris Hunt's favorite. Thaxter even dressed the part: always in black, gray, or white. As Fields observed, "She never wore any other colors, nor was there anything like 'trimming' ever seen about her; there were only the fine, free outlines, and a white handkerchief folded carefully about her neck and shoulders."[25]

Flowers, always so much a part of Celia's life, completed the aesthetic picture. As Allen Lacy writes in the introduction to *An Island Garden*: "At base Thaxter's appreciation of gardening was purely aesthetic. She loved flowers entirely for their own sake and for the sake of the pleasure they gave her. She gave wholehearted recognition to the pleasures of the senses as good in themselves."[26] Writing in the most lyrical prose of her career, Thaxter described both the flowers in her garden and the role of gardening in her life. Even the sowing of the seeds aroused her emotions: "Standing by that space of blank and motionless ground, I think of all it holds for me of beauty and delight, and I am filled with joy at the thought that I may be the magician to whom power is given to summon so sweet a pageant from the silent and passive soil."[27] Her references to magic, to beauty, delight, and joy, reflect the liberating influence of the Aesthetic Movement. In planting her seeds, nurturing her flowers, and finally transporting them to her parlor, Thaxter achieved a harmony with nature and with herself that she was unable to reach during the earlier, turbulent years of her life.

By all accounts, the flowers Thaxter displayed in her parlor were sensational. Three of Childe Hassam's paintings reproduced in *An Island Garden*—*The Altar and the Shrine* (1892), *A Favorite Corner* (1892), and *The Room of Flowers* (1894)— transport us there, and we are almost overwhelmed by the profusion of flowers in the most magnificent blend of colors—blues, yellows, reds, pinks, white. *The Room of Flowers* treats us to the whole parlor crowded with books, pictures, vases of fresh flowers, chairs, tables, a desk. Our interest is piqued by the figure of a young woman in white reclining on the sofa and reading a book. The other two pictures focus on special parts of the room. *The Altar and the Shrine* depicts a bookcase known as the altar, topped with vase after vase of poppies carefully arranged in colors from purest white to tinted shades of pink and finally rich, deep rose and crimson. In *An Island Garden* Thaxter provides a prose description of Hassam's painting:

> To the left of this altar of flowers is a little table, upon which a picture stands and leans against the wall at the back. In the picture two Tea Roses long since faded live yet in their exquisite hues, never indeed to die. Before this I keep always the fairest flowers, and this table is the shrine. Sometimes it is a spray of Madonna Lilies in a long white vase of ground glass . . . or a tall sapphire glass holds deep blue Larkspurs of the same shade . . . or a charming dull red Japanese jar holds a new Nasturtium that exactly repeats its hues.[28]

She also described *A Favorite Corner*: "Near my seat in a sofa corner . . . stands yet another small table, covered with a snow-white linen cloth. . . . On this are gathered every day all the rarest and loveliest flowers as they blossom, that I may touch them, dwell on them, breathe their delightful fragrance and adore them."[29] All in all, Thaxter devoted six pages in her book to a detailed description of how she used flowers to achieve the desired effect in her parlor.

While the sunflower was the "official" flower of the Aesthetic Movement, poppies became a conspicuous symbol as well. In the Gilbert and Sullivan operetta *Patience*, Bunthorne (the character evocative of Oscar Wilde) sings: "You will rank as an apostle in the high aesthetic band, / If you walk down Piccadilly with a Poppy or a Lily in your mediaeval hand."[30] For years, poppies have been associated with beauty, magic, and medicine: their beauty has charmed their viewers; their ability to reproduce rapidly has connected them with fertility; their medicinal qualities have been said to offer forgetfulness and sleep. We can see that they fascinated both Thaxter and Hassam, because they were the flower most frequently mentioned in *An Island Garden* and the flower Hassam most often chose to paint when he was visiting Appledore. Altogether, there are nine illustrations of poppies in the book, and Thaxter's "Plan of the Garden" listed five different kinds of poppies.

Why this fascination with poppies? Thaxter wrote that "one never can have enough of them!"[31] Attracted by their sensual beauty, she described them in sexual terms as she examined the calyx, the outer part of the flower, the stamen, the male floral organ, and the anther, which produces pollen:

> It is held upright upon a straight and polished stem, its petals curving upward and outward into the cup of light, pure gold with a lustrous satin sheen. . . . It is not enough that the powdery anthers are orange bordered with gold; they are whirled about the very heart of the flower like a revolving Catherine-wheel of fire. In the centre of the anthers is a shining point of warm sea-green, a last, consummate touch which makes the beauty of the blossom supreme.[32]

The writing of naturalist and art critic John Ruskin fueled Thaxter's interest in poppies: "John Ruskin says: 'I have in my hand a small red Poppy. . . . It is an intensely simple, intensely floral flower. All silk and flame, a scarlet cup, perfect edged all round, seen among the wild grass far away like a burning coal from Heaven's altars.'"[33] Curator David Curry called Ruskin "the most important aesthetic authority of the nineteenth century" and believed that he was a significant link between Childe Hassam and the Aesthetic Movement.[34] Thaxter enjoyed his books as early as 1854, when she wrote to Lizzie Hoxie: "Now we [she and Levi] are reading Ruskin's last volume of 'Modern Painters,' and I declare I can't tell what we have the best times over, for we sometimes lose ourselves in wonder and admiration for him and then shout with unbounded mirth at his impatient sarcasm. . . ."[35] As her interest in gardening grew, Thaxter admired Ruskin even more, particularly his scientific examination of flowers; she not only adopted his descriptive style but quoted him several times in *An Island Garden*.

However, the real clue to her fascination with poppies lies in Thaxter's own words:

> I muse over their [poppy] seed-pods, those supremely graceful urns that are wrought with such matchless elegance of shape, and think what strange power they hold within. Sleep is there, and Death, his brother, imprisoned in those mystic sealed cups. There is a hint of their mystery in their shape of sombre beauty, but never a suggestion in the fluttering blossom.[36]

The grace and beauty of the poppies, their suggestion of arcane powers and intimation of sleep and death, the juxtaposition of the mysterious shape of the flower and the vulnerability of the blossom, stimulated her senses and excited her imagination. They were nature's perfect complement to the art, music, and conversation that filled her salon.

Music, another expression of the Aesthetic Movement, resounded literally and figuratively throughout Celia Thaxter's cottage. To achieve the perfect ambience, she purchased a grand piano: "This room is made for music; on the polished floor is no carpet to muffle sound. . . . There are no heavy draperies to muffle the windows, nothing to absorb the sound."[37] Childe Hassam depicted the setting in his 1893 painting *The Sonata*. In it we see a young woman, dressed in white, her head bowed, music in hand, seated before a piano. Resting on the piano is what appears to be a yellow rose; to her left is the perimeter of a painting with a Japanese motif. In *The Sonata*, Hassam gathered the three most important aesthetic components of life at Appledore: art, music, and flowers. In "Schumann's Sonata in A Minor" Thaxter uses poetry to achieve the same effect, blending the sensuousness of the flowers and the colors of the evening to produce a kind of midsummer night's dream:

> The quiet room, the flowers, the perfumed calm,
>   The slender crystal vase, where all aflame
> The scarlet poppies stand erect and tall,
>   Color that burns as if no frost could tame.
> The shaded lamplight glowing over all,
>   The summer night a dream of warmth and balm.
>
> Outbreaks at once the golden melody,
>   "With passionate expression!" Ah, from whence
> Comes the enchantment of this potent spell,
>   This charm that takes us captive, soul and sense?
> The sacred power of music, who shall tell,
>   Who find the secret of its mastery? . . .[38]

Thaxter's interest in music surfaced early in her marriage when she took piano lessons, explaining to Sarah Weiss: "I find it rather difficult to manage domestic affairs just now, especially as I began to take my music lessons a week or two ago & if I mean to do anything I must practice. In spite of everything I am getting along nicely & only wish I could keep it up a couple of years!"[39] Years later, music came to play an even greater role in her life. Musicians were among the favored guests at Appledore; all performed during their visits to the delight of Thaxter and her guests.

Ole Bull (1810–1880), one of the most charismatic musicians to visit Appledore, was also one of the most memorable. He came to America from Norway for the first time in 1842; by then he was a well-established violin virtuoso, a protégé of the Italian violinist Paganini, and a master of the romantic tradition. His biographer Einar Haugen observed: "Bull's talent as a performer was not the only source of his popularity with his audience. He was also handsome with an irresistible personal charm."[40] In addition to performing throughout the world, he became involved in a pioneering community (which ultimately failed) in western Pennsylvania.

Ole Bull often appeared in Boston concert halls, where he was admired by Thaxter's friends, including Annie and James Fields and Henry Wadsworth Longfellow and his wife, Fanny, who wrote in her diary that he was "a new Orpheus, with a soul in his violin. When I drove home, I seemed to see twelve moons instead of one."[41] In the summer of 1869, Bull appeared at the Boston Peace Jubilee, an enormous festival celebrating the end of the Civil War, where he functioned as the concertmaster of an orchestra of 1,094 players! After the festival, he rested at Appledore House, and while there performed a concert to benefit the Norwegians who were newly arrived on the Isles of Shoals. It is easy to imagine Thaxter's fascination with this charming, attractive visitor who provided one more exciting dimension to her salon.

Music was in the air—impromptu recitals featuring soloists, trios, and piano duets occurred daily—and Celia Thaxter was in her element. Beethoven and Chopin, the darlings of the Aesthetic Movement, were the favorites, but William Mason also introduced Edward MacDowell's *Tragica* Sonata, playing it once a day until it also became popular among the guests.[42]

Why was music so important to Thaxter? Annie Fields's explanation is sensitive and insightful:

> It seemed as if the new awakening of her spirit to a conscious sense of its own independent existence came while listening to the music of Beethoven. Day after day Mr. Paine delighted to play for her and was eager to forerun her wish to hear. During the long summer mornings he would repeat her favorite sonatas (109 and 110), and her expressions of gratitude to him and to Mr. Eichberg are more touching than ever before. Up to this moment of her life she seems to have considered herself a striving, struggling, sorrowing, and oftentimes rebellious atom; one knowing only its own fatuousness and its own power of suffering; deeper, however, hidden in a half recognized consciousness, she was always able to find in the heart of nature the same response which she had felt as a little child; but her half-awakened self was a mist-driven creature longing for the light. This light she found

in listening to Beethoven, and from that moment music was more than ever a great factor in her existence.[43]

Fields's description of Thaxter as a lonely, unhappy outsider struggling to find meaning in her life is poignant. Fields recognized that music illuminated a path to a feeling of contentment that Thaxter had never known; it was the final step in Thaxter's search for her own voice, a voice she found in the Aesthetic Movement.

10 *Finale, 1888-1894*

And so the ripe year wanes.[1]

—Celia Thaxter, *An Island Garden*

*B*y THE SUMMER OF 1887 THAXTER REACHED AN UNEXPECTED AND HAPPY STAGE OF HER life: a time when she could relax and enjoy herself. John and Roland were married; Karl, happily occupied with his photography. Her parlor was filled with the artists, musicians, and friends she treasured; her garden bloomed gloriously; she wrote and painted in an atmosphere of culture and beauty. She spent all summer at Appledore, then returned with Karl to Boston for the winter.

Back on the islands for her birthday in June 1888, Thaxter wrote a cheerful note to Fields; her description of the bakers and the bootblack affirm Appledore House's status as a luxury hotel:

> My birthday—so old! 48—To think of having lived nearly half a century! It isn't five o'clock in the morning. I have just been downstairs in the bakery watching the bakers, for they make wondrous rolls and bread sticks. I had to go and see how they did it. . . . Head baker has worked in the principal Confectioners and hotels in Boston and is all accomplished and what he did with the snow-white almost aerial, sensitive mass of dough was perfectly amazing. And the bakers looked so remarkably picturesque and handsome and innocent, in differently shaped caps of absolutely snow white linen. . . . The bootblack . . . just stole past me up the stairs, to gather up the shoes at sleeper's doors— that shows how early it is. I am waiting over here at the hotel for the early six o'clock breakfast to be ready. . . .[2]

The luxurious accommodations, Thaxter's salon, and the beautiful natural surroundings assured the success of Appledore Hotel season after season. Rosamond Thaxter described the years from 1880 to 1890 as "The Golden Years."[3] Oscar and Cedric's entrepreneurship knew no bounds. After buying the Oceanic Hotel from their rival and expanding the original hotel to three buildings, connected by covered piazzas, they thought of another idea. In 1888, several longtime guests were invited to build cottages on the island while boarding at the hotel; in twenty years the property would revert to the Laightons, unless a new agreement were reached. Childe Hassam, J. Appleton Brown, Ross Turner, and several other frequent vacationers took advantage of the idea and built summer homes. Now they not only had their own homes, but they could enjoy Thaxter's parlor and garden as well as a tennis court, pier and dock, small swimming pool, and boats for yachting and sailing. In addition, according to Rosamond Thaxter, "There were rustic summer houses placed at spots where the views were most beautiful and the romantic settings inspired much reading of poetry and decorous love scenes."[4] Nightly entertainment was provided in the best Victorian tradition:

> The evening mood at the hotel was anything but quiet and sober, however. Guests always dressed for dinner to which they were summoned by the band playing tunes from Gilbert and Sullivan. Wines were enjoyed. Afterward guests dispersed over the rocks, through the parlors or to the billiard room. Many jokes and pranks were played by the old timers.[5]

During these years, Thaxter was able to enjoy her stay on the islands in ways that had been impossible earlier. Her parents and Levi were dead, and the conflicted emotions their relationships had entailed were put aside. With John and Roland married and pursuing their own lives, Karl was her only dependent. Thankfully, Celia's relationships with her younger sons had improved, and she became closer to them than when they were children.

After Levi's death, Roland had abandoned his plans to become a doctor and returned to Harvard to study entomology; he received his M.A. and Ph.D. concurrently in 1888. He married Mabel Freeman the same year and accepted a job at the Connecticut Experiment Station in New Haven, where he worked as a plant pathologist for a short time before returning to Harvard to assist Professor William Farlow, a well-known botanist. For the rest of his life he remained at Harvard and gained fame as a botanist, entomologist, and bacteriologist. He was both a teacher and a research scientist. According to Harvard professor Donald Pfister, "within his body of published research are contributions significant enough to justify several careers."[6] His father's influence can be seen in the attention he gave to scientific details in his work, and Celia's artistic bent led to the meticulous illustrations that survive today.

Two descriptions of Roland present a picture of a taciturn, obsessive man, who was nevertheless admired by his colleagues. Pfister writes:

> In addition to indigestion and malaria Thaxter suffered from the occupational disease of many brilliant scientists—he was inordinately shy. In an internal battle to cover his shyness, he put up a front that amounted to tactlessness. . . . Thaxter yearned to be "impractical" as if impractical science was the only science. . . . When he got back to Harvard he became impractical for sure. He spent the rest of his scientific life in collecting and designing a card file for the Laboulbeniales, an order of fungi parasitic on water insects.[7]

Another scientist, Carroll Dodge, says:

> During his years of teaching, nearly one thousand students worked in his laboratories. While not a brilliant lecturer, his patient laboratory teaching by the Socratic method, his insistence on accurate drawings and clear presentation made lasting impressions on all who came under his influence. . . . When one considers that poor health, due to gastric ulcers which necessitated seven abdominal operations, was almost constantly present during this period, his great success as a teacher is all the more remarkable. Undoubtedly this physical handicap accounts for some of the irritability reported by some of his former students.[8]

Roland was devoted to his wife and four children and suffered a great personal loss when his oldest son—to whom Celia had been very attached—died prematurely in 1906.

Roland's marriage and the birth of his children brought Celia great happiness. As she informed her friends the Wards: "My youngest son Roland has a professorship at Harvard and they are building a little house for themselves in Norton's Woods, near Kirkland St., and the mother and babes are staying with me till it is ready for them. I never knew what it was to be happy, I think till I became a grandmother!"[9] The following winter, however, Thaxter once again found herself in the role of caregiver. As she told her friend Clara Anthony:

> Ever since your beautiful letter came to me I have been trying to write, but I have been taking care of people all winter—first my precious

Celia and her grandson. REPRODUCED HERE BY PERMISSION OF THE
HOUGHTON LIBRARY, HARVARD UNIVERSITY.

little grandson was ill in bed a long time with the grippe, then my
beloved youngest son, his father, went down with it, and as he is so
very delicate with a burden of malaria to carry which is in itself a
grievous tax of all his powers, I trembled for his life, and flew to him
and tarried till I saw him on the road to recovery, and then sped back
again just in time to catch the eldest as he came down with the same
dread and mysterious disease, poor Karl, as you know. . . .[10]

Nevertheless, it was Roland and his family who gave Celia the normalcy she
craved all her life; she found joy in her son's career, his wife appreciated her,
and their children adored her. Her final years were enriched by their love and
devotion.

John's career as a dairy farmer finally was launched in 1884. How successful
John was as a farmer is open to question, but, fortunately, his marriage to Mary
Gertrude Stoddard, the daughter of a wealthy mill-owning family, provided
him with another source of income. He met his future wife when she and her
family visited Appledore, and, after a lengthy courtship, they were married on
June 1, 1887. Their daughter Rosamond reported, in her inimitable way: "They
got off to rather a bad start as Gertrude, instructed by her mother, pleaded she
was tired and asked for separate rooms, locking the connecting door. Things
improved when they reached Niagara Falls . . ."[11]

Ultimately, their marriage proved to be contentious; in fact, Gertrude's library included a book titled *How to Be Happy Though Married*, and in 1920 she consulted a Portsmouth attorney about her husband's conduct and obligations. But in the eyes of their only daughter, born a year after Celia's death, John was a doting and attentive father. Rosamond's biography of her grandmother begins with this dedication: "To John Thaxter, Celia's Second Son, My Blue-Eyed, Affectionate Father, I Lovingly Dedicate This Story of His Gifted And Courageous Mother."[12]

Throughout the years, Thaxter's relationship with John Greenleaf Whittier continued to strengthen and grow. The depth of their friendship is revealed in the following letter, which she wrote to him in 1889. Interestingly, the portions in italics were not reprinted in the book of Thaxter's letters edited by Annie Fields and Rose Lamb. Undoubtedly they felt her thoughts were too personal, exposing too much of the emotional side of her life, which they wished to shield from the public.

Most dear friend,

You cannot know what a joy your dear letter is to me. I have read it again and again, *every precious word of it, more glad each time, for every syllable of it. Shall I tell you—I had a kind of sorrowful feeling that you had forgotten me, or rather drifted so far away as not to care much, if any, and I love you so dearly and truly, it troubled me sore. . . .*

Yes, I had a quiet, lovely winter in Portsmouth, *a place for my poor Karl where he was happy* . . . did more writing than for years, and was well and content until about three weeks ago, when I was suddenly very ill, as I have been twice before, for no reason that anybody appears able to find out, except "overwork" the doctors say, in years past. *Nothing but morphine under the skin does any good and I never know when the bolt is going to fall and smite me, it gives me no warning. Please do not speak of it, I hate to be questioned and talked to, don't you? I know you do!* So I say as little about it as possible. I do not mind the thought of death, it means only fuller life, but there is a pang in the thought of leaving my poor Karl. But I know the heavenly Father provides for all. . . .

Never did the island look so lovely in the early spring since I was a little child playing on the rocks at White Island. . . . Sometimes I wonder if it is wise or well to love any spot on this old earth as intensely as I do this. . . .

I am going to send you with this a little copy of an old picture of Karl and myself when we were babes together, he one year old, I eighteen. *Karl copied it. Isn't it a pathetic picture, being so prophetic of our life together—poor Karl!*

Thank you for the beautiful poem you enclosed. It is most lovely. You ask what I have been writing? A great deal, for me. I wish I had sent you the April "St. Nicholas," for in it is a version I made of Tolstoy's "Where love is there is God also." . . .

Dear friend, I hope I have not wearied you with so long a letter. Please send me one little line to say if you got it and the photo. God bless you. Ever, with deep, gentle, grateful love, your CT[13]

For many nineteenth-century women, Annie Fields in particular, some things were not to be shared; one must be "armored in calm," like Alexandra, the heroine of Willa Cather's *O Pioneers!*[14] For Thaxter to admit in this letter that she thought Whittier had forgotten her, to confess that she used morphine, to so poignantly express her despair over Karl's illnesses, must have seemed inappropriate to Fields. Yet, for the modern-day reader, this letter provides a welcome insight into Thaxter's feeling and helps us to understand her in the light of our own experiences.

In 1885, Fields and Jewett invited Whittier to live with them, but, treasuring his independence and fearing that he would not like city life and would be uncomfortable because of his deafness, he refused: "It would be like having a waif from Barnum's Museum shut up in your library, and people coming to see what it looks like."[15] During the last decade of his life, he continued to see family and friends but gradually became increasingly frail and reclusive. When he wrote this letter to Thaxter in 1890, Whittier was eighty-two years old and clearly despondent. We can only imagine how saddened Celia was when she read:

My dear friend,

. . . I can say little for myself; the years grow very heavy, and my sight fails, so that my pen has to run without much direction. I can read very little and the long nights are rather tedious. Thanks for "My Lighthouse," beautiful within and without, a cheering and hopeful light shines from it. As I sit alone by my lonely hearth I think of the many charming days and evenings at the enchanted island and how much I love thee. God bless thee for all thy kindness!

With love to thy brothers I am always affectionately

thy friend, J. G. W.[16]

John Greenleaf Whittier died on September 7, 1892, four days after suffering a paralytic stroke. His legacy lived on not only in his poetry and good works but, thanks to James Fields's management of his royalties and investments, in generous gifts to his family, friends, and charitable institutions.

Childe Hassam was one of Thaxter's young friends. With him, she had a completely different relationship than with either John Greenleaf Whittier or James Fields. She was not looking for the fatherly approval she sought from them, nor did she worry about the physical illnesses that troubled the older men. More important, Thaxter's close friendship with Hassam began when her most difficult personal years were over: she and Levi had made a mutually satisfactory agreement to live apart, and she was an acclaimed poet, presiding over a fashionable salon on Appledore Island. There was an air of playful confidence about her when she met with the young artists and musicians who vacationed there each summer that was most appealing. To Hassam especially, she was a mentor and friend. As Smith College professor Ann Boutelle writes: "Thaxter's effect on Hassam's work was [also] exceptional. She introduced him to the Shoals, she created a warm and appreciative ambience for him there and as a result he adopted the Shoals as subject matter for roughly ten percent of his massive (nearly 4,000 pieces) oeuvre. Some of his most beautiful and most daring paintings were painted at the Shoals."[17]

The son of an old New England family, Hassam was born in 1859 in the Boston suburb of Dorchester. He was proud that he was related on his paternal side to William Morris Hunt and his brother, architect Richard Morris Hunt, and on his maternal side to Nathaniel Hawthorne. His first venture in the world of art was as an apprentice to a wood engraver, but soon he, like Celia, found freelance work in the burgeoning magazine industry. He produced illustrations for *Harper's*, *The Century*, *Scribner's*, and several juvenile publications. Sometime around 1878, he began to take formal drawing and painting lessons. Although his reputation as a watercolorist was growing, he continued to create illustrations, including some for Celia's poems. In 1883, Hassam made his first trip to Europe, where he toured Great Britain, France, Italy, and Spain. Upon returning to Boston, he displayed sixty-seven works in an exhibition in late 1883— apparently successfully, because the following year he married Maude Doane, a young woman from Dorchester whom he had been courting. He acquired his first studio on Tremont Street, opposite the Boston Common, and began painting in oils; he was able to support himself and Maude with the sale of his art for the rest of their lives.

Childe Hassam: Photograph by Karl Thaxter. PHOTOGRAPH,
COURTESY PORTSMOUTH ATHENÆUM.

In the spring of 1886, the Hassams left Boston for Paris, joining many other American artists attracted by the success of the Impressionist movement. This was the year of the last exhibition of the original Impressionist painters in Paris and the first large exhibit in New York. According to his biographer Donelson Hoopes, "Hassam's motives for going to Paris undoubtedly involved a keen interest in what the Impressionists were doing, but they went beyond that to his recognition of the need for refining his talent in the larger crucible of contemporary art."[18] Although the influence of Claude Monet is apparent in many of his Appledore paintings, he never went to Giverny to meet the artist. Instead he remained in Paris working diligently for three years to expand and perfect his technique and to achieve critical notice for his paintings. Upon their return to the United States in 1889, the Hassams moved to New York. It was during this time that he began spending summers at Appledore and, according to Hoopes, "created a series of paintings that invites comparison with the work of the best of the *plein air* Frenchmen."[19]

Thaxter and Hassam met in Boston, probably as early as 1877, when she began painting. His first trip to Appledore was around 1881. As he explained some years later, Thaxter convinced him to drop Frederick as his first name:

> When I was not much past twenty I met Celia Thaxter who liked, as so many others did, to paint in watercolors. She said to me one day "you should not, with an unusual name like yours, fail to take advantage of its unique character—There is a young Englishman who has just written some remarkably good stories of India. . . . His name is Joseph Rudyard Kipling—but he has the literary sense to drop the prefix. If your name is to become known, as Jane Hunt [sister of William Hunt] thinks it will, it would be better without the F." That was quite early in my career and so I became Childe Hassam and I spent some of my pleasantest summers in the Isles of Shoals and in her salon there.[20]

After his return from Paris, Hassam spent winters in New York and summers painting in New England. Thaxter provided him with a studio not far from her cottage. His enthusiasm for his life there is reflected in a letter to his friend the critic and poet George Woodbury: "Do come out here! Now! Quick! Laurence Hutton[21] is here with a lot of letters of Mark Twain—and Mrs. Thaxter's garden is beautiful, perfectly beautiful. . . ."[22]

Hassam's first Appledore paintings date from 1886: watercolors focusing on the lighthouse at White Island, Thaxter's first home. From 1890 until Celia's death in 1894, he visited the Isles of Shoals each year, enchanted by the islands and by his hostess. Together they created *An Island Garden*, published in 1894.

During the last years of her life, Thaxter's love of nature led to a vigorous campaign against the use of birds' feathers in women's hats. The Audubon Society became the perfect vehicle for her efforts. Writing to her friend Feroline Fox, she exclaimed:

> I cannot express to you my distress at the destruction of the birds. You know how I love them; every other poem I have written has some bird

for its subject, and I look at the ghastly horror of women's headgear with absolute suffering. I remonstrate with every wearer of birds. I never lose an opportunity of doing this whenever and wherever it occurs. . . . No woman worthy of the name would wish to be instrumental in destroying the dear, beautiful creatures; and for such idle folly! To deck their heads like squaws, who are supposed to know better, when a ribbon or a flower would serve their purpose just as well . . . Believe me, I, too, am engaged heart and soul in trying to save our dear birds. I don't care to head a league, because I think I can do just as much good in other ways, and I hate to drag myself into public vices any more than I can possibly help. Have you not noticed how carefully I keep out of publicity? But be sure I shall do everything in my power in other ways, quite as much as I could in the way you suggest. I will join this society whose circular you send me, and continue to work strongly, if quietly, in the cause. No one can have it more at heart than I.[23]

Despite her professed desire to avoid publicity, Thaxter could not resist a worthy cause. In 1886, she became the secretary of the Audubon Society in Waltham and campaigned vigorously for the preservation of wildlife. In February 1887, she wrote an article for the first issue of the *Audubon Magazine*. It was titled "Woman's Heartlessness" and expressed her outrage at the current fashions in women's hats: "Ah, me, my fire-flecked oriole. . . . Your beauty makes you a target for the accursed gun that shatters your lovely life . . . that your dead body may disfigure some woman's head and call all eyes to gaze upon her!"[24] The next year, in her capacity as secretary of the Appledore Audubon Society, she asked John Greenleaf Whittier and his niece Phoebe to sign bird pledges.[25]

One of Thaxter's most engaging epistolary friendships grew out of this love of birds. It was with author and naturalist Bradford Torrey, who had been born in Weymouth, Massachusetts, in 1843. He was on the editorial staff of *Youth's Companion*. His book *Birds in the Bush* had been published in 1885, and several others were written while Thaxter was still alive.

Her first letter to Torrey was classic: "By this wing which I send you, can you tell me the name of the bird who owned it?"[26] Unfortunately, Torrey's responses to Thaxter's letters have not been preserved, but he must have answered immediately because on December 16 she wrote: "Both your notes have reached me and I thank you for the information about the bird. Why is it called Kildeer plover, do you know?"[27] By May 1889, she was inviting him to come to Appledore to study the birds in person. She was also complaining to him about her brother (probably Oscar) "who has shot 3 white owls within the last few days, much to my distress! Perfectly beautiful they were, their plumage so exquisitely white and soft and clean. He sent two of them to a taxidermist to be set up, and then they sell at large prices." In addition, she requested a photograph: "Haven't you a spare photo of yourself? It is a curious feeling to write to 'a mind' entirely, in this impersonal way! Please send your shadow to me and I will send you my flowerbank and myself, a grandmother of fifty-four, and your sincere friend."[28]

In return, Torrey sent Thaxter a copy of his book of essays, *A Rambler's Lease*. Her enthusiasm knew no bounds: "I have read your beautiful book, every single word of it, with the greatest possible pleasure, and I feel like shaking hands with you *with both hands*. Not only have I read it once, but I take it up again and again for pure pleasure. I can't begin to tell you how I sympathize with your moods, with your philosophy, with all you say."[29]

Their correspondence continued in this manner for the next four years. Bradford Torrey never did come to the Shoals, and they never met when Thaxter was in Portsmouth, but they continued to exchange books and compliments. Obviously Torrey enjoyed the copy of *An Island Garden* that Celia sent him; in the spring of 1894 she wrote: "I'm so glad you like the book. It doesn't pretend to be much except a faithful chronicle of a mighty good time. As you say, enthusiasm is a good thing, and enthusiasm at sixty more valuable than at sixteen, and in another year I am going to be sixty."[30]

The last letter Thaxter wrote to her new friend foreshadowed her death: "I scribble this little line . . . to beg you, when the whirl of people passes and tranquility settles once more upon our little world, to steal a moment and slip down here and let us see you and know you, will you not? *Do*. Some of us may be slipping out of this mortal state and we shall never know each other in this particular phase of existence, which would be a pity I think!"[31]

In these letters to Bradford Torrey, there is none of the angst that characterizes her earlier correspondence, especially to her women friends. Despite her worries about Karl and her often debilitating illnesses, Thaxter found a measure of peace in her final years. For a long time the vicissitudes of nature seemed to have been reflected in her own life, but in the end the storms abated, and she was able to enjoy her world of family and friends in the beauty of her island home.

The summer of 1888 promised to be delightful. In a letter to Fields, Thaxter was uncharacteristically buoyant:

> Aunty Reed has been reading Jane Carlyle aloud to me while I painted. It is very interesting yet I must confess I did get tired of so many bed-bugs and headaches and blue pills and castor oil and sleepless nights and barking dogs. I think half of it and the bed bugs and bowel complaints would have been better unprinted. . . . It is such a pity that everything in a person's life should be dragged through the middle of the king's highway, don't you think, dearest?[32]

However, as usual the days were hectic. Thaxter's responsibilities at the hotel (principally making reservations, which called for great diplomacy) as well as caring for her garden, entertaining the many visitors to her parlor, and, of course, her literary and artistic commitments kept her constantly busy. Although she seemed happy, these tasks wore her out, and, in October, she became ill. In a letter to her friend William Ward, editor of the magazine *The Independent*, she wrote: "I have had a sudden sharp attack of illness since I wrote last which makes me fear a little about being away from any physician through the tempestuous winter, and makes my brothers fear more than myself. It yielded at last to the hypodermic injections of morphine, but neuralgic swords playing about the region of the heart and cutting and tearing across the spine are not very pleasant companions to deal with . . . this attack is very nearly a repetition of last summer's. . . ."[33] The illnesses that had plagued her in the past—heart disease, neuralgia, and what she called "nervous prostration"—were about to overwhelm her.

Once again, Fields became the recipient of a series of disturbing letters describing the next few months. In one letter Celia wrote:

> My dearest Annie,
>
> . . . I am better, but I cannot yet leave the lounge where I lie most of the day. All the time my side troubles me, high up in my left side. This afternoon I ventured to put on my clothes for a while, I have been living in my dressing gown a fortnight. I haven't much strength and my eyes look like two burned holes in a blanket. But I am getting over it, slowly. . . .
>
> . . . The Dr. said all my trouble came from exhaustion consequent on overwork, overwork for a long time, and last spring, out of all

reason. Yes, I did not take into consideration my 53 years and never spared myself, so here I am. . . .[34]

Rather than risk the uncertainties of medical help on the islands, Thaxter moved with Karl to Portsmouth for the winter. Her home on State Street was delightful: nine sunlit rooms including a parlor, bathroom, kitchen, several bedrooms, and even a "carpenter's shop" for Karl. She again seemed happy, even upbeat, writing to a friend: "I am a great deal better, and getting well fast under a treatment I discovered and apply myself. No doctors, thank you."[35] Like her friends Annie and Sarah, Celia sometimes devised her own medication; she also accepted their suggestions. In response to one recommendation from Fields, she wrote: "Thank you for the advice about hot beef tea and I'll try it again, tho' I've tried it before. But the father of all the owls seems to take possession of me o'nights!"[36] She was also willing to accept other nontraditional cures. She wrote to her friend Ada Hepworth that she had been "fighting with nervous prostration all winter" but was now feeling better "with the help of a wise old doctor who lives not far from here, who feeds me on champagne."[37] While nervous prostration—what today might be called depression—was not uncommon among nineteenth-century women, most doctors prescribed water cures at fashionable spas. Thaxter's champagne treatment was unique, but obviously effective!

By the following summer, Thaxter was strong enough to return to Appledore. In a letter to Fields, she portrayed the vitality in her parlor:

My dearest Annie:

From my sofa corner, which I hope soon to be leaving, for a seat, my own, at my painting table, I scribble a line. . . . How to tell you of life here just now! . . . Mrs. Hemenway still lingers and she has bought nearly five hundred dollars worth of Ross Turner's Bermuda pictures, four beautiful ones, they are wonderful, the color like peacocks' feathers, the water, fused jewels. . . . Mr. Mason is playing Grieg, such dreaming music. Appleton Brown is here . . . and the Hassams . . . and others whom you do not know but who turn to me, I have my hands, head and heart too full, and I wish they would come by installments and not all at once, it takes the life pretty nearly out of me to have everybody wanting all of me at once! But it doesn't last long, thank heaven.[38]

Thaxter continued with a description of her never ending war on slugs, which she elaborated upon in *An Island Garden*:

> Oh Annie, you would have laughed to see the box of toads which came for me night before last! Ninety toads, all wired over in a box and wondering what fate was in store for them, no doubt. Soon as the mowing was done all the million slugs in the grass charged into my poor garden and post haste, I sent for more of my little dusty pets, my friends, my saviors! And I turned the 90 loose in the fat slugging grounds and such a breakfast as they must have had! If there's one thing I adore more than another, it's a toad! They eat every bug in the garden![39]

Celia and Karl returned to Portsmouth in November and spent a dreary winter there. As Thaxter explained to her friend Mrs. Ward: "I have been ill all winter with nervous prostration too. I have given away all my strength all my life long and now I miss it sadly. But I trust to struggle up out of this weariness bye and bye . . . the Dr. will not let me write, but I could not refrain from replying to your sweet letter. . . . I am trying to *vegetate* and forget that I have even my moderate portion of intelligence. . . . I *must* ask you—have you Tennyson's new volume, and do you not think the last poem most beautiful? 'Across the Bar.' . . ."[40] After a lifetime of endless activity, the confinement of her illness was oppressive. Tennyson's poem gave voice to her feelings: "Sunset and evening star / And one clear call for me / And may there be no moaning of the bar / When I put out to sea. . . ."[41]

She was no better in December. Writing to William Ward, Thaxter reported: "I am better but still fastened to pepsin[42] and Vichy water and not able to sleep unless I stay out of doors pretty nearly all the time—if I do this, then I sleep at night. . . ."[43] Even more important, she was showing further signs of depression as she contemplated the loss of several of her friends: "Lily Bowditch is gone and her aunt Olivia, Dr. Henry's wife, and now young Mrs. Stone, Lucy Bowditch is seriously ill. . . . How I shall miss poor dear Lily! But we are always learning these sad lessons . . . and being taught over and over again not to let our affection twine too closely round any mortal thing, since nothing really *is* except God, the sad, sad touch of change is upon everything else. . . ."[44]

In January 1891, the restorative powers of gardening helped Thaxter. In her introduction to *An Island Garden*, she wrote, "Ever since I could remember anything, flowers have been like dear friends to me, comforters, inspirers, powers to uplift and to cheer."[45] After months of illness, her flowers comforted her once again as she began planting seeds for her summer garden: "When the snow is still blowing against the window-pane in January and February, and the wild winds are howling without, what pleasure it is to plan for summer that is to be!"[46] The seeds for pansies, dahlias, and other stronger plants could be sown in shallow boxes, but for the more delicate flowers, like the Iceland poppies, she devised another system.[47] These were placed in "rows of egg-shells close together, each shell cut off at one end, with a hole for drainage at the bottom . . . when comes the happy time for setting them out in the garden beds, the shell can be broken away from the oval ball of earth that holds their roots without disturbing them, and they are transplanted almost without knowing it."[48] Her winter gardening raised her spirits: "My upper windows all winter are filled with young Wall-flowers, Stocks, single Dahlias, Hollyhocks, Poppies, and many other garden plants, which are watched and tended with the most faithful care till the time comes for transporting them over the seas to Appledore."[49]

The visit of Roland and his family in the fall further restored Thaxter's spirits. Writing to the Wards, she described her happiness:

> When my little three years old Eliot comes to me and says with grave intensity, "Granna, I *adore* you" my cup of bliss is quite full! Then I have a little granddaughter a year old. . . . But my arms and thoughts are full all the time, and everything else goes, writing most of all![50]

Despite her poor health and lack of time for writing, Thaxter agreed to write *An Island Garden*. As she says in the "Prefatory": "Year after year the island garden has grown in beauty and charm, so that in response to the many entreaties of strangers as well as friends who have said to me, summer after summer, 'Tell us how you do it! Write a book about it and tell us how it is done, that we may go also and do likewise,' I have written this book at last. Truly it contains the fruit of much sweet and bitter experience. . . ."[51]

An Island Garden, which is still popular today, proved to be one of Thaxter's most ambitious undertakings. Illustrated by Childe Hassam, it is a combination of a how-to gardening manual, a treatise on poppies, a vendetta against slugs, and a guide to home decoration with flowers. In painstaking detail, she describes her techniques for planning her garden, preparing the soil, planting her flowers, keeping them healthy, and finally bringing them into her parlor for her

Beyond the Garden Gate. REPRODUCED HERE BY PERMISSION OF THE HOUGHTON LIBRARY,
HARVARD UNIVERSITY.

guests to enjoy. Her descriptions of the sights, sounds, and scents not only of her garden but of the islands as well are a continuing reminder of her connection to the natural world:

> And so the ripe year wanes. From turfy slopes afar the breeze brings delicious, pungent, spicy odors from the wild Everlasting flowers, and the mushrooms are pearly in the grass. I gather the seed-pods in the garden beds, sharing their bounty with the birds I love so well, for there are enough and to spare for us all. Soon will set in the fitful weather, with fierce gales and sullen skies and frosty air, and it will be time to tuck up safely my Roses and Lilies and the rest for their long winter sleep beneath the snow, where I never forget them, but ever dream of their wakening in happy summers yet to be.[52]

Writing the book proved to be an arduous task. A poignant letter to Sarah Orne Jewett reveals just how difficult it was:

> . . . I am pegging away hard on the book and I want to ask you a lot of things. I have got a little plan of the garden, as you suggested, with places of everything marked,—a sort of little map. I have got the whole thing about done, the writing, but there is much copying and arranging of parts to make a proper unity. I have been so ill since the house closed, just about *dead* with the stress and bother of things and people, and feared to slip back to the hateful state of three years ago. The doctor said, "You are going to have the whole thing over again if you are not *mighty* careful," and mighty careful I have been and I am better.[53]

Although she felt better physically, Thaxter's depression continued and made her work even more difficult. Feelings of sadness at the loss of so many friends lingered: "Dear Annie, has not Death been busy? Everybody gone. Bryant, Longfellow, Lowell, Whittier, Browning, Tennyson! Even dear Sam Longfellow has joined the mute procession, too. What an empty world it grows!"[54] She was also having trouble concentrating; as she confessed to Jewett: "Oh, you dear kind wisest and helpfulest! I thought I should remember . . . every word of your suggestions when you spoke them, but alas! I rack my stupid and empty brain in vain for most of them. . . ."[55] With Jewett's help, Thaxter completed the book. Houghton Mifflin published the first edition of one thousand copies of *An Island Garden*, with Hassam's paintings and chapter headings[56] and Sarah Wyman Whitman's gold-stamped cover in March 1894. According to Paula Blanchard, "Sarah read it through at least twice, suggesting changes and cutting, and finally helped with the copying when Celia felt too sick to do it herself."[57] Jewett's kindness, her empathy — her gift of sympathy — made Thaxter's task less daunting.

In the summer after *An Island Garden* was published, Thaxter invited her dearest friends to Appledore to walk and sail with her and visit her favorite places on the islands. Annie Fields, Childe Hassam, Ole Bull, Rose Lamb, and Sarah Jewett were among those who accompanied her.[58] In her preface to *The Poems of Celia Thaxter*, Jewett describes those last days. The friends climbed the cliffs of Star Island and rested near the Gosport church; they sailed to the lighthouse on White Island, where Celia and her family had lived so long ago; they visited the Spaniards' graves, where she recited her poem honoring the sailors' memory, and ended with a visit to all her special places on Appledore Island:

> It was midsummer, and the bayberry bushes were all a bright and shining green, and we watched a sandpiper, and heard the plaintive cry that begged us not to find and trouble its nest. Under the very rocks and gray ledges, to the far nests of the wild sea birds, her love and knowledge seemed to go. She was made of that very dust, and set about with that sea, islanded indeed in the reserves of her lonely nature, with its storms and calmness of high tides. . . .[59]

Celia Thaxter died on August 26, 1894. She had gone to bed early and died at dawn the following morning. Annie Fields described how her body lay in her parlor on "a bed of sweet bay . . . prepared by her friends Appleton Brown and Childe Hassam. . . . William Mason once more played the music from Schumann which she chiefly loved."[60] Her funeral service was conducted by her dear Portsmouth friend the Reverend James De Normandie; then her closest friends accompanied her body to the family burial ground. Annie's tribute expressed the feelings of all who were gathered there that day: "It was indeed a poet's burial, but it was far more than that: it was the celebration of the passing of a large and beneficent soul."[61]

Daring: A Postscript

As you have seen, I am a writer who came of a sheltered life. A sheltered life can be a daring life as well. For all serious daring starts from within.[1]

—EUDORA WELTY, *One Writer's Beginnings*

DARING IS NOT THE FIRST ADJECTIVE THAT COMES TO MIND WHEN WE THINK OF CELIA Thaxter. Sheltered, yes, but not daring. Although she had deep admiration for John Greenleaf Wittier, she never became a political activist; in fact, she appeared detached from politics. While she was certainly against slavery, she has never been identified as an abolitionist. Her name never arises in the annals of the women's suffrage movement. And surely the notorious Victoria Woodhull, who was only five years younger than Thaxter and who shared her interest in Spiritualism, was never invited to Appledore.[2] Thaxter's only real political action took place in the arena of the Audubon Society with her protest against the use of bird feathers in women's hats.

Yet, if we examine Celia Thaxter's life closely, the word daring belongs. From the time she was four years old and landed on the shores of White Island, she faced physical danger from the storms that battered the islands. Despite the protection of her intrepid parents and the solidly built lighthouse, the weather was a constant threat. The thought of Celia at age five or six waiting on the lighthouse dock with a lantern to guide her father's return reminds us of her bravery.

Another kind of daring—perhaps risk taking is a better description—was her decision at sixteen to marry Levi Thaxter and move to the mainland. Leaving behind her family and all that was familiar, Thaxter embarked on a new life where even the existence of trees and horses seemed unusual. But her most courageous decision came in 1880 when she separated from Levi and, in effect, declared her independence. Her decision to break bonds of home and mother-hood defied the nineteenth-century norm, which was to live within your hus-band's home under all circumstances. Bravely, Thaxter embarked on a new life, earning money for herself and her family, pursuing her career in art, maintain-ing her island salon — and still remaining within the bounds of propriety.

The Aesthetic Movement gave voice to Thaxter's daring. It empowered her to pursue a new career and added another dimension to her life. No longer content to be among the "pots and kettles,"[3] she chose the more satisfying roles of artist, gardener, and doyenne of a sophisticated salon.

And finally, Thaxter was not content to accept the disregard for the natural world that she saw around her. She not only joined the Audubon Society and spoke out against "the heartlessness of women"[4] but both *Among the Isles of Shoals* and *An Island Garden* are testaments to her unique relationship with nature. Had she lived longer, more avenues for daring would have been opened to her, and she would not have hesitated to pursue them. "For all serious daring starts from within."[5]

NOTES

ABBREVIATIONS

AF   Annie Fields and Rose Lamb, eds., *Letters of Celia Thaxter*
CL   Cedric Laighton, *Letters to Celia*
DT   Donna Titus, *By This Wing*
HL   Houghton Library, Harvard University, Cambridge, Mass.
LH   Longfellow House, Cambridge, Mass.
ML   Morgan Library
OL   Oscar Laighton, *Ninety Years at the Isles of Shoals*
PA   Portsmouth Atheneum, Portsmouth, N.H.
RT   Rosamond Thaxter Collection

INTRODUCTION (pp. 1–5)

1. AF, iii.

2. Celia Thaxter, *Among the Isles of Shoals*, 7–8.

3. Celia Thaxter, *Among the Isles of Shoals*, 14–15.

4. Celia Thaxter, *Among the Isles of Shoals*, 27.

5. Rutledge, *The Isles of Shoals in Lore and Legend*, 2.

6. Rutledge, *The Isles of Shoals in Lore and Legend*, 19.

7. Rutledge, *The Isles of Shoals in Lore and Legend*, 10.

8. Rutledge, *The Isles of Shoals in Lore and Legend*, 33.

9. Their fate is sadly reminiscent of Aleutian Islanders and Japanese Americans during World War II. Although Shoalers were not placed in internment camps,

they were forced to leave their homes for unfounded reasons based on suspicion and prejudice.

10. Celia Thaxter, *Among the Isles of Shoals*, 67.

11. Celia Thaxter, *Among the Isles of Shoals*, 68.

12. Celia Thaxter, *Among the Isles of Shoals*, 55.

13. Sarton, *Mrs. Stevens Hears the Mermaids Singing*, 174.

14. OL, 139.

1. HOME IN A LIGHTHOUSE (pp. 7–19)

1. Thomas Laighton, *Journals*, PA.

2. "Rotation," *Portsmouth Journal*, September 28, 1839.

3. Rutledge, *The Isles of Shoals in Lore and Legend*, 61.

4. Rosamond Thaxter, *Sandpiper*, 57.

5. Rutledge, *The Isles of Shoals in Lore and Legend*, 65.

6. Westbrook, *Acres of Flint*, 133.

7. "The Candidates in District No. 1," *Portsmouth Journal*, March 9, 1839.

8. A chronology of Thomas Laighton's political career: 1837, State Senate; 1839, State Senate; 1841, New Hampshire House of Representatives, the Board of Selectmen in Portsmouth; 1842, New Hampshire House of Representatives.

9. "Poet Dead," *Boston Post*, August 28, 1894.

10. Jewett, *Best Short Stores*, 108–9.

11. Jewett, *Best Short Stores*, 113.

12. Jewett, *Best Short Stores*, 112.

13. Jewett, *Best Short Stores*, 114.

14. Thoreau, *The Heart of Thoreau's Journals*, 16.

15. Albee, "Memories of Celia Thaxter," 163–64.

16. Thomas Laighton, *Journals*, PA.

17. Thomas Laighton, letter to Eliza Laighton, October 4, 1856, RT.

18. Celia Thaxter, *Among the Isles of Shoals*, 120–21.

19. Celia Thaxter, *Among the Isles of Shoals*, 121.

20. Celia Thaxter, *Among the Isles of Shoals*, 122.

21. Celia Thaxter, *Among the Isles of Shoals*, 121.

22. Celia Thaxter, *Among the Isles of Shoals*, 132.

23. Celia Thaxter, *Among the Isles of Shoals*, 140.

24. Celia Thaxter, *Among the Isles of Shoals*, 140.

25. Celia Thaxter, *Among the Isles of Shoals*, 143.

26. Celia Thaxter, *Among the Isles of Shoals*, 134.

27. Celia Thaxter, *Poems*, 26.

28. Celia Thaxter, *Among the Isles of Shoals*, 122.

29. Celia Thaxter, letter to Annie Fields, March 14, 1876, RT.

30. Grossman, "'Uncle Oscar.'"

31. Rosamond Thaxter, *Sandpiper*, 12.

32. CL.

33. Cedric Laighton, letter to Celia Thaxter, January 22, 1860, CL, 3.

34. OL, 99.

35. Paula Blanchard, *Sarah Orne Jewett*, 182–83.

2. ENTER: LEVI THAXTER (pp. 20–33)

1. Celia Thaxter, letter to Rose Lamb, September 1889, AF, 165.

2. Rosamond Thaxter, *Sandpiper*, 16.

3. Donahue, "Celia Thaxter's World," 75.

4. Parloa, *The Appledore Cook Book*, 14.

5. Levi Thaxter, letter to Thomas Wentworth Higginson, January 19, 1842, HL bMS AM 1162.10.

6. Elizabeth Peabody (1811–1893) was the sister-in-law of both Nathaniel Hawthorne and Horace Mann. She was an outspoken advocate of social and educational reform, establishing the first kindergarten in the United States. She hosted Margaret Fuller's famous "conversations," and her bookstore became a meeting place for the Boston Transcendental Club as well as The Brothers and Sisters.

7. Thomas Wentworth Higginson, letter to Annie Fields, Cambridge, Mass., January 1898 in Thomas Wentworth Higginson, *Letters and Journals* (Boston: Houghton Mifflin, 1921).

8. Levi Thaxter, Sr., letter to Lucy Titcomb, July 15, 1856, RT.

9. Levi Thaxter, letter to Thomas Wentworth Higginson (1843?), HL bMS AM 1162.10.

10. Levi Thaxter, letter to Christopher Riley, April 3, 1846, HL 47M-360.

11. Levi Thaxter, letter Christopher Riley, New York, New York, May 4, 1846, RT.

12. Thomas Laighton, *Journals*, July 26, 1846.

13. Wells, *Dear Preceptor*, 60.

14. Higginson, *Letters and Journals*, 24.

15. OL, 15.

16. Rutledge, *The Isles of Shoals in Lore and Legend*, 73.

17. OL, 20–21.

18. Isles of Shoals Box 2, PA.

19. OL, 22.

20. OL, 25.

21. OL, 24.

22. OL, 29.

23. OL, 34.

24. OL, 33.

25. *New Hampshire Journal*, September 2, 1848.

26. *My History is America's History*.

27. Rosamond Thaxter, *Sandpiper*, 28.

28. Hawthorne, *American Notebooks*, 512.

29. Hawthorne, *American Notebooks*, 538.

30. Dr. Henry Bowditch, letter to Mrs. Bowditch, August 10, 1858, PA.

31. Dr. Henry Bowditch, letter to Mrs. Bowditch, August 10, 1858, PA.

32. Dr. Henry Bowditch, letter to Mrs. Bowditch, August 18, 1858, PA.

33. Dr. Henry Bowditch, letter to Mrs. Bowditch, August 14, 1858, PA.

34. Dr. Henry Bowditch, letter to Mrs. Bowditch, August 18, 1858, PA.

35. John Greenleaf Whittier, letter to Lucy Larcom, July 21, 1861, RT.

36. Wells, *Dear Preceptor*, 63–64.

37. Wells, *Dear Preceptor*, 63.

38. Rutledge, *The Isles of Shoals in Lore and Legend*, 76.

39. Thomas Laighton, *Journals*, October 7, 1848.

40. Thomas Laighton, *Journals*, October 8, 1848.

41. Thomas Laighton, *Journals*, November 22, 1848.

42. Thomas Laighton, *Journals*, November 22, 1848.

43. Rutledge, *The Isles of Shoals in Lore and Legend*, 77.

44. *Boston Post*, August 27, 1894.

45. Thomas Laighton, *Journals*, December 1848.

46. OL, 38.

47. Rosamond Thaxter, *Sandpiper*, 29.

48. Wells, *Dear Preceptor*, 70.

49. Celia Thaxter, letter to Jennie Usher, March 2, 1851, RT.

50. Celia Thaxter, letter to Jennie Usher, March 2, 1851, RT.

51. Rosamond Thaxter, *Sandpiper*, 35.

3. THE EARLY YEARS, 1851–1860 (pp. 34–43)

1. Higginson, *Letters and Journals*, 28.

2. Rosamond Thaxter, *Sandpiper*, 36.

3. Rosamond Thaxter, *Sandpiper*, 38.

4. Hawthorne, *American Notebooks*, 665.

5. Hawthorne, *American Notebooks*, 516.

6. Hawthorne, *American Notebooks*, 516.

7. Hawthorne, *American Notebooks*, 516.

8. Hawthorne, *American Notebooks*, 537.

9. Celia Thaxter, letter to Margie Curzon, 1850s, RT.

10. Celia Thaxter, letter to Sarah Weiss, March 5, 1854, RT.

11. Celia Thaxter, letter to Oscar Laighton, February 12, 1856, RT.

12. Rosamond Thaxter, *Sandpiper*, 49.

13. Levi Thaxter. MS 58, Box 3, PA.

14. Rosamond Thaxter, *Sandpiper*, 50.

15. Celia Thaxter, letter to Oscar Laighton, February 15, 1856, RT.

16. Celia Thaxter, letter to Sarah Weiss, January 4, 1857, RT.

17. Rutledge, *The Isles of Shoals in Lore and Legend*, 83–84.

18. Celia Thaxter, letter to E. C. Hoxie, May 25, 1856, AF, 3.

19. Celia Thaxter, letter to E. C. Hoxie, January 18, 1857, AF, 4–6.

20. Woolf, *Women and Writing*, 143.

21. Celia Thaxter, letter to E. C. Hoxie, March 28, 1857, AF, 9.

22. Celia Thaxter, letter to Sarah Weiss, May 31, 1857, RT.

23. Celia Thaxter, letter to Sarah Weiss, May 31, 1857, RT.

24. Celia Thaxter, letter to E. C. Hoxie, November 22, 1857, RT.

25. Cedric Laighton, letter to Celia Thaxter, Appledore, January 1, 1852, RT.

26. Celia Thaxter, letter to Elizabeth Hoxie, January 20, 1859, AF, 15–16.

27. Celia Thaxter, letter to E. C. Hoxie, Newtonville, November 22, 1857, AF, 13.

28. Celia is referring to Lizzie's sister and her friend from Artichoke Mills, Margie Curzon.

29. Celia Thaxter, letter to E. C. Hoxie, January 30, 1859, AF, 15–16.

30. Cedric Laighton, letter to Celia Thaxter, May 27, 1860, CL, 5.

4. New Horizons, 1861 (pp. 44–51)

1. Celia Thaxter, *Poems*, 1.

2. Celia Thaxter. *Poems*, 1.

3. Celia Thaxter, letter to her family, in Lyman Rutledge, *The Isles of Shoals in Lore and Legend*, 86.

4. AF, xiii.

5. Rosamond Thaxter, *Sandpiper*, 61.

6. Celia Thaxter, letter to Sarah Weiss, September 1861, RT.

7. Donovan, "Celia Thaxter," 228.

8. Celia Thaxter, *Poems*, 18–19.

9. Gollin, *Annie Adams Fields*, 114.

10. Brooks, *Literature in New England*, 478.

11. Tryon, *Parnassus Corner*, 2.

12. Gollin, *Annie Adams Fields*, 51.

13. Austin, *Fields of the Atlantic Monthly*, 31.

14. Donovan, *New England Local Color Literature*, 39.

15. In *The American Scene*, Henry James wrote: "Here, behind the effaced anonymous door, was the little ark of the modern deluge . . . here still the long drawing-room that looks over the water and toward the sunset with a seat for every visiting shade . . . and relics and tokens so thick on its walls as to make it positively, in all the town, the votive temple to memory." James, *The American Scene*, 244–45.

16. Hedrick, *Harriet Beecher Stowe*, 294.

5. Coming of Age, 1862–1868 (pp. 52–68)

1. Celia Thaxter, letter to Sarah Weiss, July 2, 1852, RT.

2. Celia Thaxter, letter to James T. Fields, October 25, 1862, AF, 26.

3. Celia Thaxter, letter to Mary Lawson, summer 1860, RT.

4. John Thaxter, letter to Celia Thaxter, April 9, 1863, RT.

5. Celia Thaxter, letter to Sarah Weiss, February 1862, RT.

6. Celia Thaxter, letter to Sarah Weiss, March 1861, RT.

7. Celia Thaxter, letter to Lizzie Hoxie, April 24, 1862, AF, 28–29.

8. Celia Thaxter, letter to Lizzie Hoxie, April 24, 1862, AF, 28–29.

9. Goodman, *Jean Stafford*, 158.

10. Vallier, *Poet on Demand*, 22.

11. Vallier, *Poet on Demand*, 20.

12. Celia Thaxter, *Among the Isles of Shoals*, 33.

13. Celia Thaxter, *Poems*, 24–25.

14. Celia Thaxter, *Among the Isles of Shoals*, 143–44.

15. Celia Thaxter, *Poems*, 6–10.

16. Kate Field (1838–1896) was an author, lecturer, and journalist.

17. Celia Thaxter, letter to Kate Field, August 10, 1863, RT.

18. Celia Thaxter, letter to Kate Field, August 10, 1863, RT.

19. Parloa, *The Appledore Cook Book*, 204.

20. William Mason, *Memories of a Musical Life*, 251.

21. Celia Thaxter, letter to Lucy Larcom, Shoals, September 6, 1863, RT.

22. Isles of Shoals Box 2, PA.

23. Myron Mandel, who is an attorney, reached this conclusion after doing research at the Portsmouth Atheneum.

24. Celia Thaxter, letter to James T. Fields, October 25, 1862, AF, 26.

25. Celia Thaxter, letter to James T. Fields, September 23, 1862, RT.

26. Annie Fields's Diary, January 5, 1867, HL.

27. Rosamond Thaxter, *Sandpiper*, 83.

28. Celia Thaxter, letter to unknown recipient, April 6, 1867, RT.

29. Whittier, *Complete Poetical Works*, 243.

30. In 1833, when only twenty-six, he published his first antislavery pronouncement, *Justice and Expediency*; early in 1834 he was appointed an agent of the American Anti-Slavery Society, and later in that year he was elected to the state legislature from his hometown of Haverhill, Massachusetts. After John Brown's raid at Harper's Ferry in 1859, the most important statement of Whittier's political and social views appeared in an article titled "The Lesson of the Day."

31. Whittier, *Complete Poetical Works*, 243.

32. Whittier, *Complete Poetical Works*, 186.

33. Celia Thaxter, letter to John Greenleaf Whittier, November 15, 1863, HL bMS AM 1844.

34. Pollard, *John Greenleaf Whittier*, 364.

35. Warren, *New and Selected Essays*, 244.

36. John Greenleaf Whittier, letter to Celia Thaxter, 11th month 24, 1872, RT.

37. John Greenleaf Whittier, letter to Celia Thaxter, 8th month 24th, 1867, RT.

38. John Greenleaf Whittier, letter to Celia Thaxter, 3rd month 29th, 1867, RT.

39. Celia Thaxter, Autograph File 172, HL.

40. Heineman, *Restless Angels*, 2

41. Celia Thaxter, letter to Sarah Weiss, n.d. 1852, RT.

42. Celia Thaxter, letter to Mary Lawson, April 6, 1867, RT.

43. Ralph Waldo Emerson, *Complete Essays and Other Writings*, 90.

44. Whitman, *Poetry and Prose*, 165.

45. In a letter to a friend, Celia expressed her disapproval of Whitman: "He *does* drag great things into the mire, oh he *does*! There are great things here and there, but suddenly your foot goes through the wholesome surface of the earth into a cesspool, it is loathsome to me—I don't want to read him. I never want to touch his work. And yet I know he has done fine and wonderful things. But you are never sure of him, never, never. You don't know where he is going to take you. "Pagan" indeed! and of the goats, goatish!" Celia Thaxter, letter to Clara Anthony, May 18, 1892, RT.

46. Gilligan, *In a Different Voice*, 173.

47. Heilbrun, *Writing a Woman's Life*, 18.

48. Douglas, *The Feminization of American Culture*, 96.

49. Annie Fields, ed. *Letters of Sarah Orne Jewett*, 11.

6. The Difficult Years, 1868–1877 (pp. 69–93)

1. Celia Thaxter, *Stories and Poems for Children*, 13.

2. Celia Thaxter, letter to Mary Lawson, January 1868, RT.

3. Celia Thaxter, letter to Annie Fields, October 4, 1891, RT.

4. Celia Thaxter, letter to Annie Fields, February 22, 1876, RT.

5. Levi Thaxter, *Journals, 1868–1869*, MS, RT.

6. Celia Thaxter, letter to James T. Fields, April 3, 1876, RT.

7. Celia did not seem to be embarrassed to ask for help from Annie. On March 8, 1876, she wrote: "I am waiting to get a check from St. Nicholas in return for a little poem, "Marjorie," which Mrs. Dodge accepted and then I'll send you my debt, my dearest Annie for the paper. . . ."

8. Celia Thaxter, letter to E. C. Hoxie, March 1869, AF, 40.

9. Celia Thaxter, letter to E. C. Hoxie, January 1870, AF, 43–44.

10. Celia Thaxter, letter to Elizabeth Hoxie, December 8, 1871, RT.

11. Celia Thaxter, *Poems*, 18–19.

12. James T. Fields, letter to Celia Thaxter, June 8, 1874, RT.

13. Vallier, *Poet on Demand*, 76.

14. Celia Thaxter, *Poems*, 61.

15. Fetterley, "Theorizing Regionalism," 41.

16. Fetterley, "Theorizing Regionalism," 44.

17. Fetterley, "Theorizing Regionalism," 48.

18. Littenberg, "From Transcendentalism to Ecofeminism," 141.

19. Littenberg, "From Transcendentalism to Ecofeminism," 148.

20. Fetterley, "Theorizing Regionalism," 40.

21. Celia Thaxter, *Among the Isles of Shoals*, 15.

22. Celia Thaxter, *Among the Isles of Shoals*, 92.

23. Celia Thaxter, *Among the Isles of Shoals*, 92.

24. Celia Thaxter, *Among the Isles of Shoals*, 96.

25. Melville, *Billy Budd and Other Stories*, 161.

26. Celia Thaxter, *Among the Isles of Shoals*, 163.

27. Celia Thaxter, *Among the Isles of Shoals*, 169.

28. Mary Abigail Dodge (1833–1896).

29. Celia Thaxter, letter to Gail Hamilton, January 14, 1867, RT.

30. Erica Weiss, "Children's Periodicals in the United States During the Nineteenth Century and the Influence of Mary Mapes Dodge," 4. http://www.facstaff.bucknell.edu/gcarr/19cUSWW/MMD/weiss.html

31. "Introduction to *The Youth's Companion*." *Nineteenth-Century American Children & What They Read: Some of Their Magazines*, 4. http://www.merrycoz.org/

32. Celia Thaxter, *Stories and Poems for Children*, 3.

33. Celia Thaxter, *Stories and Poems for Children*, 10.

34. Celia Thaxter, *Stories and Poems for Children*, 11.

35. Celia Thaxter, *Stories and Poems for Children*, 13.

36. Celia Thaxter, *Stories and Poems for Children*, 14–21.

37. Celia Thaxter, *Stories and Poems for Children*, 50.

38. Jackson, "September," 78.

39. Celia Thaxter, *Stories and Poems for Children*, 114.

40. Celia Thaxter, *Stories and Poems for Children*, 139.

41. Celia Thaxter, *Stories and Poems for Children*, 165.

42. Celia Thaxter, *Stories and Poems for Children*, introduction.

43. Rosamond Thaxter, *Sandpiper*, 104.

44. Rosamond Thaxter, *Sandpiper*, 103.

45. William Mason, *Memories of a Musical Life*, 253.

46. Excerpt from U.S. Census of Kittery, 1870, Box 2, PA.

47. OL, 74.

48. Celia Thaxter, *Among the Isles of Shoals*, 184.

49. Celia Thaxter, "A Memorable Murder," 604.

50. Celia Thaxter, "A Memorable Murder," 604.

51. Celia Thaxter, "A Memorable Murder," 608.

52. Celia Thaxter, "A Memorable Murder," 610.

53. Arnica is a plant used for treating bruises.

54. Celia Thaxter, "A Memorable Murder," 612.

55. Celia Thaxter, letter to Annie Fields, February 23, 1875, RT.

56. Rutledge, *Moonlight Murder at Smuttynose*, 43.

57. Gail Hamilton was an author as well as an editor of *St. Nicholas*. There is no record of Celia's reaction to this dispute.

58. Gollin, *Annie Adams Fields*, 163.

59. George Emerson, *The Last Farewell to His Pupils*, 20.

60. Letter to the Editor, "Out-door Aid for the Poor," *Boston Herald*, August 14, 1888.

61. Celia Thaxter, letter to Annie Fields, January 7, 1877.

62. Celia Thaxter, letter to Annie Fields, October 10, 1877.

63. Celia Thaxter, letter to Annie Fields, March 14, 1876, RT.

64. Celia Thaxter, letter to Annie Fields, April 4, 1876, RT.

65. Celia Thaxter, letter to Annie Fields, May 5, 1876, RT.

66. Celia Thaxter, letter to Annie Fields, January 7, 1877, RT.

67. Celia Thaxter, letter to Annie Fields, January 17, 1877, RT.

68. Celia Thaxter, letter to Annie Fields, January 17, 1877, RT.

69. Celia Thaxter, letter to Annie Fields, August 15, 1877, RT.

70. Celia Thaxter, letter to Annie Fields, November 14, 1877, RT.

71. Celia Thaxter, letter to Annie Fields, November 19, 1877, RT.

72. Dickinson, "1136," in *Final Harvest*, 250.

73. Celia Thaxter, letter to Annie Fields, November 25, 1877, RT.

74. Celia Thaxter, letter to Annie Fields, November 27, 1877, RT.

75. Levi Thaxter, letter to John Thaxter, March 28, 1876, RT.

76. Levi Thaxter, letter to John Thaxter, March 20, 1877, RT.

77. Levi Thaxter, letter to John Thaxter, September 9, 1877, RT.

78. Levi Thaxter, letter to John Thaxter, May 20, 1877, RT.

79. Levi Thaxter, letter to John Thaxter, March 20, 1877, RT.

80. Levi Thaxter, letter to John Thaxter, June 19, 1877, RT.

81. Levi Thaxter, letter to John Thaxter, August 5, 1877, RT.

82. Levi Thaxter, letter to John Thaxter, September 27, 1877, RT.

83. Levi Thaxter, letter to John Thaxter, October 21, 1877, RT.

84. Levi Thaxter, letter to John Thaxter, October 9, 1877, RT.

7. New Beginnings, 1878–1886 (pp. 94–114)

1. Browning, *Aurora Leigh*, 396.

2. Levi Thaxter, letter to John Thaxter, June 19, 1877, RT.

3. Celia Thaxter, letter to John Thaxter, June 17, 1878, RT.

4. Celia Thaxter, letter to John Thaxter, December 27, 1881, RT.

5. Celia Thaxter, letter to Sarah Weiss, n.d., RT.

6. Celia Thaxter, letter to Charlotte Dana, July 2, 1885, RT.

7. Celia Thaxter, letter to John Thaxter, June 14, 1877, RT.

8. Celia Thaxter, letter to John Thaxter, January 15, 1882, RT.

9. Celia Thaxter, letter to John Thaxter, June 23, 1885, RT.

10. Celia Thaxter, letter to John Thaxter, December 21, 1880, RT.

11. Roland Thaxter, letter to John Thaxter, May 3, 1878, RT.

12. Celia Thaxter, letter to Rose Darrah, August 5, 1882, RT.

13. Celia Thaxter, letter to John Thaxter, February 19, 1882, RT.

14. Celia Thaxter, letter to Mr. and Mrs. Wm. Ward, January 18, 1883, RT.

15. Rosamond Thaxter, *Sandpiper*, 124.

16. Celia Thaxter, letter to Annie Fields, September 4, 1878, RT.

17. Brooks, *Literature in New England*, 161.

18. Rosamond Thaxter, *Sandpiper*, 170.

19. Webster, *William Morris Hunt*, 151.

20. Celia Thaxter, letter to Annie Fields, July 19, 1879, AF, 94.

21. Celia Thaxter, letter to Annie Fields, Shoals, n.d., 1879, AF, 95.

22. Record, "Sweeping View of History," B1–2.

23. Celia Thaxter, letter to John Thaxter, May 2, 1880, RT.

24. Celia Thaxter, letter to John Thaxter, May 4, 1880, RT.

25. Celia is referring to a cook who had been hired to care for "the boys."

26. Celia Thaxter, letter to John Thaxter, May 12, 1880, RT.

27. Browning, *Aurora Leigh*, 396.

28. Welter, *Dimity Convictions*, 21.

29. Tennyson, *Idylls of the King*, 136.

30. OL, 108.

31. OL, 110.

32. OL, 111.

33. OL, 130–31.

34. Celia Thaxter, letter to Annie Fields, December 8, 1880, RT.

35. Celia Thaxter, letter to Annie Fields, November 1880, AF, 106.

36. Celia Thaxter, letter to Annie Fields, January 13, 1881, RT.

37. Celia Thaxter, letter to Annie Fields, December 31, 1880, RT.

38. Celia Thaxter, letter to John Field, March 6, 1881, ML.

39. Celia Thaxter, letter to E. C. Hoxie, March 28, 1857, AF, 9.

40. Rosamond Thaxter, "Thou Whom Eyes Saw Never," RT.

41. Levi Thaxter, *Literary World*, March 11, 1882, 78–79.

42. Brooks, *Literature in New England*, 53.

43. E. L. P., *Boston Transcript*, 1881.

44. Letter to the Editor, *Boston Daily Advertiser*, April 1882.

45. Ryals, *Life of Robert Browning*, 12.

46. Rosamond Thaxter, quoted in "Address to the Massachusetts Historical Society."

47. Ryals, *Life of Robert Browning*, 55.

48. E. L. P., *Boston Transcript*, 1880.

49. Celia Thaxter, letter to Roland and John Thaxter, July 3, 1881, RT.

50. Celia Thaxter, letter to Julius Eichberg, October 1882, AF, 133.

51. Celia Thaxter, letter to Annie Fields, Thanksgiving Day, 1882, RT.

52. Celia Thaxter, letter to John Thaxter, December 30, 1883, RT.

53. Harvard College Library Clipping Sheet, May 31, 1884, Harvard University Archives.

54. Orr, *Life and Letters of Robert Browning*, 335.

55. Celia Thaxter, letter to Mrs. Clara Anthony, April 26, 1892, RT.

56. Celia Thaxter, letter to E. C. Hoxie, Newtonville, January 18, 1857, AF, 5.

57. Celia Thaxter, letter to Anne Ritchie, January 27, 1880, RT.

8. ANNIE AND SARAH (pp. 115–28)

1. Paula Blanchard, *Sarah Orne Jewett*, 137.

2. Celia Thaxter, letter to Annie Fields, October 23, 1881, RT.

3. At the height of her professional career, on her fifty-third birthday, Sarah was thrown from her carriage when her horse slipped as it descended a hill. She suffered a concussion and damage to her neck from which she never fully recovered. Annie stayed with her after the accident until she appeared to be improving. Then, shortly after her return to Boston and possibly as the result of the stress of worry over Sarah, Annie suffered a mild stroke. For the next three months, each woman was confined to her own home filled with anxiety about her friend. In April 1903 Sarah was finally able to go to Boston, but, by October, more than a year after the accident, it was apparent that her health was not improving. For the next six years, until her death in 1909, she was more or less an invalid. Sometimes she was able to write letters, but any serious writing was out of the question. Except for a four-month vacation to Europe in 1903, probably on doctor's orders, Annie spent as much time as possible with her.

4. Celia Thaxter, letter to Bradford Torrey, January 28, 1890, DT, 36.

5. Paula Blanchard, *Sarah Orne Jewett*, 24.

6. Paula Blanchard, *Sarah Orne Jewett*, 66.

7. By the time of publication of *The Country of the Pointed Firs* Sarah had spent the previous fourteen years with Annie Fields, and, as Marjorie Pryse observes: "Jewett 'outgrew' her fears of the loss of friendship *Deephaven* records, but did not outgrow female friendship as both the frame for and motivating force behind her fiction" ("Archives of Friendship," 63).

8. Jewett, *Deephaven*, 251.

9. Paula Blanchard, *Sarah Orne Jewett*, 137.

10. Nickname for Sarah.

11. Celia Thaxter, letter to Annie Fields, December 27, 1881, RT.

12. Paula Blanchard, *Sarah Orne Jewett*, 182–83.

13. Littenberg, "From Transcendentalism to Ecofeminism," 140.

14. Celia Thaxter, *Among the Isles of Shoals*, 30–31.

15. Jewett, *Country of the Pointed Firs*, 99–100.

16. Todisco, "By Pen and Spade," 34–35.

17. Paula Blanchard, *Sarah Orne Jewett*, 197.

18. Celia Thaxter, letter to Rose Lamb, March 1892, Autograph File AL 3633.5.10, HL.

19. Jewett, *Country of the Pointed Firs*, 29.

20. Celia Thaxter, *Among the Isles of Shoals*, 173–74.

21. Jewett, *Country of the Pointed Firs*, 186.

22. Jewett, "The White Heron," in *Best Short Stories*, 83.

23. Jewett, *Best Short Stories*, 84.

24. Jewett, *Best Short Stories*, 86.

25. Jewett, *Best Short Stories*, 90.

26. Celia Thaxter, *Stories and Poems for Children*, 230–32.

27. Celia Thaxter, letter to Annie Fields, March 14, 1876, RT.

28. Sarah Orne Jewett, letter to Sarah Whitman, August 29, 1894, AF.

29. Jewett, *Country of the Pointed Firs*, 35.

30. Goldsmith, *Other Powers*, xiii–xiv.

31. Goldsmith, *Other Powers*, 35.

32. Celia Thaxter, letter to John Greenleaf Whittier, January 1885, bMS AM 1844, HL.

33. Cranston, *HPB*, 119.

34. Ellwood, *Theosophy*, 2.

35. Celia Thaxter, letter to John Greenleaf Whittier, 1884, AF, 141–42.

36. Howe, *Memories of a Hostess*, 130.

37. Celia Thaxter, letter to Mrs. Ward, May 17, 1887, RT.

38. Celia Thaxter, letter to Feroline Fox, June 1885, AF, 144.

9. The Aesthetic Movement: Finding a Voice (pp. 129–43)

1. McDowell, "Childhood Memories of Celia Thaxter," 125–26.

2. Wilde, "House Decoration."

3. *Britannica on Line*.

4. Jewett, "The Flight of Miss Betsey Lane," in *Best Short Stories*, 205.

5. Jewett, *Best Short Stories*, 209.

6. Burke et al., *In Pursuit of Beauty*, 220.

7. Cather, *My Antonia*, 163.

8. Brandimarte, "Somebody's Aunt and Nobody's Mother," 213.

9. Brandimarte, "Somebody's Aunt and Nobody's Mother," 217.

10. Brooks, *Literature in New England*, 148.

11. Celia Thaxter, letter to Annie Fields, spring 1877, RT.

12. Cedric Laighton, letter to Celia Thaxter, January 24, 1864, CL, 63.

13. Celia Thaxter, letter to Feroline Fox, September 22, 1874, AF, 58–59.

14. Woloch, *Women and the American Experience*, 275.

15. Harvey Green, *The Light of the Home*, 107.

16. Anderson, "Celia Thaxter and Her Gardens," 121.

17. Celia Thaxter, letter to Annie Fields, February 24, 1877, RT.

18. Celia Thaxter, letter to Annie Fields, November 2, 1881, AF, 125–126.

19. Celia Thaxter, letter to Annie Fields, spring 1877, RT.

20. Stephan, *One Woman's Work*, 100.

21. Wilde, "House Decoration," 128.

22. Mary Warner Blanchard, *Oscar Wilde's America*, 107.

23. Celia Thaxter, *An Island Garden*, 104.

24. Celia Thaxter, letter to James T. Fields, October 25, 1862, RT.

25. AF, ix.

26. Celia Thaxter, *An Island Garden*, xi.

27. Celia Thaxter, *An Island Garden*, 27–28.

28. Celia Thaxter, *An Island Garden*, 96–97.

29. Celia Thaxter, *An Island Garden*, 99.

30. Martyn Green, ed., *Treasury of Gilbert & Sullivan*, 225.

31. Celia Thaxter, *An Island Garden*, 50.

32. Celia Thaxter, *An Island Garden*, 76–77.

33. Celia Thaxter, *An Island Garden*, 81.

34. Curry, *Childe Hassam*, 86.

35. Celia Thaxter, letter to E. C. Hoxie, January 1857, AF, 5–6.

36. Celia Thaxter, *An Island Garden*, 83.

37. Celia Thaxter, *An Island Garden*, 94.

38. Celia Thaxter, *Poems*, 184–85.

39. Celia Thaxter, letter to Sarah Weiss, Newton, January 7, n.d., RT.

40. Haugen and Cai, *Ole Bull*, xxii.

41. Haugen and Cai, *Ole Bull*, 85.

42. Caleb Mason, *The Isles of Shoals Remembered*, xiii.

43. AF, 138–139.

10. Finale, 1888–1894 (pp. 144–61)

1. Celia Thaxter, *An Island Garden*, 126.

2. Celia Thaxter, letter to Annie Fields, June 29, 1888, RT.

3. Rosamond Thaxter, *Sandpiper*, 194.

4. Rosamond Thaxter, *Sandpiper*, 196.

5. Rosamond Thaxter, *Sandpiper*, 195.

6. Pfister, "Roland Thaxter and Myxobacteria," 1.

7. Pfister, "Roland Thaxter and Myxobacteria," 7.

8. Dodge, "Roland Thaxter," 6.

9. Celia Thaxter, letter to Mr. and Mrs. Ward, November 22, 1891, RT.

10. Celia Thaxter, letter to Clara Anthony, February 9, 1892, RT.

11. Rosamond Thaxter, *Aunt Rozzie Remembers*.

12. Rosamond Thaxter, *Sandpiper*, v. In later life, John waged a battle in his community to garner support for the League of Nations. This was an unpopular cause among many New Englanders, who feared that the United States might lose control over the price of textiles and other exports. His enthusiasm led to yet another conflict in his life, this time with a local high school, whose principal wrote him:

    > Traip Academy is supported not only by the adherents to the League of Nations, but its opponents as well. We do not permit politics to extend in any way into the Academy. You can easily see, therefore, that it will be impossible to use your issue, which is undoubtably [*sic*] one of the big political issues of the day. I am, therefore, returning your data with thanks and also informing you that we can neither at this, or any future time, use lectures or plays on the League of Nations. Thanking you for your favors of the past I am, Yours truly, C. P. Steward, Jr. Principal.

    John died in August 1929; according to his obituary he was "74 years, eight months and 19 days." The obituary ended: "He was an able man, who preferred to live quietly and in the enjoyment of country life, and manifestly had that love of nature and scholarship one might expect from the son of such talented parents." Even in his death, John was misunderstood and was seen through the lens of his parents' lives, not his own.

13. Celia Thaxter, letter to John Greenleaf Whittier, April 11, 1889, RT.

14. Cather, *O Pioneers!* 135.

15. John Greenleaf Whittier, letter to Annie Fields, October 2, 1885, in Pollard, *John Greenleaf Whittier*, 447.

16. John Greenleaf Whittier, letter to Celia Thaxter, November 23, 1890, RT.

17. Boutelle, "'A Crescent That Shall Orb into a Sun,'" 115.

18. Hoopes, *Childe Hassam*, 13.

19. Hoopes, *Childe Hassam*, 15.

20. Caleb Mason, *The Isles of Shoals Remembered*, March entry.

21. Laurence Hutton was an author and drama critic who wrote about literature and the theater.

22. Childe Hassam, letter to George Woodbury, August 1, n.d., bMS AM 1587, HL.

23. Celia Thaxter, letter to Feroline Fox, April 1886, AF, 145–46.

24. Celia Thaxter, "Woman's Heartlessness," 282.

25. Celia Thaxter, letter to John Greenleaf Whittier, June 24, 1888, bMS AM 1844, HL.

26. Celia Thaxter, letter to Bradford Torrey, December 7, 1888, DT, 11.

27. Celia Thaxter, letter to Bradford Torrey, Portsmouth, December 16, 1888, RT.

28. Celia Thaxter, letter to Bradford Torrey, November 10, 1889, DT, 28.

29. Celia Thaxter, letter to Bradford Torrey, December 13, 1889, DT, 29.

30. Celia Thaxter, letter to Bradford Torrey, Shoals, April 17, 1894, DT, 92.

31. Celia Thaxter, letter to Bradford Torrey, Shoals, July 20, 1894, DT, 93–94.

32. Celia Thaxter, letter to Annie Fields, June 28, 1888, RT.

33. Celia Thaxter, letter to William Hayes Ward, October 11, 1888, RT.

34. Celia Thaxter, letter to Annie Fields, October 17, 1888, RT.

35. Celia Thaxter, letter to M. L. Padelford, December 12, 1888, AF.

36. Celia Thaxter, letter to Annie Fields, October 4, 1891, RT.

37. Celia Thaxter, letter to Adaline Hepworth, April 8, 1890, AF, 174.

38. Celia Thaxter, letter to Annie Fields, July 15, 1889, RT.

39. Celia Thaxter, letter to Annie Fields, July 15, 1889, RT.

40. Celia Thaxter, letter to Mrs. Ward, April 17, 1890, RT.

41. Tennyson, "Crossing the Bar," 771.

42. Pepsin is a digestive enzyme found in the gastric juice of stomach secretions; an extract of pepsin from the stomachs of calves, pigs, et cetera, was used as a digestive aid.

43. Celia Thaxter, letter to William Ward, December 25, 1890, RT.

44. Celia Thaxter, letter to William Ward, December 25, 1890, RT.

45. Celia Thaxter, *An Island Garden*, v.

46. Celia Thaxter, *An Island Garden*, 15.

47. Celia's eggshells were forerunners of today's moss "Jiffy Pots."

48. Celia Thaxter, *An Island Garden*, 16.

49. Celia Thaxter, *An Island Garden*, 17.

50. Celia Thaxter, letter to Mr. and Mrs. Wm. Ward, November 22, 1891, RT.

51. Celia Thaxter, *An Island Garden*, vii.

52. Celia Thaxter, *An Island Garden*, 126.

53. Celia Thaxter, letter to Sarah Orne Jewett, September 1893, RT.

54. Celia Thaxter, letter to Annie Fields, October 1892, AF, 193.

55. Celia Thaxter, letter to Sarah Orne Jewett, February 5, 1893, RT.

56. "In the original edition, Hassam's paintings and chapter headings were reproduced by chromolithography, an expensive and painstaking process of color
printing in use during the second half of the nineteenth century. The litho-
graphic artist who copied the original work of art many have used as many as
thirty stones to make one color reproduction. The chromolithographs for *An
Island Garden* were made at Armstrong & Company, which had merged with
Houghton Mifflin in 1875." From the publisher's note in *An Island Garden*.

57. Paula Blanchard, *Sarah Orne Jewett*, 269.

58. Rosamond Thaxter, *Sandpiper*, 240.

59. Jewett, preface to Celia Thaxter, *Poems*, viii.

60. AF, 221.

61. AF, *Letters of Celia Thaxter*, 222.

DARING: A POSTSCRIPT (pp. 162–63)

1. Welty, *One Writer's Beginnings*, 104.

2. Woodhull, according to her biographer Barbara Goldsmith, was not only a
well-known Spiritualist, but also "the 'high priestess' of free love, the crusading
editor, the San Francisco actress and part-time prostitute, the founder of the
first stock brokerage firm for women, the disciple of Karl Marx, the blackmailer,
the presidential candidate, the sinner, the saint." Goldsmith, *Other Powers*, 7.

3. Celia Thaxter, letter to James T. Fields, October 25, 1862, AF, 26.

4. Celia Thaxter, "Woman's Heartlessness," 281–82.

5. Welty, *One Writer's Beginnings*, 104.

BIBLIOGRAPHY

WORKS OF CELIA THAXTER

Among the Isles of Shoals. Boston: James R. Osgood, 1873.
An Island Garden. 1894. Boston: Houghton, Mifflin, 1988.
"A Memorable Murder." *Atlantic Monthly*, May 1875, 602–15.
The Poems of Celia Thaxter. Boston: Houghton Mifflin, 1899.
Stories and Poems for Children. Boston: Houghton Mifflin, 1883.
Verses. Boston: Lathrop, 1891.
"Woman's Heartlessness." In *Nineteenth-Century American Women Writers*, Karen Kilcup, ed. Oxford: Blackwell, 1997, 281–82.

SECONDARY SOURCES

Albee, John. "Memories of Celia Thaxter." In *The Heavenly Guest*, Oscar Laighton, ed. Andover, Mass.: Smith and Coutts, 1935, 161–74.
Anderson, Mrs. Larz, "Celia Thaxter and Her Gardens." In *The Heavenly Guest*, Oscar Laighton, ed. Andover, Mass.: Smith and Coutts, 1935, 115–23.
Austin, James. *Fields of the Atlantic Monthly.* San Marino, Calif.: Huntington Library, 1953.
Blanchard, Mary Warner. *Oscar Wilde's America.* New Haven, Conn.: Yale University Press, 1998.
Blanchard, Paula. *Sarah Orne Jewett: Her World and Work.* Boston: Addison-Wesley, 1994.
Booth, Edwina. *Edwin Booth.* New York: Century, 1984.
Boutelle, Ann Edwards. "'A Crescent That Shall Orb into a Sun': The Art and

Friendship of Celia Thaxter and Childe Hassam." *Overhere: A European Journal of American Culture* 17:2 (winter 1997): 115–31.

Bowditch, Dr. Henry. "Pilgrimage to Appledore: 1858." MS 58. Atheneum, Portsmouth, N.H.

Brandimarte, Cynthia. "Somebody's Aunt and Nobody's Mother: The American China Painter and Her Work, 1870–1920." *Winterthur Portfolio* 23:4 (winter 1988): 204–24.

Brighton, Ray. "Laighton Exiled Himself to the Isles of Shoals." *Portsmouth Herald*, January 7, 1990.

Britannica on Line. 1999. Encyclopedia Britannica, January 5, 2000. hhttp://www .britannica.com

Brooks, Van Wyck. *Literature in New England: Indian Summer, 1865–1917*. 1936. Garden City, N.Y.: Garden City Publishing, 1944.

Browning, Elizabeth Barrett. *Aurora Leigh*. In *Norton Anthology of Literature by Women*, Sandra Gilbert and Susan Gubar, eds. New York: Norton, 1985, 391–401.

Buell, Lawrence. *The Environmental Imagination*. Cambridge, Mass.: Harvard University Press, 1995.

———. *New England Literary Culture*. Cambridge: Cambridge University Press, 1986.

Burke, Doreen, et al. *In Pursuit of Beauty: Americans and the Aesthetic Movement*. New York: Metropolitan Museum of Art, Rizzoli. 1986.

"The Candidates in District No. 1." *Portsmouth Journal*, March 9, 1839.

Cather, Willa. *My Antonia*. 1918. New York: Penguin, 1994.

———. *O Pioneers!* 1913. Boston: Houghton Mifflin, 1941.

Conway, Jill. *When Memory Speaks*. New York: Random House, 1998.

Cranston, Sylvia. *HPB: The Extraordinary Life and Influence of Helena Blavatsky, Founder of the Modern Theosophical Movement*. New York: G. P. Putnam's Sons, 1993.

Curry, David. *Childe Hassam: An Island Garden Revisited*. New York: Norton, 1990.

Dickinson, Emily. *Final Harvest*. Boston: Little, Brown, 1961.

Dodge, Carroll. "Roland Thaxter." In *Annales de Cryptogamie Exotique*. July 1933. Tome 6, fasc. 1. Laboratoire de Cryptogamie du Muséum National d'Historie Naturelle, 6.

Donahue, Marie. "Celia Thaxter's World." *Down East*, August 1976, 72+.

Donovan, Josephine. "Celia Thaxter." In *Guide to American Women Writers*, Lina Mainiero, ed. New York: Ungar, 1979, 226–28.

———. *New England Local Color Literature: A Woman's Tradition*. New York: Ungar, 1983.

Douglas, Ann. *The Feminization of American Culture*. New York: Doubleday, 1977.

Eastlake, Charles. *Hints on Household Taste*. London: Longmans, Green, 1872.

Ellwood, Robert. *Theosophy: A Modern Expression of the Wisdom of the Ages*. Wheaton, Ill.: Theosophical Publishing House, 1986.

E. L. P. (reporter). *Boston Transcript*, 1880.

———. *Boston Transcript*, 1881.

Emerson, George. *The Last Farewell to His Pupils.* Boston: C. P. Moody Printer, 1855.

Emerson, Ralph Waldo. *The Complete Essays and Other Writings of Ralph Waldo Emerson.* New York: Modern Library, 1950.

Faderman, Lillian. *Surpassing the Love of Men: Romantic Friendship and Love from the Renaissance to the Present.* New York: Morrow, 1981.

Fetterley, Judith. "Theorizing Regionalism: Celia Thaxter's *Among the Isles of Shoals.*" In *Breaking Boundaries,* Sherrie Inness and Diana Royer, eds. Iowa City: Iowa Univesity Press, 1997, 38–53.

Fields, Annie. *Authors and Friends.* Boston: Houghton Mifflin, 1896.

———, ed. *Letters of Sarah Orne Jewett.* Boston: Houghton Mifflin, 1911.

———, ed. *Whittier: Notes of His Life and of His Friendships.* New York: Harper, 1893.

Fields, Annie, and Rose Lamb, eds. *Letters of Celia Thaxter.* Boston: Houghton, 1896.

Gerdts, William. *American Impressionism.* New York: Artabras Publishers, 1984.

Gilligan, Carol. *In a Different Voice: Psychological Theory and Women's Development.* Cambridge, Mass.: Harvard University Press, 1982.

Goldsmith, Barbara. *Other Powers: The Age of Suffrage, Spiritualism, and the Scandalous Victoria Woodhull.* New York: Knopf, 1998.

Gollin, Rita. *Annie Adams Fields.* Amherst: University of Massachusetts Press, 2002.

Goodman, Charlotte. *Jean Stafford: The Savage Heart.* Austin: Texas University Press, 1990.

Green, Harvey. *The Light of the Home.* New York: Pantheon, 1983.

Green, Martyn, ed. *Martyn Green's Treasury of Gilbert & Sullivan.* New York: Simon & Schuster, 1985.

Grossman, Max R. "'Uncle Oscar'—His Death at 99¾ Made 100,000 Persons Mourn." *Boston Sunday Post,* April 9, 1939.

Harvard College Library Clipping Sheet, May 31, 1884. Harvard University Archives, Cambridge, Mass.

Harvard Quinquennial Catalogue of the Officers and Graduates, 1636–1930. Cambridge, Mass.: Harvard University Press, 1930.

Haugen, Eniar. "Celia Thaxter and the Norwegians of the Isles of Shoals." In *Fin(s) de Siècle in Scandinavian Perspective: Studies in Honor of Harald S. Naess,* Faith Ingwersen and Mary Norseng, eds. Columbia, S.C.: Camden House, 1993, 172–77.

Haugen, Eniar, and Camilla Cai. *Ole Bull: Norway's Romantic Musician and Cosmopolitan Patriot.* Madison: University of Wisconsin Press, 1993.

Hawthorne, Nathaniel. *The American Notebooks.* Columbus: Ohio State University Press, 1972.

Hedrick, Joan. *Harriet Beecher Stowe: A Life.* New York: Oxford University Press, 1994.

Heilbrun, Carolyn. *Writing a Woman's Life.* New York: Norton, 1988.

Heineman, Helen. *Restless Angels: The Friendship of Six Victorian Women.* Athens: Ohio University Press, 1983.

Hesterberg, Carol. "Roland Thaxter and the Farlow." *Newsletter of the Friends of the Farlow* (fall 1995): 1–3.

Higginson, Thomas Wentworth. *Letters and Journals of Thomas Wentworth Higginson.* Boston: Houghton Mifflin, 1921.

Hill, May Brawley. *Grandmother's Garden: The Old-Fashioned American Garden, 1865–1915.* New York: Harry Abrams, 1995.

Honan, Park. *Authors' Lives.* New York: St. Martin's Press, 1990.

Hoopes, Donelson. *Childe Hassam.* New York: Watson-Guptill, 1979.

Horsfall, James. *Annual Review of Phytopathology* 19 (1979): 29–35.

Howe, M. A. DeWolfe. *Memories of a Hostess.* Boston: Atlantic Monthly Press, 1922.

Howells, William Dean. *Literary Friends and Acquaintance.* New York: Harper, 1900.

Jackson, Helen Hunt. "September." In *Favorite Poems: Old and New,* Helen Ferris, ed. New York: Doubleday, 1957, 78.

James, Edward, Janet James, and Paul Boyer, eds. *Notable American Women.* Cambridge, Mass.: Harvard University Press, 1971.

James, Henry. *The American Scene.* Bloomington: Indiana University Press, 1968.

Jewett, Sarah Orne. *Best Short Stores of Sarah Orne Jewett.* Camden, Maine: Yankee Books, 1988.

———. *The Country of the Pointed Firs.* New York: Norton, 1982.

———. *Deephaven.* Boston: James Osgood, 1877. Boston: Houghton Mifflin, 1895.

Kelly, Catherine. *In the New England Fashion.* Ithaca, N.Y.: Cornell University Press, 1999.

Kilcup, Karen, ed. *Nineteenth-Century American Women Writers.* Oxford: Blackwell, 1997.

Laighton, Cedric. *Letters to Celia.* Boston: Star Island, 1972.

Laighton, Oscar. *Ninety Years at the Isles of Shoals.* 1930. Boston: Star Island, 1988.

Laighton, Oscar, ed. *The Heavenly Guest with Other Unpublished Writings.* Andover, Mass.: Smith and Coutts, 1935.

Laighton, Thomas. *Journals, 1833–1849.* MS, Atheneum, Portsmouth, N.H.

Lambourne, Lionel. *The Aesthetic Movement.* London: Phaidon, 1996.

Letter to the Editor, "Out-door Aid for the Poor." *Boston Herald,* August 14, 1888. From Fields's Addenda Box 11, Huntington Library, San Marino, Calif.

Littenberg, Marcia. "From Transcendentalism to Ecofeminism: Celia Thaxter and Sarah Orne Jewett's Island Views Revisited." In *Jewett and Her Contemporaries: Reshaping the Canon,* Karen Kilcup and Thomas Edwards, eds. Gainesville: University Press of Florida, 1999, 37–152.

Mandel, Norma Haft. "Annie Fields and the Gift of Sympathy." Ph.D. diss., City University Graduate Center, 1996.

Mason, Caleb. *The Isles of Shoals Remembered: A Legacy from America's First Musicians' and Artists' Colony.* Boston: Tuttle, 1992.

Mason, William. *Memories of a Musical Life.* New York: Century, 1901.

McDowell, Maude Appleton, "Childhood Memories of Celia Thaxter." In *The Heavenly Guest,* ed. Oscar Laighton. Andover, Mass.: Smith and Coutts, 1935, 124–28.

Melville, Herman. *Billy Budd and Other Stories.* New York: Penguin, 1987.

"Memorial to Annie Fields by The Associated Charities of Boston, 1915." Houghton Library, Harvard University, Cambridge, Mass.

My History Is America's History: A Millennium Project of the National Endowment for the Humanities. American History Files: Vacations and Resorts, May 16, 2001. http://www.myhistory.org/history_files/vacation_and_resorts.html

Neff, Emily, and George Shockelford. *American Painters in the Age of Impressionism*. Houston: Museum of Fine Arts, 1995.

Nineteenth-Century American Children & What They Read: Some of Their Magazines. http://www.merrycoz.org

Orr, Mrs. Sutherland. *Life and Letters of Robert Browning*. Boston: Houghton Mifflin, 1891.

Parloa, Maria. *The Appledore Cook Book: Containing Practical Receipts for Plain and Rich Cooking*. Boston: Graves and Ellis, 1872.

Pfister, Donald. "Roland Thaxter and Myxobacteria." In *Myxobacteria*, vol. 2, Martin Dworkin and Dale Kaiser, eds. Washington, D.C.: American Society for Microbiology, 1993.

"Poet Dead." *Boston Post*, August 28, 1894.

Pollard, John. *John Greenleaf Whittier: Friend of Man*. Hamden, Conn.: Archon, 1969.

Portsmouth Herald, August 19, 1929.

Pryse, Marjorie. "Archives of Friendship and the Way Jewett Wrote," *The New England Quarterly* 66 (March 1993): 47–67.

Record, Jody. "Sweeping View of History: Champernowne Farm, Once Home to Poet Celia Thaxter, for Sale." *The Union Leader* (Manchester, N.H.), May 9, 1998, B1–2.

Reeve, F.D. "Islands, Cities, and Flowers." *Gettysburg Review* 4 (summer 1991): 454–59.

Rose, Phyllis. *Parallel Lives: Five Victorian Marriages*. New York: Vintage, 1984.

"Rotation." *Portsmouth Journal*, September 28, 1839.

Rutledge, Lyman. *The Isles of Shoals in Lore and Legend*. 1965. Boston: Star Island, 1971.

———. *Moonlight Murder at Smuttynose*. 1958. Boston: Star Island, 1988.

Ryals, Clyde de L. *The Life of Robert Browning: A Critical Biography*. Oxford: Blackwell, 1993.

Sarton, May. *Mrs. Stevens Hears the Mermaids Singing*. New York: Norton, 1965.

Scheele, Carl. *Neither Snow nor Rain. . . . The Story of the United States Mails*. Washington, D.C.: Smithsonian Institution Press, 1970.

Spofford, Harriet. *House and Hearth*. New York: Dodd, Mead, 1891.

———. *A Little Book of Friends*. Boston: Little, Brown, 1916.

Stephan, Sharon, ed. *One Woman's Work: The Visual Art of Celia Laighton Thaxter*. Portsmouth, N.H.: Peter Randall, 2001.

Tennyson, Alfred Lord. "Crossing the Bar." In *The Norton Anthology of Poetry*, Alexander Allison et al., eds. New York: Norton, 1975, 771.

———. *Idylls of the King*. New York: Heritage Club, 1939.

Tharp, Louise Hall. *The Peabody Sisters of Salem*. Boston: Little, Brown, 1950.

Thaxter, Levi. *Journals, 1868–1869*. Rosamond Thaxter Collection.

———. Letter. *Literary World*, MS, March 11, 1882, 78–79.

Thaxter, Rosamond. "Address to the Massachusetts Historical Society." 1952. Rosamond Thaxter Collection.

———. *Aunt Rozzie Remembers*. Published privately, n.d.

———. *Sandpiper: The Life and Letters of Celia Thaxter*. 1969. Portsmouth, N.H.: Peter Randall, 1999.

———. "Thou Whom Eyes Saw Never." Published privately, n.d.

Thoreau, Henry David. *The Heart of Thoreau's Journals*. 1927. New York: Dover, 1961.

Titus, Donna Marion. *By This Wing: Letters by Celia Thaxter to Bradford Torrey*. Manchester, N.H.: J. Palmer, 1999.

Todisco, Patrice. "By Pen and Spade." *Hortus: A Gardening Journal* (summer 1990): 34–44.

Torrey, Bradford. "A November Chronicle." *Atlantic Monthly* 61 (1888): 589–94.

Tryon, William. *Parnassus Corner: A Life of James T. Fields, Publisher to the Victorians*. Boston: Houghton Mifflin, 1963.

Turner, Jane, ed. *The Dictionary of Art*, vol. 14. New York: Grove's Dictionaries, 1996.

Vallier, Jane. *Poet on Demand*. Portsmouth, N.H.: Peter Randall, 1994.

Warren, Robert Penn. *New and Selected Essays*. New York: Random House, 1989.

Webster, Sally. *William Morris Hunt, 1824–1879*. Cambridge: Cambridge University Press, 1991.

Weinberg, Barbara, Doreen Bolger, and David Curry. *American Impressionism and Realism*. New York: Metropolitan Museum of Art, 1994.

Wells, Anna. *Dear Preceptor: The Life and Times of Thomas Wentworth Higginson*. Boston: Houghton Mifflin, 1963.

Welter, Barbara. *Dimity Convictions*. Athens: Ohio University Press, 1976.

Welty, Eudora. *One Writer's Beginnings*. Cambridge, Mass.: Harvard University Press, 1984.

Westbrook, Perry. *Acres of Flint*. Washington, D.C.: Scarecrow Press, 1951.

Whitman, Walt. *Poetry and Prose*. New York: Library of America, 1982.

Whittier, John Greenleaf. *The Complete Poetical Works*. Cambridge, Mass.: Riverside, 1984.

Whittker, Robert. *Land of Lost Content: The Piscataqua River Basin and the Isles of Shoals. The People. Their Dreams. Their History*. Dover, N.H.: Alan Sutton Publishing, 1994.

Who Was Who in American Art, Peter Falke, ed. Madison, Conn.: Sound View Press, 1985.

Wilde, Oscar. "House Decoration." In *Essays and Lectures by Oscar Wilde*. London: Methuen, 1908. http://www.burrows.com/founders/house.html

Woloch, Nancy. *Women and the American Experience*. Boston: McGraw-Hill, 2000.

Woolf, Virginia. *A Room of One's Own*. San Diego: Harcourt, 1981.

———. *Women and Writing*. San Diego: Harcourt, 1972.

INDEX

Note: The initials CLT refer to Celia Laighton Thaxter. LLT refers to Levi Thaxter. The designation "*p*" refers to illustrations.